THE FIRST BOOK OF JEWISH JOKES

THE FIRST BOOK OF JEWISH JOKES

The Collection of L. M. Büschenthal

Edited by Elliott Oring

Translated by Michaela Lang

With annotations by Anastasiya Astapova,
Tsafi Sebba-Elran, Elliott Oring, Dan Ben-Amos,
Larisa Privalskaya, and Ilze Akerbergs

INDIANA UNIVERSITY PRESS

Bloomington and Indianapolis

This book is a publication of

Indiana University Press
Office of Scholarly Publishing
Herman B Wells Library 350
1320 East 10th Street
Bloomington, Indiana 47405 USA

iupress.indiana.edu

© 2018 by Elliott Oring

All rights reserved

No part of this book may be reproduced or utilized in any form or by any means, electronic or mechanical, including photocopying and recording, or by any information storage and retrieval system, without permission in writing from the publisher. The paper used in this publication meets the minimum requirements of the American National Standard for Information Sciences—Permanence of Paper for Printed Library Materials, ANSI Z39.48-1992.

Manufactured in the
United States of America

Library of Congress Cataloging-in-Publication Data

Names: B?uschenthal, Lippmann Moses, 1784-1818, author. | Oring, Elliott, 1945- editor. | Lang, Michaela, translator.
Title: The first book of Jewish jokes : the collection of L. M. Buschenthal / edited by Elliott Oring ; translated by Michaela Lang, with annotations by Anastasiya Astapova, Tsafi Sebba-Elran, Elliott Oring, Dan Ben-Amos, Larisa Privalskaya, and Ilze Akerbergs.
Description: Bloomington : Indiana University Press, 2018. | Includes bibliographical references and index.
Identifiers: LCCN 2018019097 (print) | LCCN 2018021736 (ebook) | ISBN 9780253038357 (e-book) | ISBN 9780253038319 (hardback : alk. paper) | ISBN 9780253038326 (pbk. : alk. paper)
Subjects: LCSH: Jewish wit and humor. | Jewish wit and humor—History and criticism.
Classification: LCC PN6231.J5 (ebook) | LCC PN6231.J5 B86 2018 (print) | DDC 818/.602—dc23
LC record available at https://lccn.loc.gov/2018019097

1 2 3 4 5   23 22 21 20 19 18

Contents

vii
Foreword

ix
Acknowledgments

Part I: Introduction

3
1. On Jewish Jokes and the Collection of Lippmann Moses Büschenthal

27
2. The Jews in the Century of Büschenthal

Part II: The Texts

51
3. Collection of Witty Notions from Jews as a Contribution to the Characterization of the Jewish Nation/L. M. Büschenthal

99
4. Texts from The Friend of the Jews or Selected Anecdotes, Pranks, and Notions of the Children of Israel/Judas Ascher

135
Appendix I: Büschenthal Texts Taken from Judas Ascher, *Der Judenfreund*

139
Appendix II: Sources of Joke Analogues

147
References

155
Index

Foreword

THE FIRST BOOK *of Jewish Jokes*, at its core, is a translation of a collection of jokes published in 1812 by Lippmann Moses Büschenthal: *Sammlung witziger Einfälle von Juden, als Beyträge zur Characteristik der Jüdischen Nation* (Collection of witty notions from Jews as a contribution to the characterization of the Jewish nation).[1] To title anything as the "first," "original," "earliest," or "archetypical" is likely to invite reactions pointing to a host of earlier instances. In this case, the title of the book is offered as a deliberate provocation. An outpouring of specimens of earlier Jewish joke books is welcome. While there is no dearth of articles and books—scholarly and popular—published on the Jewish joke and Jewish humor more generally, this literature proceeds virtually without any reference to historical sources. This translation of Büschenthal's *Sammlung* (collection) is designed to stimulate the search for even earlier examples of Jewish joke books that contribute to an understanding of the development of jokes and anecdotes that are characterized as distinctively Jewish.

The title *The First Book of Jewish Jokes* is not only provocative; it is demonstrably false. Although Büschenthal's *Sammlung* had been identified by a prominent Germanist as the first Jewish joke book (Gilman 2012, 6), many of Büschenthal's jokes are acquired from an earlier source: *Der Judenfreund, oder auserlesene Anekdoten, Schwänke, und Einfälle von Kindern Israels* (The friend of the Jews, or selected anecdotes, pranks, and notions of the Children of Israel) published in 1810 under the name of Judas Ascher. Three-quarters of the jokes in Büschenthal's *Sammlung* are taken word-for-word from Ascher's *Der Judenfreund*.[2] Undoubtedly, other joke books are out there. Even Ascher refers in his foreword to a pamphlet, *Anekdoten von guten Juden* (Anecdotes of good Jews), but these books have yet to be identified and made available. Nevertheless, Büschenthal's collection is, at present, the first book of Jewish jokes that can be attributed to a known author/compiler. Judas Ascher would appear to be a pseudonym. His name is not found in any encyclopedia of German authors, nor does his name seem to be associated with any other book than *Der Judenfreund*.³

Accompanying the translation of Büschenthal's *Sammlung* is a translation of all the texts in Ascher that Büschenthal did not include in his own book. The reader is actually getting a translation of two early books of Jewish jokes. A table indicating which jokes in the *Sammlung* come from *Der Judenfreund* follows the translations. Also included in this volume is an essay on the nature and problems of Jewish joke scholarship and an essay on the situation of the Jews in central and western Europe in the century leading up to the publication of Büschenthal's and Ascher's joke anthologies. Finally, the jokes in the *Sammlung* are annotated; that is to say, an effort has been made to search for analogues to the jokes in order to get some sense of how many of them appear in later Jewish joke collections. Since there are no comprehensive indices of joke types as there are of folktales, ballads, or legends, the search for analogues is necessarily a hit-and-miss affair. Nevertheless, the search might offer some sense of the extent to which Büschenthal's texts do or do not survive in what is perceived to be a more contemporary Jewish joke inventory.

To characterize the *Sammlung* as "the first book of Jewish jokes" is, no doubt, something of an exaggeration, although not by much. The purpose of the title is to rouse scholarly interest in the Jewish joke. Hopefully, it will also entice readers whose interests are something other than scholarly. Such readers need to be forewarned that Büschenthal's book is unlikely to prove a resource for increasing one's personal repertoire of humorous materials. Most of the jokes are not of a kind likely to be retold to friends and acquaintances. In a few cases, the humor may escape comprehension altogether. It is hoped, however, that those who have an interest in Jewish jokes for their entertainment value will still find them interesting. After all, they were published over two hundred years ago. They are the product of an age with a different philosophical outlook, when different historical forces were in play, and when the social and material circumstances of the Jews in Europe were significantly different from what they are today.

Notes

1. A digital copy of the original work can be found at http://sammlungen.ub.uni-frankfurt.de/judaicaffm/content/pageview/7020489 (accessed June 17, 2017).

2. The WorldCat database identifies only nine libraries in four countries that have Büschenthal's *Sammlung* in their holdings: Germany (4); United States (1); Switzerland (1); United Kingdom (3). WorldCat identifies twenty libraries in six countries with copies of *Der Judenfreund*: Germany (11), United States (4), Israel (2), Netherlands (1), Switzerland (1), United Kingdom (1).

3. Judas Ascher's name does not appear in the twenty-six-volume work *Neue Deutsche Biographie* (1952–2013), the ten-volume *Dictionary of German Biography* (1995–2000), the thirteen-volume *Deutsche Biographische Enzyklopädie*, or the four-volume *Bibliographica Judaica: Verzeichnis jüdischer Autoren deutscher Sprache* (1981).

Acknowledgments

THIS VOLUME IS an act of collaboration, and there are a number of people to be thanked for their contributions to the project. First and foremost is Michaela Lang, who translated Büschenthal's *Sammlung* in its entirety as well as those texts in Judas Ascher's *Der Judenfreund* that Büschenthal did not incorporate into his volume. Dr. Anastasiya Astapova, research fellow, Institute of Cultural Research and Arts, University of Tartu, Estonia, surveyed the Russian Jewish joke literature; Dr. Tsafi Sebba-Elran, lecturer, Department of Hebrew and Comparative Literature, University of Haifa, Israel, searched the Hebrew collections of Alter Druyanow, Shimon Ernst, and Dov Sadan; Dan Ben-Amos, professor of folklore and Asian and Middle Eastern Studies, University of Pennsylvania, examined Immanuel Olsvanger's *Rosinkess mit Mandlen*; Larisa Privalskaya perused J. Chana Rawnitzki's *Yidishe Witzn*; and Dr. Ilze Akerbergs looked at the Latvian collection *Latvju tautas anekdotes* compiled by P. Birkerts and the Lithuanian collection *Lietuvių samojus* by Jonas Balys. Dr. Inta Carpenter edited the two supplementary essays, and Kathleen Stocks and Norman Klein proofread the entire book. My sincerest thanks to James R. Dow, professor emeritus of German at Iowa State University; Susanne Müller of the European Ethnology Section of the University of Vienna Library; Wolfgang Mieder, professor of German at the University of Vermont, Burlington; Dr. Eddy Portnoy of the Max Weinreich Center for Advanced Jewish Studies at YIVO; and Sarah Quill at the Herman B. Wells Library at Indiana University, Bloomington, for supplementary information and references.

THE FIRST BOOK OF JEWISH JOKES

Part I
INTRODUCTION

CHAPTER 1

On Jewish Jokes and the Collection of Lippmann Moses Büschenthal

A "Jewish joke" is not a social fact, something out there in the world, but rather a constructed category. It is the construction that constitutes the social fact. Not every joke told about Jews would be considered a Jewish joke. A hostile anecdote about Jews told by Gentiles would be regarded as a piece of anti-Semitism and not a Jewish joke (Freud 1960, 111; also Ausubel 1948, 265). Conversely, a joke told by Jews about the number of lawyers or psychologists it takes to screw in a lightbulb would likely be regarded as an instance of joke telling with nothing particularly Jewish about it. Much, it would seem, depends on the nature of the jokes themselves and an assessment of the motivations of the tellers.

I would date the beginnings of the serious discussion of the Jewish joke to Freud's book *Jokes and Their Relation to the Unconscious*, first published in Vienna in 1905. Freud employed a substantial number of Jewish examples in his analysis of joke construction and joke purposes (1960, 16–116).[1] More importantly, Freud made a comment on an aspect of Jewish jokes that has stuck in the imagination of subsequent joke scholars and commentators:

> A particularly favourable occasion for tendentious jokes is presented when the intended rebellious criticism is directed against the subject himself, or to put it more cautiously, against someone in whom the subject has a share—a collective person, that is (the subject's own nation for instance). The occurrence of self-criticism as a determinant may explain how it is that a number of the most apt jokes . . . have grown up on the soil of Jewish popular life. They are stories created by Jews and are directed against Jewish characteristics. . . . Incidentally, I do not know whether there are many other instances of a people making fun to such a degree of its own character. (1960, 111–12)

Opinions had been expressed on Jewish humor prior to Freud. Hermann Adler, chief rabbi of London, published an essay on Jewish humor in 1893 and had even noted its self-critical aspects (468). But Adler's concern was to defend the Jewish people against charges of humorlessness made by Thomas Carlyle (1795–1881) and Ernest Renan (1823–1892) rather than to define or characterize the nature of Jewish jokes or to analyze Jewish humor per se. Set within the framework of his psychoanalytic psychology, Freud established the discussion of

3

Jewish jokes on an entirely new footing. Jewish jokes emerged as potentially significant social and psychological phenomena. Freud's disciples would eventually distill Freud's casual observation about the self-critical tendencies of the Jewish joke into a thesis of Jewish masochism (Bergler 1956, 111; Reik 1962, 220–221; Grotjahn 1966, 22–23).² Since then, few commentators have been able to avoid depicting Jewish jokes as self-mocking, self-deprecating, and even self-hating (e.g., Revel 1943, 547; Simon 1948, 46; Ausubel 1948, 265; Mikes 1971, 102–104; Bermant 1986, 242–243; Schwarzbaum 1968, 26; Telushkin 1992, 77–82; Eilbirt 1993, 141–148; Wisse 2013, 7–11, 34, 106; but see Oring 1992, 122–134; Davies 2002, 17–49).

After Freud, the discussion of the Jewish joke became sustained and serious. A substantial literature developed. Efforts were made to characterize the Jewish joke and identify its distinctiveness. Jewish jokes were said not merely to employ Jewish characters, settings, and practices but also to express Jewish sensibilities (Telushkin 1992, 16). They are jokes without which, it was claimed, Jewish culture could not be understood (Nador 1975, 3). "In nothing is Jewish psychology so vividly revealed as in Jewish jokes" (Rosten 1970, xxiii).

Typically, the label *Jewish joke* is used to refer to a class of jokes believed to have arisen in the Jewish communities of Europe—particularly eastern Europe—and to express something fundamental about the nature and character of those communities (Revel 1943, 546; Cray 1964, 344; Golden 1972, 13; Nador 1975, 3; Davies 1986, 76; Nevo and Levine 1994, 16; Ziv 1986, 11; Fischman 2011, 48; Telushkin 1992, 16). It was the product of the Yiddish language—its intonations, syntax, and style—and the realities of life in the Pale of Settlement. It was a form of expression "born in the Empire of the Czars" (Mikes 1971, 102). In other words, Jewish jokes are considered to be exceptional and distinguishable from the jokes and anecdotes of the Lithuanians, Belarusians, Russians, Ukrainians, and Poles among whom the Jews lived. The jokes of the Sephardim and the Jewish communities of the Middle East, however, were not considered part and parcel of the Jewish joke repertoire. They were excluded because they had not been regarded as substantially different from those found in the Arab, Turkish, or Persian societies in which Jews were submerged (Ben-Amos 1991, 36; Wisse 2013, 20). So while the jokes of Jews in North Africa and the Middle East were held—rightly or wrongly—to be part and parcel of North African and Middle Eastern oral literary culture, the jokes of the Jews of Europe were regarded as a fundamentally different and distinguishable kind of expression. Even jokes from Israel were excluded from the Jewish joke category unless they derived from eastern European sources (e.g., Druyanow 1963). Israeli jokes, and Israeli humor more generally, were apprehended as different and largely ignored. Some commentators did not regard Israel as an apt environment for the production of humor or Israelis as being a funny people (Landmann 1962, 198; Mikes 1971, 114; Bermant 1986, 152; Telsuhkin 1992, 173; Wisse 2013, 30–35; but see Oring 1981).

Although the Jewish joke has been attributed to the communities of eastern Europe, there is also a sense among scholars that the Jewish joke sprang from a more ancient tradition. Something of a cottage industry has developed that is devoted to identifying instances of humor in the Bible, Talmud, and rabbinic literature. For some scholars, these endeavors are merely meant to demonstrate that Jews produced and consumed humor throughout their history as a people. In the nineteenth century, it was claimed that the Jews lacked humor, and as has been noted, some of the efforts to uncover humor in early Jewish sources were designed to challenge this characterization (Adler 1893; Chotzner 1905; Isaacs 1911; Radday and Brenner 1990). For others, however, the claim—explicit or implied—is that the contemporary Jewish joke and Jewish humor *evolved* from this much older tradition (Bermant 1986, 4; Ilan 2009; Brodsky 2011, 25; Wisse 2013, 22; Friedman and Friedman 2014). While there are certainly instances of humor among ancient and early and late medieval Jews—as there are among most peoples both ancient and modern—the identification of jokes or humorous expressions in ancient sources is not a straightforward affair. Some of the proposed identifications seem tenuous and unconvincing (Oring 2015). Absent a report of laughter or smiling in response to a purportedly humorous expression, the claim that a piece of ancient text is humorous is a perilous enterprise.[3] Furthermore, what are called "Jewish jokes" today seem worlds away from most of the expressions that are claimed to be humorous in the Bible, Talmud, and rabbinic literature. They seem far more similar in structure and style to jokes found in European cultures generally. Nevertheless, if a claim is made for the distinctiveness of the Jewish joke in relation to the oral humorous literature of Europe, it makes sense that some scholars might seek an explanation for that distinctiveness by situating it in a culture and tradition with roots in a non-European past.

The Jewish joke is said to be distinctive in ways other than the self-criticism identified by Freud. One claim is that Jewish jokes were of superior quality. Jews were held to be particularly astute in joke making, and their jokes were "more acute, more profound, and richer in expression" than the jokes of other peoples (Landmann 1962, 194; Mikes 1971, 111; Alexander Moszkowski quoted in Revel 1943, 545). Jews were said to have a "pre-eminence" in the field of humor production (Bermant 1986, 4). Aesthetic appreciation, however, invokes vague standards of evaluation. What, after all, constitutes a "more acute," "more profound," or "richer" expression? Absent specific, well-defined criteria, the assessment is likely to be entirely subjective. Furthermore, people, times, and tastes change. What might be considered profound in one generation may seem utterly conventional or even jejune in the next, assuming it can be understood at all.

Jewish jokes were also said to operate according to a peculiar logic—a logic that descends from or parodies the style and methods of Talmudic study and interpretation. Jewish jokes have been characterized as having a "crazy logic" or a "logical rigor gone over the edge" (Cohen 1999, 45–68). A variety of commentators have noted a tendency in the Jewish joke to engage in impossible argument, elaborate reasoning, and hair splitting (Untermeyer 1946, 521–526; Simon 1948, 43–45; Reik 1962, 114–116; Altman 1971, 141; Nador 1975, 5; Bermant 1986, 240–241; Davies 1986, 76; Raskin 1992, 30–32; Telsuhkin 1992, 41–61; Shloyme Bastomski in Gottesman 2003, 88; Druyanow in Bar-Itzhak 2010, 130, 132; Finkin 2011, 91–94).

Perhaps the last great distinction of the Jewish joke has nothing to do with the structure or content of jokes per se. It rather has to do with the fact of joking itself. Given the history of the Jewish people and their unceasing persecution, the Jews should really have had no reason to joke at all (Richman 1952, 4; Richman 1954, xi; Learsi 1961, 12–13; Skikne 2009, 44). The fact that they did and do joke would suggest either that they possess some special inner resource—some irrepressible spirit that the jokes express—or that the jokes have some compensatory function to perform that would be absent in groups whose joking was cultivated under happier conditions. One view is that the jokes are directed against their oppressors and are defensive or even retaliatory (Adler 1893, 458; Revel 1943, 545; Simon 1948, 46; Druyanow 1963: 1, ix; Schwarzbaum 1968, 23; Davies 2002, 17–49; Druyanow in Bar-Itzhak 2010, 136). Another view is that the jokes are a triumph of the spirit under impossible conditions ("Review" 1876, 81–82; Adler 1893, 458; Davidson 1907, xix; Rohatyn 1911, 11; Ausubel 1948, xx; Richman 1952, 4; Richman 1954, xiv; Ausubel 1967, 22; Schwarzbaum 1968, 23; Rosten 1970, xxiii; Mikes 1971, 104; Samuel 1971, 210–211; Niger 1972, 43; Novak and Waldoks 1981, xiii; Ziv 1986, 11; Alter 1987, 25; Druyanow in Bar-Itzhak 2010, 134).[4] This notion is often voiced in the phrase "laughter through tears," which supposedly marks the Jews as singular in the spectrum of joking nations.

Unfortunately, none of these descriptions have been established through sustained, methodical research. No one has done the comparative work to determine whether what are called "Jewish jokes" are, in fact, distinctive beyond their use of Jewish characters, locales, observances, and behaviors and the fact that Jews—although not exclusively Jews—tell and enjoy them (see Nevo 1991). Scholars are aware that Jewish jokes and stories have older non-Jewish analogues and sources, but the relationships are invariably established in terms of individual texts rather than on the basis of bodies of material (Richman 1952, 4–11; Schwarzbaum 1968, 27–36; Raskin 1992). It is difficult to know whether Jewish joking is more self-critical than the joking of other groups because the principle is evidenced casually and anecdotally through the use of a small set of joke examples (but see Davies 2002, 17–75). The same can be said for the idea that Jewish jokes habitually present a logic different from the jokes of other peoples. There are a few jokes that are regularly trotted out to evidence this proposition as well, but systematic comparisons have yet to be done. Also, there is little information on humor and joking in oppressed populations, so it is difficult to ascertain whether "laughter through tears" is a distinctly Jewish kind of expression.

It is possible that the descriptions that have been offered are accurate and can actually serve to characterize the large body of jokes that have been called "Jewish." It seems a doubtful proposition, but it is possible. What is more certain is that at present there exists more of a *mythology* of the Jewish joke than a sober and substantive representation of it. A mythology may sometimes prove to be true, but it would be foolish to simply accept such truth on faith.

My definition of the Jewish joke lies elsewhere. Whether the jokes of Jews are literary formations peculiar to the Jewish people or not, the key question is how did the genre of the joke become attached to Jews in the first place? When and where did this happen? And why did Jews adopt the joke genre as a symbol of their nationhood? When did "The People of the Book" become "The People of the Joke"? My definition of the "Jewish joke" is any joke that has been "conceptualized as uniquely, distinctly, or characteristically reflective of, evocative of, or conditioned by the Jewish people and their circumstance" (Oring 1983, 262; 1992, 114–15). Whether such conceptualizations are accurate is beside the point. The definition of "Jewish joke" lies in the act of ascription of the label and not in the joke itself. Jewish jokes, then, are not old jokes about Jewish characters or old Jews telling jokes, but the idea that certain jokes, joke qualities, and even joke-performance styles are regarded as distinctly Jewish. With this definition, the whole question of the Jewish joke becomes a sociological and historical rather than a literary question.

Consequently, whatever jokes were to be found in the Bible, Talmud, or Midrash were not Jewish jokes. As far as is known, this humor was never regarded by the writers and compilers of these texts as anything more than jokes and witticisms. They were not considered typically Jewish. They were not considered representations of Jewish character or signs of peoplehood. In the late nineteenth and early twentieth centuries, however, such jokes were excavated from these age-old texts to evidence an ancient connection between jokes and the Jewish people. In that act of excavation, in that effort to construct a history or pseudo-history of Jewish humor, those jokes—if they actually were jokes—became Jewish jokes.

When and where did the connection between Jews and jokes come into being? When and where did the jokes of Jews become "Jewish jokes"? There seem to be no collections of jokes about Jewish characters in typical Jewish circumstances compiled by Jews that go back to the Middle Ages. Undoubtedly, the rabbis would have condemned such collections as frivolous and *betul torah* (a neglect of Torah study)—a serious transgression—yet such joke collections exist for the Arab and Persian Middle Ages (Omar 2004, 1:319–22), and Muslim religious authorities would unlikely have been any more favorably disposed toward frivolity, irreverence, and misspent time than the early rabbis (Schwarzbaum 1968, 20).[5] From a historical standpoint at least, it might seem to be the Persians and Arabs who might claim a privileged connection to jokes and joking rather than the Jews.

The earliest dates for collections of jokes about Jews in Yiddish are generally later than Sigmund Freud's 1905 *Jokes and Their Relation to the Unconscious*. There is a Yiddish book of jokes that was published in Vilna in 1823, *Hundert un eyni anekdotin* (One hundred and one anecdotes).⁶ This is a very early date. The book is in Martynas Mažvydas National Library in Vilnius but is not widely available. The blurb on a digital copy of the title page of the book notes, however, that "most of the anecdotes are translations from French and Polish into easy to understand Yiddish" (YIVO Vilna). Two sample jokes appear on the web page. One concerns a Turk who finds himself in Poland in wintertime. When he tries to pick up a stone from the street to throw at an angry dog, he finds it frozen and curses the Poles for forging their stones into the ground. There is a version of this joke about a Frenchman in Russia (Teitelbaum 1945, 322; Spalding 1969, 4). The story can be found in John Taylor's *Wit and Mirth* printed in London in 1628 and goes back at least as far as 1258 in Sa'di Shirazi's *Gulistan* (Clouston 1888, 78–79 Sa'di 1258). The other joke is about an exchange of fire between British and French cannoneers at the Battle of Minorca (one of the Balearic Islands off the east coast of Spain) in 1756 (YIVO Vilna). This book of jokes would not seem to be a book of jokes by or about Jews but a more general book of jokes that was translated into Yiddish. The dates of books of jokes in Yiddish about Jews and characterized as "Jewish" seem to be of a much later date.⁷

In 1912, S. An-ski (Shlomo Zanvil Rappoport [1863–1920]) conducted an ethnographic expedition to seventy Jewish communities in Volhynia and Podolia (largely present-day Ukraine) and collected some 1,800 folktales, legends, and proverbs; 1,500 songs; and 1,000 melodies. He photographed synagogues and gravestones, as well as individual villagers, and brought back some 700 pieces of folk art and items of material culture (Bar-Itzhak 2010, 28–30). In 1914, An-ski compiled a questionnaire for an ethnographic program for the study of Jewish folklore and folklife, which contains 2,087 questions (Deutsch 2011, 103–313). Only 10 questions in the survey specifically ask about jokes. They focus largely on matters of courtship and marriage and the relationship between students and teachers. Whatever else An-ski's program might signify, it would not seem that An-ski, the reigning expert on Yiddish folklore and ethnography at that time—the "father" of Jewish ethnography (Kugelmass 2006)—considered jokes a major genre of eastern European Jewish folklore or regarded them as a touchstone of Jewish communal life.⁸

Jokes seem to play only a very small part in the reminiscences of life in the Pale of Settlement. There are mentions of pranks played on the holidays of Simchas Torah (Rejoicing in the Torah), Chanukah, and Purim (Miller 1980, 23–25; Wengeroff 2010, 114) and references to the rhymes of the *badkhonim* (wedding jesters) (Lifschutz 1952; Bisberg-Youkelson and Youkelson 2000, 114) and to *purim shpiln* (Purim plays) (Roskies and Roskies 1975, 232–34), but references to verbal jokes hardly appear at all. Far more central to the memoirs, autobiographies, and memory books are matters of poverty, fights, divorces, nicknames, and the abuses by teachers of their charges in *kheder* (elementary religious school).⁹

In fact, the early calls for the collection of Yiddish folklore in the early twentieth century emphasized the gathering of folk songs rather than jokes. For the early Jewish folklorists, songs were the authentic expressions of the Jewish soul (Gottesman 2003, 31–49). Only in the 1920s and 1930s do collections of oral Yiddish jokes appear. How then did jokes suddenly come to be regarded by Jewish folklorists as the *key* to the "spiritual recesses of the Jewish people" (Druyanow quoted in Bar-Itzhak 2010, 116)? The deep connection of jokes with the Jewish people of eastern Europe seems suspicious. The Jewish joke, as we have defined it, would not first seem to be a product of the Pale of Settlement. In fact, with all the popular and scholarly literature devoted to Jewish jokes and Jewish humor, some very basic questions have yet to be asked, let alone answered.

A clue about the special connection of Jews with jokes and humor comes from early nineteenth-century German sources. *Judenwitz*—a term that combines a word used to denote a Jew (*Jude*) with one that is used to signify wit or a joke (*Witz*)—was central to the literary debates unfolding in the first decades of the nineteenth century. There are indications that the concept, if not the term, was already employed in the late eighteenth century (Chase 2000, 2). The term as a whole was not meant to signify what we would today call the "Jewish joke" or "Jewish humor." Rather, the term connoted a style of discourse that was deemed caustic, mercenary, destructive, and merely clever and that was held to be characteristic of Jewish writers. *Witz* referred more to a wisecrack than a joke. It is not clear, however, when the term first came into general usage or whether Jews employed it to characterize their own oral discourse. It was regarded by German literati, however, as part of a Jewish conspiracy to take over German culture. Philosophically, *Witz* was not considered a subset of *Humor*. *Humor* was held to be inclusive, deep, and involve a "benevolent appreciation of life's general absurdity." *Humor* was a term applied to the expressions of autonomous national cultures like those of Germany or England, while *Witz* was regarded as something submerged and antithetical to the cultural mainstream (Chase 2000, 2–17).

Judenwitz was employed as a term of opprobrium (although the Jewish authors who were the central targets of the accusation—Moritz Gottlieb Saphir, Ludwig Börne, and Heinrich Heine—were widely read and often appreciated). It is possible that the term was ultimately accepted by Jews and turned into a positive attribution.[10] In any event, it would seem the uniting of Jews and *what we would today call "humor"* occurred in late eighteenth- and early nineteenth-century central Europe, and perhaps it is from the charge of *Judenwitz* that the idea that jokes and humor were distinctive attributes of the Jewish people was born.

It was in this milieu that Lippmann Moses Büschenthal published his book *Sammlung witziger Einfälle von Juden, als Beyträge zur characteristik der Jüdischen Nation* (Collection of witty notions about Jews, as a contribution to the characterization of the Jewish nation) in 1812. Little is known about Büschenthal. He was born in 1784 in Bischheim, Alsace, a town only a few kilometers outside the city of Strasbourg. Almost five hundred Jews were living in Bischheim at that time (Roth 1972, 4:1055).[11] Jews were not permitted to live in Strasbourg until 1791, two years after the French Revolution. Büschenthal married Debora Auerbach, the granddaughter of David Sinzheim. Sinzheim was the rabbi who formulated the responses of the Assembly of Jewish Notables to the twelve questions that Napoleon posed about Judaism. He was subsequently appointed president of the Grand Sanhedrin convened by Napoleon and became chief rabbi of France in the Central French Consistory during his reign (see chap. 2). Sinzheim was the head of a yeshiva in Bischheim that moved to Strasbourg after 1791, and it seems likely that Büschenthal would have attended it. Büschenthal would later become the leader of congregations in Breslau and Berlin; however, these were not traditional synagogues, and it is not clear whether Büschenthal was actually ordained as a rabbi. If he was, he was not as traditional as Sinzheim. Büschenthal married to please his father, had four children, and was divorced in 1813 (Goedeke 1938, 63–64; Heuer 1996, 353; "Büschenthal" 1840, 60). After a period in Paris, Büschenthal made his way east to Neuwied on the east bank of the Rhine (near Koblenz) and then to Elberfeld (present-day Wuppertal), where he became a newspaper editor (Killy 1995, 2:213). It was in Elberfeld that his joke book was published in 1812. Elberfeld was then a part of the Grand Duchy of Berg created by Napoleon in 1808 (Lefebvre 1969, 231). Jews had been expelled from Elberfeld in 1794 and were only readmitted when the area came under French rule (Roth 1972, 16:677). Büschenthal was a *maskil* (a participant in the Jewish Enlightenment and a promoter of secular knowledge and literature [see chap. 2]), and from 1807 to 1819, he contributed Romantic poetry to the movement's flagship journal, *Sulamith: Eine Zeitschrift zur Beförderung der Kultur und Humanität unter den Israeliten* (Sulamith: Journal for the advancement of culture and humanism among the Israelites).[12] He also published a Hebrew translation of Friedrich Schiller's "Ode to Joy" (Kilcher 2007, 48–60). In 1798, Büschenthal published a psalm in Hebrew celebrating Napoleon's escape from an attempted assassination (Schechter 2003, 301; "Napoleon Bonaparte" 1801, 461–62).[13] In 1802, he and Wolf Heidenheim published an ode in Hebrew and German on the occasion of Napoleon's trip through areas of the lower Rhine to Jewish communities near Koblenz ("Büschenthal" 1840, 60). In 1806, he wrote, again with Heidenheim, a poem in Hebrew and German dedicated to and praising Karl von Dalberg, whom Napoleon had elevated to prince primate of the Confederation of the Rhine and grand duke of Frankfurt (see chap. 2). Many Jews were enamored of Napoleon and many wrote poems in his honor (Schechter 2003, 226), but it was not uncommon for some of Napoleon's appeal to wane with the reversal of his fortunes and the restoration of the Bourbons (Szajkowski 1954, 229n53). In 1814, Büschenthal moved to Vienna, where he was employed as an editor and literary advisor, and then to Breslau, where he served as a *Prediger* (preacher) before moving to another position in Berlin. He died in Berlin in 1818 (Heuer 1996, 353; Goedeke 1938, 63–64).

Büschenthal's joke collection is important for a number of reasons. First is its early date—1812. Second, the book is in good German, not Yiddish, and except for some *Oy vay*s (German: "Au wai[h]"; jokes #38, #47), *eppes*es (joke #85) and intonations in the mouths of some joke characters, it is devoid of Yiddishisms. Third, the jokes are presented not as merely entertaining stories but as expressions that reveal aspects of the character of the Jewish people. While Büschenthal was not the first to suggest that a nation's humor might reflect attributes of its character, he seems to be the first to make this claim for Jews and specifically on the basis of jokes.

On the title page of his book, Büschenthal states he "recorded" or "noted down" the jokes (*aufgezeichnet*), which might suggest that he compiled them from oral rather than written sources. This was not the case. Eighty of the texts (75.5%) in his book were taken word-for-word from Judas Ascher's *Der Judenfreund, oder auserlesene Anekdoten, Schäwanke, und Einfälle von den Kindern Israels* (The friend of the Jews, or selected anecdotes, pranks, and notions of the Children of Israel) published in Leipzig two years before. (The particular jokes appropriated from Ascher by Büschenthal are indicated in appendix I.) The sources for the first twenty-six jokes in the *Sammlung* (collection) that Büschenthal did not plagiarize from Ascher are unknown at present. Judas Ascher is also an unknown. His name is associated only with *Der Judenfreund*, and it is not possible to say with absolute certainty, despite his name, that he was Jewish.[14]

It is possible, however, to discern the audience for whom Büschenthal's *Sammlung* was intended. It was intended for both Jews and Gentiles. Because it is in German, it would have been accessible to Germans and to those Jews who embraced the *Haskalah* (Jewish Enlightenment) program and had learned German. A majority of traditional, religious Jews could read Hebrew and Yiddish written in Hebrew letters, but often they could not read German written in Gothic letters. Büschenthal's book also includes a small number of texts that include explanatory materials regarding fasting (joke #3), life cycle terminology (joke #13), the restrictions on the foods a Jew could eat in a restaurant (joke #26), Talmud study (joke #41), and Jewish ingenuity in escaping difficult situations (joke #46). Such details would seem unnecessary in a book directed solely at a Jewish audience. Although the last two in this series of texts are taken from Ascher's *Der Judenfreund*, the first three texts are found only in Büschenthal. Several anecdotes about Moses Mendelssohn (jokes #61, #64, #69, and #104) that appear both in Ascher and Büschenthal were also published anonymously in the journal *Sulamith* in 1812 ("Anekdoten" 1812). That is the same year that Büschenthal published his collection and the year he started to contribute to this Haskalah periodical, so it seems reasonable to suppose that it was Büschenthal who submitted them.

In his very brief introduction to the *Sammlung*, Büschenthal claims to be an impartial observer who is publishing jokes that display both the positive and negative traits of the Jews. This is true. There are joke texts in which the Jew is clever and others in which he is deceitful, a rogue, or an utter fool. Büschenthal also states in this introduction that the Jews have long been recognized as a quick-witted and funny people. It seems important to establish a time line for the perception of Jews as smart, clever, and funny. While Büschenthal claims the image to be a long-standing one, when the Jews first came to be broadly identified for their wit and humor remains unclear.[15] Büschenthal also asserts that the Jews became a funny people because of the centuries of oppression they had endured. All through the eighteenth century, oppression was the factor employed by both Jewish and Gentile champions of Jewish toleration and emancipation to account for what were perceived to be deformities in the Jewish character. Remove the oppression and normalize their participation in society they argued, and Jews would become respectable and productive citizens like anyone else (see chap. 2). Büschenthal claimed oppression gives rise to conditions of necessity and weakness, which in turn give rise to cunning, and "cunning is the mother of wit." This would seem to be the very first published theory of Jewish humor.[16]

It is important to register that not every text in Büschenthal would be considered a joke by today's standards. Many, indeed most, are jokes, but some should be characterized today as comic or merry tales. They are meant to be humorous but don't have true punchlines (Oring 1989, 349–364; 1992, 81–93). There is even a text that seems to contain no comic element at all (joke #37). This caveat is even more necessary when looking at Asher's *Der Judenfreund*. Ascher includes jokes and comic tales but also what today might be called legends and true-crime reports. While these texts do not constitute anywhere near a majority in his anthology, they are nevertheless well represented. Today the term *anecdote* is generally employed to refer to an amusing incident concerning a known contemporary or historical personage. In the eighteenth century, however, the term generally referred to an account of some unpublished historical or striking incident. (The term itself comes from the Greek and Latin [*an* + *ekdotos* = unpublished]). So the subtitle of Ascher's book does not mislead; it does not promise that everything contained within it will prove to be amusing.

Büschenthal's collection contains 106 jokes and anecdotes. Almost every joke involves a Jewish character in some kind of interaction. In about a third of the jokes, a Jew seems to get the better of a fellow Jew—usually in word but sometimes in deed. In almost half (45%), a Jew gets the better of a Gentile. In only 3 jokes do Gentiles seem to get the better of a Jew. This categorization is somewhat loose. For example, in one joke (#79), an army officer pays off his debt but forces the Jewish moneylender to eat his promissory note at knife point. When the officer seeks to borrow from the Jew again, the Jew agrees but only if the note is written on gingerbread. I count this joke as a "victory" for the Jew. Although he does not prevail physically, he gets the humorous last word. Table 1.1 outlines the interactions.

Table 1.1 Joke Interaction in Büschenthal

Category	Jokes	Number of jokes	Percentage of total
Jew > Jew	1, 3, 4, 13, 14, 21, 22, 29, 37, 42, 48, 52, 58, 59, 60, 61, 63, 65, 66, 68, 77, 78, 80, 86, 89, 92, 97, 98, 100, 101, 106	31	29.2
Jew > Gentile	2, 6, 7, 8, 9, 10, 11, 12, 15, 16, 17, 19, 23, 24, 25, 26, 28, 30, 33, 34, 35, 36, 38, 39, 40, 46, 51, 54, 55, 57, 62, 64, 67, 69, 73, 74, 75, 76, 79, 81, 84, 85, 87, 88, 90, 91, 99, 103, 105	49	46.2
Gentile > Jew	27, 31, 93	3	2.8
Self-Stupidity	5, 41, 43, 44, 45, 47, 53, 56, 70, 71, 72, 82, 94, 95, 96	15	14.2
Uncertain	18, 20, 32, 49, 50, 81, 102, 104	8	7.5
Total		106	100

> = victor in exchange with

The *jokescape* in table 1.2 characterizes the jokes in terms of the scenarios, actions, events, and personnel that are represented in an attempt to give a snapshot of the compilation as a whole.

Without comparing the jokescapes from different Jewish joke books, it is difficult to assess whether this distribution of texts is typical or not. The attempt to classify individual jokes, even by topic, is far from a straightforward affair.[17] Determining who the victor is in a social interaction is somewhat easier but by no means clear-cut. Without an explicit methodology for how a joke is to be classified and without multiple ratings by different judges, it is hard to know whether the classifications would be reliable and comparisons based on them valid. Nevertheless, they do allow us to see that jokes about confrontations with Gentiles, money lending, business dealings, deceit, rabbis (although they are not major figures), the rich, sex and pregnancy, fasting, baptism, doctors, and marriage are regularly found both in Büschenthal as well as in later corpuses of Jewish jokes. In Büschenthal's book, however, jokes are rare or absent that invoke biblical or rabbinic quotations, as are jokes about biblical events or characters,[18] the *Schadchen* (marriage broker), betrothal, weddings, domestic arrangements,[19] Jewish mothers,[20] the *Schnorrer* (beggar),[21] restaurants, and inns,[22] drinking and drunkenness, the cantor, the synagogue, the house of study, Talmudic sophistry, the Messiah, *melamdim* (teachers of children), *apikorsim* (heretics) and atheists, Hassidim, the Jewish body,[23] death and burial, heaven, the Torah, and God—except, in this last case, in interactions with Christian clergy who are ridiculing Jewish belief or trying to convert a Jew (e.g., jokes #6 and #15). An inspection

Table 1.2 Jokescape for Jokes in Büschenthal

Category	Jokes	Number of jokes	Percentage of total
Christians (dispute with/ attempted conversion by)	[6], 10, 14, 15, 39, [57], 74	7	6.6
High culture	18, [51], 56, 72, 95, 96, 97, 98	8	7.5
Moses Mendelssohn	61, [64], 68, 69, [104]	5	4.7
Army/soldiering	[24], [32], 36	3	2.8
Cowardice	[24], [51]	2	1.9
Rich Jews/miserliness	4, 29, [49], 60, [63] [65], 86	7	6.6
Marriage/family	3, [22], [43], 70, 100	5	4.7
Jews abused/ridiculed (verbal/physical)	[2], 7, [17], 19, 26, 28, [31], [34], [39], [45], [51], [52], [62], [64], [66], 67, 71, [79], [83], [88], [103]	21	19.8
Baptized Jews	75, 76	2	1.9
Money lending/borrowing	[31], [33], [37], 40, [49]. [63] 77, [78], [79], [87], [88]	11	10.4
Horses/riding/postal coaches	5, 9, [45], 82, 84, [89], [103], 106	8	7.5
Sex/pregnancy/scatology	[12], [22], 58, 93	4	3.8
Theater	[2], [33], [34]	3	2.8
Government figures and institutions:			
Kings, Princes Dukes, Barons	8, [9], [32] [39], [87]	5	4.7
Courts/Legal/Police	1, [23], 30, [37], [52], 54, [62], [80], 85, [91], [105]	11	10.4
Bureaucrats	55, [83]	2	1.9
Customs/Passports/ Gatekeepers	[12], 16, [25], [38], [39]	5	4.7
Jewish custom/observance	3, [6], 13, [20], 53	5	4.7
Rabbis	[9], [22], 41, [42]	4	3.8
Scholarship	[42], [43]	2	1.9
Haskalah	[20], 21	2	1.9
Market/fair	[11], [44], [46], 47, [78]	5	4.7
Theft/fraud by Jew	[27], 35, [37], [80], [105]	5	4.7
Other tricks by a Jew	[11], [17], [25], [38], [46], [89], [90], [91], [105]	9	8.5

(*Continued*)

Table 1.2 (Continued)

Category	Jokes	Number of jokes	Percentage of total
Jew tricked	[27], [37]	2	1.9
Business	[44], 48, 67, 73, 101	5	4.7
Medicine/doctors	[49], 50, [57], [65], [66], [90]	6	5.7
Chess	59, [104]	2	1.9
Defective language	[23]	1	0.94
Serious texts	[37]	1	0.94
Other	81, 92, 94, 99, 102	5	4.7
Total		163	153

Note: Total jokes in book = 106
Total joke texts classified = 163
Percentage = Number of texts classified/jokes in book
Jokes in brackets are classified in more than one category

of other Jewish joke collections actually reveals relatively few analogues to the jokes in Büschenthal's compilation (see appendix II). The number of jokes about postal coaches, passports and customs, civil courts, and moneylending might prove striking to the contemporary reader. But as Jews were almost exclusively restricted in their occupations to moneylending and trade, this emphasis in the jokes should not be surprising. Jews often traveled great distances to attend markets and fairs (Glückel 1977), and even the poorest Jews might engage in moneylending as a means of earning or supplementing a meager livelihood.[24] Also, moneylending and business dealings would continually involve them in legal disputes.

In Büschenthal's book, there are no jokes that evidence any kind of crazy or perverse logic. The closest thing to a joke involving such logic is the joke about a cat that is weighed because it is blamed for having eaten the eleven pounds of meat that was meant for lunch (#102). The tale, however, is found in early Middle Eastern collections and is known throughout Europe and North Africa (Uther 2011, Type 1373). It appears as a Hodja Nasreddin story (Downing 1965, 10). As for self-critical stories, Jewish characters in the jokes are sometimes foolish (e.g., #22, #45), sometimes verbally or physically abused (e.g., #31, #79), sometimes devious and dishonest (e.g., #46, #80, #91). Are these self-critical jokes? Except for their Jewish characters and situations, they do not seem particularly different from jokes in other corpuses that involve fools or scoundrels. Until there is an unambiguous definition of the self-critical joke and comparisons are made across cultural boundaries, the concept will remain uncertain and basically unusable (see Davies 2002, 17–49).

Table 1.3 Joke Interaction in Ascher Texts *Not* Appropriated by Büschenthal

Category	Jokes	Number of jokes	Percentage of total
Jew > Jew	217, 221, 243, 333, 344	5	6.3
Jew > Gentile	224, 226, 249, 263, 264, 271, 280, 292, 299, 317, 325, 336, 353	13	16.3
Gentile > Jew	203, 205 206, 208, 209, 212, 219, 222, 223, 230, 236, 245, 250, 254, 260, 268, 279, 289, 291, 297, 323, 340, 347, 348, 349, 351, 354, 355, 358, 360	30	37.5
Self-stupidity	210, 225, 227, 231, 238, 251, 253, 265, 269, 284, 288, 326, 328, 329, 331, 332, 343, 346, 350	19	23.8
Uncertain	201, 202, 204, 228, 247, 252, 282, 293, 301, 307, 320, 337, 339	13	16.3
Total		80	100

> = victor in exchange with

Jokes #27–106 in Büschenthal were lifted word-for-word from Judas Ascher's 1810 publication.[25] While the lifting of jokes from other joke books regularly goes on even today, the extent of Büschenthal's appropriation seems striking. (It was not uncommon in the eighteenth century, however, for authors to reproduce entire scholarly articles by other authors and publish them under their own names.) Furthermore, Büschenthal did not bother to change the wording of the jokes he appropriated (except slightly in joke #66). Only jokes #1–26 seem to be Büschenthal's own contribution to the volume.

Büschenthal's jokes have been numbered 1–106 for ease of reference. (The jokes are not numbered in the original German text. Page numbers referencing the 1812 German publication are inserted in brackets in the translation of Büschenthal's book. The original page numbers in the 1810 publication of Ascher's *Der Judenfreund* are provided at the conclusion of each Ascher text.) Ascher's book contains 160 texts. They have been given numbers from 201 to 360. Consequently, any joke with a number higher than 200 is immediately identifiable as being from Ascher.

Büschenthal's selective appropriation of Ascher's texts may offer some insight into the motivations for his volume. Which texts did Büschenthal reject for his own volume? What seem to be his principles of selection? (All the texts in *Der Judenfreund* that Büschenthal did not use in his own book are translated in chap. 4). Tables 1.3 and 1.4 categorize the interaction and jokescape of those texts

Table 1.4 Jokescape for Jokes in Ascher *Not* Appropriated by Büschenthal

Category	Jokes	Number of jokes	Percentage
Christians (dispute with/ attempted conversion by)		0	0.0
High culture	[260], 288, 326, 328, [329], [343], 346, 332, [350], [354]	10	12.5
Moses Mendelssohn		0	0.0
Army/soldiering	[225], [227], 231	3	3.8
Cowardice	[227], [269], [358]	3	3.8
Rich Jews/miserliness	[260], [343], [350]	3	3.8
Marriage/family	[208], [247], 253, [293], 333	5	6.3
Jews abused/ ridiculed (verbal/physical)	[203], [205], [209], [212], [226], 230, [260], [263], [268], [280], [289], [325], 336, [358], [360]	15	18.8
Baptized Jews	[206], [208], [293], 297, [323], 344,	6	7.5
Money lending/ borrowing	[219], [221], [224], 228, [236], 252, 271, [291], [293], 301, 317, [325], 347, [351], [354]	15	18.8
Horses/riding/postal coaches		0	0.0
Sex/pregnancy/scatology	[247], [251]	2	2.5
Theater	201, [210], [289]	3	3.8
Government figures and institutions			
Kings, Princes Dukes, Barons	[209], [225], [226], [251], [280], [325], [349], 353	8	10.0
Courts/Legal/Police	[205], 222, [264]	3	3.8
Bureaucrats	[263], [325]	2	2.5
Customs/Passports/ Gatekeepers	[268]	1	1.3
Jewish custom/ observance	282, 299, [349]	3	3.8
Rabbis	243, [245]	2	2.5
Cantors	320	1	1.3
Scholarship	[212]	1	1.3
Market/fair	[249], [250], [254], [284]	4	5.0
Theft/fraud by Jew	[219], [221], [224], [236], [249], [254], [264], 292, 348, [355], [360]	11	13.8

(*Continued*)

Table 1.4 (Continued)

Category	Jokes	Number of jokes	Percentage
Other tricks by a Jew		0	0.0
Jew tricked	223, [245], [250], [291], [323], [351]	6	7.5
Business	[284], [291], [293], [323]	4	5.0
Medicine/doctors	265, 337	2	2.5
Chess		0	0.0
Defective language	[210], 339, [238], [307], [329], 331	6	7.5
Haskalah	[217]	1	1.3
Flogging and execution	[238], [245], [249], [355]	4	5.0
Dueling	[269], [358]	2	2.5
Serious texts	[202], [203], 204, [205], [206], [217], [219], [221], 224, 232, [355]	11	13.8
Other	[202], 279, [307], 340	4	5.0
Total texts in classification		141	176.3

Note: Total jokes in Ascher not utilized by Büschenthal = 80
Total joke texts classified = 141
Percentage = Number of texts classified/total number of texts not utilized
Jokes in brackets are classified in more than one category

in Ascher, but only those that Büschenthal did not include in his collection (total = eighty texts).

Again, the jokescape in table 1.4 only provides a snapshot of those eighty jokes in Ascher that Büschenthal *did not include* in his book. Percentages, consequently, are reckoned only with respect to those eighty texts, not the total number of texts in Ascher. Nevertheless, certain points become immediately obvious. Texts on certain topics in Ascher are entirely avoided by Büschenthal, notably those that involve flogging, execution, and dueling. There are also subjects in Ascher that Büschenthal appropriates entirely (hence a zero for the category in the above jokescape): those about Moses Mendelssohn; disputes with Christians; those about horses, riding, and postal coaches; and those about chess. (There are only two of the latter and one is also a Mendelssohn anecdote). Finally, there are a good number of "serious" texts in Ascher of which Büschenthal makes no use. The notion of a "serious" text is slightly ambiguous, but virtually all of Büschenthal's texts include some obvious comic element: a play on words, a trick, a retort, a piece of obvious stupidity. Only joke #37 in Büschenthal (#233 in Ascher) seems to be a serious account of a fraud perpetrated by one Jew on another. Other serious texts in Ascher concern the mutilation of a corpse by Jews (#202), the physical neglect by an archbishop of an injured Jew (#203), cannibalism (#204), the conviction of a Jew for avoiding a stone thrown at him by a Christian (#205), the instruction by a Jewish doctor who converted to Christianity that the money he earned fraudulently in his lifetime be returned at his death (#206), the betrayal (and consequent ushering to an early grave) of a generous and enlightened Jew by his brother (#217), other frauds perpetrated by one Jew on another (#219, #221, #224), and the true account of theft and murder by a Jew (#355). There seem to be no mitigating humorous motifs in these texts, and none of these texts finds their way into Büschenthal's book. Joke #236, however, which also unfolds as a serious account of fraud, does have a mitigating comic element in the final line, which is why I have not categorized it as "serious." Even so, Büschenthal does not use it. Except for that one serious text about fraud (#233), Büschenthal includes no others in his volume.[26] All other accounts of fraud in the collection include some comic element.

At the conclusion of Ascher's volume, there are five poems that address the bad character of Jews and their love of money or caricature Jewish hawkers and tradesmen (see chap. 4). Each of these verses has a comic aspect; nevertheless, Büschenthal makes no use of them, and they find no place in his collection. (They are translated at the end of those Ascher texts that Büschenthal did not utilize although without identifying numbers.)

Following the presentation of the jokes in Büschenthal's book, there are two curious appendices. The first is a short biography of the hard life and misadventures of one Nehemie (Nehemiah) Jehuda Leib, a Jew from Streikow (Stryków), Poland (see chap. 3), a town that came under Prussian rule with the Second Partition of Poland in 1792. The second is a firsthand account by Nehemie Jehuda Leib of the very same events (see chap. 3). The autobiographical account is longer and more detailed. Neither of the accounts contains any comic incidents or motifs. Nehemie states that he wrote his narrative to explain his actions to the court before which he was tried and condemned to a life of hard labor. He also states that he wrote his narrative in Yiddish and then translated it into German, a language in which, apparently, he was not fluent, as his account reveals numerous grammatical and punctuation errors. His narrative is dated June 6, 1790, in Saarmund and is followed by the phrase "Jüdische Unterschrift," that is, "Jewish signature," indicating that the original manuscript was signed in Hebrew letters.

Büschenthal appropriated these accounts of Nehemie Jehuda Leib word-for-word from Ascher. As it turns out, Ascher seems to have lifted these accounts— also word-for-word—from *Kriminalgeschichten: Aus gerichtlichen Akten gezogen* (Stories of criminals: Drawn from court records) published in Berlin in 1792.[27] Neither Büschenthal nor Ascher offers any explanation for the inclusion of these biographical materials in their books.

There is, however, some thematic connection between Büschenthal's joke collection and Nehemie's biography and autobiography. The biographies show

how oppression created the necessity that led to Nehemie's crime and subsequent punishment. Part of that oppression was the result of his employers—Jewish employers—who did not pay him what they owed and even had him arrested when he tried to leave their employ. But a part of Nehemie's problems stemmed from the body tax (*Leibzoll*) Jews had to pay when entering and leaving towns and cities or crossing jurisdictional boundaries.[28] As Nehemie followed his employers, who had abandoned him without funds, he could not afford to pay these taxes. He repeatedly had to pawn his clothes. This need induced him to rob a Jewish traveling companion, which led to his downfall. Indeed, the chapter title in the *Kriminalgeschichten*—which neither Ascher nor Büschenthal cite in their accounts—is "Raub, von einem Juden verübt, um den Leibzoll bezahlen können" (Robbery perpetrated by a Jew in order to pay the body tax). If this theme is the justification for including these narratives in his joke book, Büschenthal could easily have made that connection clear. Nevertheless, if the Jews are driven to their crimes and misdemeanors by persecution, it is a curious object lesson that it is not Gentiles but Nehemie's fellow Jews who are portrayed in this account as his most constant oppressors.

Büschenthal's publisher, Heinrich Büschler, was an established and prolific enterprise in Elberfeld in the early decades of the nineteenth century. They published books on German history (including school books), religion, travel (pilgrimage), education, logic, and even midwifery. But they published Büschenthal's book "in Kommission" and thus were only the distributors of the book with no involvement or investment in its editing or production. There is no evidence that they published any other books in this period dealing with Jews or Jewish subjects. Perhaps Büschenthal's book was printed at the newspaper where he was said to have worked in Elberfeld and was then contracted to be distributed by H. Büschler.

It is also possible that Büschenthal published his largely pirated book of Jewish jokes because he actually wanted to *revise* the publication of Judas Ascher and *replace* it with his own. Büschenthal might have felt that Ascher's publication contained too many texts that not merely depicted Jews in a poor light but, in some cases, vilified them. So Büschenthal may have set out to rewrite Ascher's book by incorporating new jokes that displayed the wit and ready repartee of Jews (#1–26) while editing out the more odious anecdotes. This might explain why Büschenthal seems to have had no compunctions in appropriating so many of Ascher's texts word-for-word, and why Büschenthal did not even acknowledge *Der Judenfreund* as a source of his material. He might not have wanted to call attention to Ascher's publication. The data that speak against this hypothesis are those texts in Ascher that Büschenthal did not incorporate into his own volume that could also have been used to demonstrate the penchant of Jews for witty comments, clever retorts, and silly and unthreatening behaviors (e.g., jokes #231,

#251, #263, #269, #271, #288, #307, #325). Why did Büschenthal not appropriate these texts in his book as well?

If the Jewish joke is one conceptualized as a joke associated with and distinctive of the Jewish people, what we have in Büschenthal's *Sammlung* is an early collection of Jewish jokes—perhaps the first that can be attributed to an identifiable author. Whether the jokes are truly distinctive is less important than the fact of the characterization itself. At the time Büschenthal compiled his collection, a connection had been made in the wider German culture between Jews and wit, if only in a negative, indeed insidious, way. As it stands now, the notion that Jews have a distinctive body of jokes, jokes that are reflective of their character and sensibilities, seems to first come about in Germany—not eastern Europe. Furthermore, the connection between jokes and the Jews is first made by those who are a part of the Jewish Enlightenment and not by those who were enmeshed in traditional religious communities and worldviews.

Büschenthal also offers the first published theory of the Jewish joke. His theory is rooted in the character of the Jews themselves: oppression creates necessity and weakness, which in turn give rise to cunning—the mother of wit (1812, iii; chap. 3, foreword).[29] Cunning, however, is not merely the basis for the wit of a joke; Jewish cunning and deceit are explicitly depicted in many texts in the collection itself. That is why, from Büschenthal's perspective, they can serve as a characterization of the Jewish nation. In the mid- to late twentieth century, commentators would also point to oppression as the source of the Jewish joke and Jewish humor, but these later commentators would see that oppression as kindling either an irrepressible Jewish spirt that allowed Jews to laugh despite their circumstances or regard that oppression as creating a humor that would serve as a mode of consolation for a suffering people. Twentieth-century commentators did not and would not have conceived of that oppression as giving rise to a cunning and deceitful national character, a character that was then reflected in their humorous stories.

What needs to be grasped, however, is that the deformed character of the Jew in the eighteenth and early nineteenth century was a viewpoint that was not only maintained by haters of Jews. It was accepted by advocates of Jewish emancipation as well as by their opponents. It was also accepted by many Jews, especially enlightened Jews, in this period. In 1767, two Jews from Metz wanted to open some shops in Lorraine, and they had special licenses to do so. The local authorities, however, refused to recognize their licenses. The Jews retained the lawyer Pierre-Louis Lacretelle to represent them (Schechter 2003, 78). In the course of making his case, Lacretelle argued that these Jews should be regarded as citizens, and he defended the morality of the Jews. But when he addressed the widespread belief that Jews regularly cheated Gentiles, he referred to the oppression of the Jews as the cause: "They have been . . . pursued in turn by calumny, hatred and fanaticism. . . . Ashamed of himself, and always brought back to himself by his need, he concentrates on the love of gold. . . . He cheats them [the Gentiles] with avidity, for he is pushed to do so by the necessity of living; he cheats them with joy for this is the only advantage he can obtain over them" (80). In other words, Lacretelle, who is pleading the cause of the Jews, unquestioningly accepts their perfidy, although he justifies it in terms of the conditions that Christian society has imposed on them. Almost twenty-five years later, at the time of the French Revolution, when the citizenship of the Jews was being debated, Abbé Henri Grégoire, who was one of the main architects of the emancipation of the Jews in France, wrote that the Jews were "contemptible," "frauds," "thieves," and "parasites." "No one has taken the art of deceit further than the Jews, and of lying in wait for misfortune, in order to fall basely on their victims" (88). Such words make it difficult to distinguish today the defenders of Jews from their enemies.

While it is not possible to say with certainty how Büschenthal viewed the Jews, a clue is perhaps to be had from one of his friends, Leopold Zunz. Zunz (1794–1886) claimed that he gave up the opportunity of a position as a rabbi in Breslau in favor of his friend Büschenthal (Meyer 1967, 214n13).[30] Zunz founded the Verein für Kultur und Wissenschaft des Judens (Society for Jewish culture and science) along with Eduard Gans and Moses Moser in 1819, the year after Büschenthal's death. The point of the society was to study Judaism from a scientific, philosophical, and historical point of view in an effort to foster the sense of Judaism as a culture and to integrate that culture into Western civilization. The society was also meant to suggest ways to reform Jewish character, the structure of Jewish society, and Jewish worship (Elon 2002, 110). In one of the first meetings of the society, Zunz—the only founding member of the society who did not convert to Christianity—outlined some of the problems that needed to be addressed, including that of the psychological constitution of Jews. According to Zunz, Jews believed they were chosen by God. They were conceited, superstitious, intolerant, too cerebral, physically lazy, hucksters, avaricious, greedy, and disdainful of science, and they believed it was permissible to cheat Gentiles (113). This is the description not merely of an enlightened Jew but a leader of enlightened Jews in early nineteenth-century Berlin. It is not necessary to impute self-hatred to Zunz or his colleagues in the society to explain such views. Nor is it necessary to accept this characterization as simply an introjection of the prejudices of what today would be called anti-Semites. It is possible, after all, that there were a substantial and visible number of Jews who did, in fact, cheat their Gentile customers and who did look down on their Gentile neighbors. Furthermore, as enlightened Jews, they were characterizing those Jews from whom they felt divorced both in spirit and world view. If their rejection was of traits they perceived to be characteristic of *others*—Jewish or not—it cannot be properly called self-hatred even if their characterization might prove to have been exaggerated or mistaken (Oring 1992, 134).

It seems likely that Büschenthal shared the views of his enlightened colleagues. He too would have been critical of characteristics spawned in the traditional Jewish communities of western Europe, though they were wrought by the forces of an intolerant, unjust, and sometimes brutal Christian society. While Büschenthal did not allow the more defamatory texts in Ascher's *Der Judenfreund* into his *Sammlung*, the jokes that he did include were, nevertheless, intended to hold certain Jewish behaviors—most notably, moneylending and sharp business practice—up for derision and ridicule. At the same time, he was careful to register the unjust conditions that engendered such practices. The volume as a whole could convey a message as well: there exists a population of Jews—Jews like Büschenthal himself—who understood such behaviors and characteristics to be immoral and unacceptable. After all, only a Jew who was alienated from these kinds of behaviors and who could laugh at them might attach his name to a joke collection such as this.

What is important about Büschenthal's *Sammlung witziger Einfälle von Juden* is not the answers that it provides but the questions that it raises. The discussion of Jewish jokes and Jewish humor to date has not entirely been an intellectual one. That is to say, it has not proceeded from a critical engagement with the question of what constitutes a Jewish joke, from a serious attempt to subject the corpus of what are designated as Jewish jokes to broad, comparative scrutiny, from a critical assessment of the reasons for the publication of the earliest collections of Jewish jokes, or from a scrupulous search for historical documents and sources. In general, what has been assumed is exactly that which remains to be proved: that the Jewish joke is something distinctive in the jokelore of Europe; that it is an outgrowth of an ancient tradition of Jewish humor in the Talmud, the rabbinic literature, and even the Bible; that it first crystallizes in the villages and towns of eastern Europe; and that it is a mode of defense and consolation. All of these assumptions *might* prove true but all remain to be convincingly demonstrated. To date, the Jewish joke as a concept has been largely celebratory rather than scholarly. We do not know nearly enough about Jewish jokes and Jewish humor, and what is needed is that scholars go out and learn. Hopefully, the translation and publication of Büschenthal's *Sammlung witziger Einfälle von Juden* will prove to be the first small step in this process.

Notes

1. For a thorough discussion of Freud and his relationship to Jewish jokes, see Oring (1984; 2003, 116–28).
2. They were aware, however, of the positive aspects of these jokes as well.
3. The arguments that are made for the presence of humor in the Bible are sometimes tortured: "The foremost and perhaps the only aim of the Bible is the moral improvement of the world, essentially an educational undertaking. . . . To achieve success, all verbal weapons are

permitted . . . [and] there is no sharper sword than humour. . . . Hence, humour is indispensable" (Radday 1990, 32).

4. Freud suggested that humor might display "a triumph of the ego," but the idea is certainly expressed by other commentators on the Jewish joke without the psychoanalytic framing (1960, 229).

5. See Davidson (1907, xx–xxi) on the reaction of the rabbis to parody.

6. This book is part of the YIVO Vilna Collections Project. Haim Schwarzbaum is aware of this book, but he does not appear to have seen it, as he seems to believe it to be a book of Jewish jokes (Schwarzbaum 1968, 87n60).

YIVO (Institute for Jewish Research) is based in New York City. It was established in Vilna (Vilnius) in 1925 for the study of all aspects of Jewish life. It moved to New York at the outbreak of the Second World War. Many of its collections were destroyed. What was recovered by the US Army was transferred to the New York site but much disappeared or was absorbed into libraries and archives in the various countries of eastern Europe.

7. The bibliography in Alter Druyanow's magisterial collection of Jewish jokes *Sefer ha-bediḥah ve-ha-ḥidud* (The book of the joke and the witticism) includes few references from before the twentieth century (1963, 3:392–403).

8. Nor do jokes appear in his *Gezamelte Schriften* (Collected writings), although children's songs do (An-ski 1920–25).

9. One exception would seem to be Hirsz Abramowicz's memoir, set in the period before World War I but composed around 1925 after he left eastern Europe. Most of his examples are about the ignorance of rural Jews in the jokes of townsfolk (Abramowicz 1999, 59, 64–65, 68–69, 83).

10. Minorities and stigmatized populations often transform negative epithets and images into positive—sometimes aggressively positive—characterizations and representations (Oring 1992, 130–32). See Moritz Saphir's own response to the term *Judenwitz* (quoted in Chase 2000, 242).

11. Some sources give his birth year as 1782 ("Büschenthal" 1840, 60; Heuer 1996, 353), but the obituary written by Leopold Zunz would seem to support the 1784 date, which is the one more commonly cited (Zunz 1818–19, 265).

12. The name changed to *Sulamith: Eine Zeitschrift zur Beförderung der Kultur und Humanität unter der jüdischen Nation* about the time Büschenthal began to contribute to it.

13. This was probably the bomb attack on Napoleon on Christmas Eve 1800 that killed twenty-six people but missed the carriage in which Napoleon was riding (Broers 2014, 255).

14. Ascher does refer, however, to "his fellow believers" in the foreword of his book.

15. Sander Gilman wrote a book analyzing the image of the "smart Jew," but his sources for the image start only in the late nineteenth century (Gilman 1996, 33–59). Gilman is aware of Büschenthal's book but does not consider it a relevant source (2012, 58). François Hell (1731–1794) mentions the "wit and false taste of the Jews" in his diatribe against the Jews published in *Observations d'un Alsacien sur l'affaire présente des Juifs d'Alsace* (Observations of an Alsatian on the present matter of the Jews of Alsace) in 1779, and Philippe-François de Latour-Foissac makes the claim that no one has "ever doubted their [the Jews'] intelligence" in his *Cri du citoyen* (Outcry of a citizen), an ambivalent defense of the Jews, published in 1786 (quoted in Schechter 2003, 70, 78).

16. Büschenthal also claims that for the same reason, women have had resort to deceit, but he does not ask why women were not likewise considered fonts of wit and humor.

17. I classified all these jokes on a least two separate occasions, and the results were not identical.

18. Joke #43, about an illustration of Moses, is something of an exception, although Moses is not really a character in the joke.

19. Except for joke #70.

20. Jokes #95 and #96 involve Jewish mothers, but they are really about Jewish pretensions to aesthetic sensibilities and refined taste.

21. There is one joke about a beggar (#29) and a joke about Jews borrowing money and escaping or attempting to escape repayment (joke #90), but that is not the same as a *Schnorrer*, who earns his living from begging.

22. Joke #26 is about a restaurant in an inn.

23. Joke #23 is about a Jewish stutterer although he is not the target of the joke. Mendelssohn's hunchback and stutter is mentioned, and Mendelssohn makes a joke of it by comparing himself to both Aesop and Demosthenes (#68). These traits, however, are uniquely Mendelssohn's and are not attributed to Jews in general. There are no jokes in Büschenthal about Jewish noses, limps, bleary eyes, sexuality, diabetes, or other diseases.

24. They also traveled great distances to arrange marriages, but there are no texts in either Büschenthal or Ascher about arranging marriages.

25. Joke #66 in Buschenthal (#283 in Ascher) are analogues, but there are some differences in the texts.

26. The fraud that is described in this text is perpetrated by one Jew on another. Fraud is not something that Jews as a rule perpetrate against Gentiles, but something that scoundrels perpetrate against any available victim.

27. Earlier versions appear in Klein 1791, 131–69. The autobiography is the same as in Ascher and Büschenthal, but the biography is different.

28. This tax was abolished both in France in 1784 and Prussia in 1788. Joseph II of Austria abolished it in 1782, but it was reinstituted ten years later (Roth 1972, 1588–89). Even when the tax was officially abolished, it was often maintained locally or reinstituted under another name.

29. In 1834, Moritz Gottlieb Saphir would also claim oppression to be the mother of Jewish wit, but he saw that oppression as giving rise to sarcasm rather than deceit (Chase 2000, 242).

30. The 1906 edition of the *Jewish Encyclopedia* states that Zunz withdrew his candidacy for a position as the preacher of the Hamburg Temple, but there is no indication that Büschenthal went to Hamburg, though he was a preacher in Breslau (Singer and Hirsch 1909).

CHAPTER 2

The Jews in the Century of Büschenthal

LIPPMANN MOSES BÜSCHENTHAL was born in 1784, the middle of the penultimate decade of the eighteenth century. It was a century that initiated tremendous change for the Jews of western and central Europe. The changes were social, political, legal, economic, and religious. It took, however, more than a century for many of these changes to fully materialize, and there were many setbacks along the way. Furthermore, the changes were not evenly distributed: for example, the Jews first acquired civil rights in France in 1791, but they did not acquire comparable rights in Germany until almost a century later.

At the beginning of the eighteenth century, the Jewish communities of Europe continued in some ways that had been established in the Middle Ages. The communities were autonomous and isolated. They had their own leadership, judicial and governmental structures, religious schools, economy, and houses of worship. There was no integration of the Jewish community into the larger state. Relations with the political authorities were conducted through community representatives, the *shtadlanim* (sing. *shtadlan*; intercessor, lit. persuader, effort maker). Individual and community behavior was severely circumscribed. The obligation was to abide by the numerous restrictions imposed on Jews and to pay the multitude of taxes exacted from them by the free cities, the princes, and the emperor. Jews, for example, were required to pay a tax on crossing the border of a state or entering a town, a tax that was otherwise only paid on livestock (*Leibzoll, péage*). A Jew on the highway might be forced to pay a dice tax—a tax designed to atone for the casting of dice for Jesus's clothing at his crucifixion. This tax was only abolished in eastern France in 1784 (Roth 1972, 15:839; Elon 2002, 24–25).[1]

Jews were prohibited from engaging in a range of occupations although those occupations might vary in different locales. For the most part, Jews were forbidden to own land or engage in agriculture, they could not occupy posts in the army or civil service, and they could not go to a university. Crafts that required guild membership were closed to them. Overall, Jews were restricted to moneylending, banking, dealing in gold and precious stones, peddling, and commerce. Wealthy Jews engaged in these businesses on a large scale, and some of them became influential in the courts of various princes, kings, and emperors by offering credit, luxury goods, or provisioning armies. They were called *Hofjuden* (court Jews), and these men often served as *shtandlanim* for the community as well. Most Jews, however, engaged in petty trading in regional markets, and many roamed the countryside with packs on their backs hawking their wares. Not an insignificant number were beggars, and some were robbers and highwaymen (Elon 2002, 28–31).

Jews were also enjoined from living in certain areas. Any privilege accorded a Jew was granted only in exchange for some kind of payment. In Prussia, for example, a wealthy Jew might qualify for residence in a city like Berlin by making a substantial payment. Such Jews were "protected." These payments had to be renewed annually. In 1750, an ordinance differentiated between "ordinary" and "extraordinary" Jews. Ordinary Jews had the right of domicile, and they could bequeath that right to only one of their children who was then permitted to marry. Other children could not marry. Extraordinary Jews (the sense of the terms *ordinary* and *extraordinary* are the reverse of their American colloquial usage) were, in theory, the employees of ordinary Jews. They had the right of domicile; however, they could not bequeath that right, and their children could not marry while they were in residence. Their children would have to leave the city if they wanted a family of their own. Many ordinary Jews enlarged the list of their household members and staffs in order to make urban residence possible for other Jews. Often these extraordinary Jews were employees only in name, and they engaged in small trade on their own accounts (Dubnov 1971, 4:205–6).

There were also taxes on marriage licenses and certificates, and parents of a marrying couple were required to purchase and export goods from royal factories even if they lost money on the transaction. In Prussia, a porcelain tax was instituted where porcelain of a certain value had to be purchased from the royal factory on the occasion of a marriage, the buying of a house, or other significant occasion. The pieces that were purchased were not chosen by the purchasers but assigned to them by the factory (Dubnov 1971, 4:207).

Jews could not live anywhere in the city. In some cities, like Frankfurt, residence was restricted to a ghetto that they could not leave either at night, on Sundays, or on Christian holidays. A painting commemorating the murder of a Christian child, supposedly killed by Jews in 1475 with awls thrust into the boy's wounds, was installed by the Frankfurt municipality on the way to the ghetto. It was refurbished in 1677 and 1709 and was only removed when the bridge tower was torn down in 1801 (Keller 1966, 366).

Jewish ghettos were overcrowded, dark, and dilapidated, yet the dwellings were expensive. In Berlin, Jews were not confined to a particular area, but their population was closely regulated. In many cases, Jews might not be permitted to reside in a city at all. They might be permitted to enter for the purpose of business—as in Vienna or Strasbourg—but they could be prohibited from staying overnight. At best, they could buy a pass that allowed them to reside for a short period of time while they conducted their affairs.

As in the Middle Ages, Jews could be expelled from cities or provinces en masse. While Jews were never expelled from the German states all at once as they had been from England, Spain, Portugal, and France, expulsions from cities and provinces occurred on a regular basis. In some sense, such expulsions also shaped occupational choices. Jews traded in money, valuables, and knowledge—extremely portable forms of wealth. Even when they were finally given opportunities to enter into new occupations, Jews were often reluctant to abandon their traditional livelihoods.

In 1744, Austrian empress Maria Theresa ordered the evacuation of all Jews from Prague by the end of January. The remainder of the province of Bohemia was to be evacuated by the end of June. Although the expulsion was delayed a month or two, Prague was emptied in the dead of winter. Thousands of Jews waited on the outskirts of the city until the June deadline mandated for the evacuation of the province as a whole. They had nowhere to go. Pressure was brought on the Austrian monarch by outside governments, and in 1748, the whole expulsion was reviewed and finally rescinded. A similar evacuation order was given to the Jews of Moravia, although the deadlines were extended and ultimately became moot with the reversal of the decree (Dubnov 1971, 4:193–97).

In 1737, in an effort to reduce the Jewish population of Berlin, Frederick Wilhelm I of Prussia decreed that no more than 120 Jewish families could remain in the city. Frederick the Great was equally antipathetic to an increasing Jewish population. With his conquest of the greater part of Silesia, he ordained that only 12 Jewish families could remain in the city of Breslau (Dubnov 1971, 4:203–4). The expulsions, the taxes, and the restrictions on Jewish marriage were efforts, in part, to limit the Jewish population. Yet with the continual wars of conquest, domains were occupied and annexed that contained large numbers of Jewish inhabitants. With the various partitions of Poland at the end of the eighteenth century, hundreds of thousands of Jews found themselves under Prussian, Austrian, and Russian domination.

Late in the century, several hundred Jews were to be banished from the city of Dresden. Moses Mendelssohn wrote a letter to a friend who was the head of the chamber of commerce there, and the expulsion order was rescinded (Dubnov 1971, 4:223). The Duchy of Mecklenburg was completely closed to Jews with some inroads being made only in mid-century. There were few Jews in southern Germany. The largest concentration was some four hundred families in the city of Firt on the outskirts of Nürnberg, a community that descended from the Nürnberg Jewish community that was destroyed in 1499 (225). Jews had been expelled from France in 1394. They began returning in the sixteenth century, but they came to the cities of Bordeaux and Bayonne as New Christians fleeing the Inquisitions in Spain and Portugal and blended into its economic life.[2] They eventually returned to practicing Judaism openly (Hertzberg 1968, 15–17). The Jews of Metz were acquired by France when the city was conquered in 1552. The largest population of Jews under the French crown were the inhabitants of Alsace and Lorraine, territories acquired by France in wars between 1567 and 1681 (Hertzberg 1968, 15–20; Dubnov 1971, 4:253; Roth 1972, 16:677). These Jews spoke Yiddish, and most would not learn French until after the Revolution (Hertzberg 1968, 140). For the most part, they were not permitted to reside in the body of France or even in cities like Strasbourg. On the eve of the Revolution, Jews constituted perhaps only 0.2 percent of the population of the entire kingdom (Schechter 2003, 7).

Jews were expelled from Bremen, Lübeck, and Elberfeld (in 1784), Warsaw (in 1788, when it was under Prussian control), and numerous other cities even into the nineteenth century. The first Jew was officially admitted to Sweden only in 1774. Jewish residency there was subsequently restricted to three cities—Stockholm, Göteberg, and Norrköping—and by 1803, there were sixty-nine families living in Stockholm (Dubnov 1971, 4:489–90).

While the previous discussion generally describes the situation of Jews in France and in the German states roughly between the Oder and the Rhine in the eighteenth century, there were places that were more and less favorable to Jews. Those Jews who found themselves in the Holstein city of Altona (a suburb of Hamburg but under Danish sovereignty) were permitted to build a synagogue, were given business licenses, and were protected by the Danish kings (Dubnov 1971, 4:488). Holland was religiously tolerant and became a haven for Jews who were expelled from Spain and Portugal or had fled the Inquisition. Jews in Holland had religious freedom and could worship openly, although they were barred from various occupations and were not allowed to enroll in state schools. On the other hand, the Jews of Rome lived in a ghetto, and they were required to pay the salaries of those who guarded the gates of the ghetto; wear distinctive clothing; support the "catechumen house," which prepared Jews for baptism; submit to compulsory preaching, yield to the forced conversion of their children; and submit to public humiliations during carnival (4:277–82). In 1775, Pope Pius VI proclaimed his "Edict against Jews," which restored many restrictions that had been eased in the course of the century so that Jews could no longer engrave their tombstones, recite the Psalms too loudly, travel through the city in carriages, or stay in resorts in the suburbs of the city (4:284). Misery is relative, however, as *conversos* were still being tortured and burned in Spain and Portugal well into the middle of the eighteenth century.[3] The Inquisition was not abolished on the Iberian Peninsula until after the first three decades of the nineteenth century (Keller 1966, 331–34; Hertzberg 1968, 268; Dubnov 1971, 4:302–6).

If the eighteenth century perpetuated some of the conditions under which Jews were compelled to live in the Middle Ages, new forces were at work as well. There was also a call for the emancipation of the Jews. Throughout the century, this call was intellectually engaged, though it was largely inconsequential as Jews were not granted rights as citizens in Europe until the very end of the century;

first in France after the Revolution, and in the two decades that followed in areas conquered by French armies in the Netherlands, German states, and Italy.

Already in the sixteenth and seventeenth centuries, there had been calls for religious toleration. Jean Bodin (1530–1596) opposed religious compulsion and held that matters of religion did not affect the state. In *Colloquium heptaplomeres de rerum sublimium arcanes abditis* (Colloquium of the seven about the secrets of the sublime), Bodin maintained that true religion is tolerant of all religions (Lindfors, "Jean Bodin"). In 1644, Roger Williams in *The Bloudy Tenent of Persecution, for Cause of Conscience Discussed in a Conference between Truth and Peace* argued for the freedom of religious conscience and for the separation of church and state. "The government of the civil magistrat extendth no further than over the bodies and goods of their subjects, not over their souls" (Williams 1644, 202–3). Many of the early calls for religious toleration were prompted by the wars between Catholic and Protestants that culminated in the Thirty Years' War, a war that devastated continental Europe between 1618 and 1648 and caused, directly or indirectly, millions of deaths. To some extent, the argument for the toleration of the Jews was a corollary of the call for toleration aroused by internecine Christian conflicts (Hertzberg 1968, 20). The toleration of Jews was very much a sideshow, however. Jewish toleration was often a rhetorical trope in the discussion of Catholic, Lutheran, Calvinist, Anglican, and Dissenter toleration. If a case could be made for the toleration of Jews or Muslims, then toleration should certainly be extended to fellow Christians (Marshall 2006, 8).[4]

The calls for Jewish toleration were largely products of the eighteenth century and the Enlightenment. The term *Enlightenment* (*le Siècle des Lumières*; *Aufklärung*) was coined almost after the movement it was meant to designate was over, but the movement was characterized by the effort to establish knowledge on the basis of observation and reason—critical reason, not abstract rational speculation—rather than on revelation or ancient authority (Gay 1966, 139–40). There is no exact date for its beginning. Some would date its beginning to 1687 with the publication of Isaac Newton's *Philosophiae naturalis principia mathematica*, but it had clear antecedents in the works of Niccolò Machiavelli (1469–1527), Jean Bodin, Francis Bacon (1561–1626), Galileo Galilei (1564–1642), Johannes Kepler (1571–1630), Thomas Hobbes (1588–1679), René Descartes (1596–1650), Baruch Spinoza (1632–1677), John Locke (1632–1704), Pierre Bayle (1647–1706), and others (Gay 1966, 12–20; Gay and the editors 1969, 14–17; Pagden 2013, 29–64). Nature, religion, law, morals, and society were phenomena to be investigated and explained empirically and critically without recourse to supernatural or metaphysical postulates.

Enlightenment thinkers—*philosophes*[5]—held that the world was governed by universal principles and that these principles could be uncovered through rational inquiry. Deism, the theological outlook adopted by a number of philosophes, presumed the existence of a God who set the world in motion. After that initial creation, however, God no longer engaged in its operation or maintenance. The laws by which it operated might be discovered through reason. In this world view, there was no place for prophecy, miracles, original sin, confession, sacraments, prayer, or propitiatory ritual. These were simply superstitions. The philosophes were hostile to Christian superstition as well as Jewish. What was valuable in religion was what man might arrive at by the use of reason: generosity, compassion, truth, justice—the leading of a moral, virtuous life (Gay 1966, 38–40; Brinton 1967; Meyer 1967, 19–20).

Enlightenment thinkers also held that humans everywhere were essentially the same. Individuals were autonomous, rational, and moral beings. Differences that stemmed from local conditions could be overcome as these conditions were subjected to rational scrutiny. Humans were basically good, and humanity as a whole ultimately perfectible. By virtue of their basic equality, individuals should have the liberty to make their own political, moral, and aesthetic choices. Government should, to some extent, depend on the consent of the governed, and all should stand equally before the law (Lukes 1973, 5, 7, 20, 78; Honderich 1995, 236).

Consequently, Enlightenment thinkers trumpeted religious toleration. Like Bodin before him, John Locke felt that religious toleration was the mark of the true church. The care of souls was not the province of civil magistrates. The government's only concern should be preserving and promoting the life, liberty, and property of the commonwealth's citizens (Locke 1824 [1689], 5:9–11).

Enlightenment views were not necessarily widely shared, however. When Gotthold Ephraim Lessing's *Die Juden* (The Jews) was staged in 1754, it caused a stir. The main character in that drama saves a baron from highwaymen, exposes the baron's Christian servants as the robbers, and ultimately reveals himself to be a Jew. When the baron offers the Jew all of his wealth, the Jew asks only that his nation be judged "more mildly and less sweepingly" (Robertson 1999, 4–35). Critics found the plot implausible, for they could not believe that Jews could evince even "a modicum of virtue and honesty" (Keller 1966, 355). Lessing felt, however, that it was "barbarous to make a distinction among nations, all of whom were created by God and endowed with reason. . . . Only one who is inhuman or cruel is a barbarian" (356). Just two years before his death in 1781, Lessing would produce an even more forceful play—*Nathan der Weise* (Nathan the wise)—which depicted a wise, tolerant, and virtuous Jew as its central character.[6]

Being a philosophe did not necessarily guarantee a favorable attitude toward Jews. While Voltaire (1694–1778) declared that Christians should stop persecuting and exterminating Jews and wrote scathingly of the Inquisition, he had a fierce antipathy for Judaism. It was rooted in his sense of the Bible as the book of a particularistic religion, steeped in unreason, and which depicted Hebrews committing the most barbarous behaviors. The Bible was the basis for Christianity of which he was also thoroughly contemptuous. Furthermore, he scorned the Jews for their usury, exclusivity, and their inability to interact genially with other peoples (Chisick 2002, 588–89). He was disparaging and dismissive of the poor Jews of Alsace, "who sell old clothes . . . [and] are the greatest scoundrels who have ever sullied the face of the globe" (Hertzberg 1966, 284–85). Voltaire has one of his characters, Memmius, declare to Cicero: "I would not be in the least surprised if these people would not someday become deadly to the whole human race" (300). While on the one hand, Voltaire preached tolerance, even for Jews, he seemed to find them fundamentally intolerable as people (Sutcliffe 1998, 109).[7]

The Enlightenment directly affected the Jews as well. In 1743, Moses Mendelssohn (1729–1786) sought entry to the city of Berlin to continue the religious studies he had pursued with Rabbi David Fränkel (1704–1762) back in his home city of Dessau. Once in Berlin, Mendelssohn met Jews who helped him to learn French, English, Latin, Greek, and mathematics. With these tools, he read philosophy and began to compose treatises of his own. He gave an early manuscript to Lessing, whom he had befriended, in order to solicit his opinion. When he later asked what Lessing thought of it, Lessing gave him a bound copy of it. Lessing had turned it over to a third friend, Friedrich Nicolai (1733–1811), a bookseller, who published it. *Philosophical Dialogues* (1755) was applauded not only for its ideas but also for its literary style. Other works soon followed. *Phaedon, or the Immortality of the Soul in Three Dialogues* (1767) became a best seller.

While Mendelssohn was not the first Jew to acquire secular knowledge, he was the first since Spinoza, whose philosophical works were widely read in Christian society. He was the first to publish in German. He achieved great celebrity and was called the "German Socrates." In 1771, Mendelssohn was elected to the Prussian Academy of Science, but Frederick II refused to ratify the election because Mendelssohn was a Jew. Scholars and thinkers visited his home or solicited his opinion through correspondence (Elon 2002, 39–40). For many philosophes, Mendelssohn was the proof of Enlightenment claims: all humans were capable of reason, were educable and perfectible, and shared equally in a common humanity.

Mendelssohn's work had a profound effect on Jewish society. His emphasis on the dictates of reason and of secular learning earned him the title "Father of the *Haskalah*"—Father of the Jewish Enlightenment. He was instrumental in advocating Hebrew—biblical Hebrew—as a language for literary expression and philosophical inquiry while demoting Yiddish as a jargon that diminished the moral character of the Jewish people. He translated the Bible with traditional commentaries into German—all written in Hebrew characters—so that Jews who knew no Hebrew could read it. (Most Jews could not read texts written in Gothic or Latin characters.) He supported the organization of a *Freischule* (free school) in Berlin for the education of Jewish boys with a curriculum that deemphasized the Talmud in favor of the Bible and that taught German, French, history, science, and mathematics.

David Friedländer (1750–1834), a protégé of Mendelssohn, sought to make German the language of instruction, to teach only ethical portions of the Bible, and to educate boys and girls together (Roth 1972, 7:1439). Under Mendelssohn's supervision, Friedländer composed a German translation of the Hebrew prayer book, although it was not published until after Mendelssohn's death. By the end of the century, Friedländer had become a spokesman for the Prussian Jewish community. Ultimately, he became something of a deist dedicated to the pure monotheism of Moses without the ceremonial law, which he felt was not a product of reason but of historical circumstance.

Friedländer imagined that enlightened Jews and Protestants might unite around this religion of reason as both were rooted in morality. In an anonymous, open letter, he even suggested to the enlightened pastor Wilhelm Abraham Teller, who was head of the Berlin Consistory of the Protestant Church, that Jews might join the Lutheran Church if they were not required to recognize the divinity of Christ or undergo baptism. His proposal aroused a great deal of debate but was ultimately rejected. Friedländer advocated reform of the Jewish liturgy and was a precursor—as was Haskalah ideology in general—of the Reform Judaism that was to arise in Germany in the nineteenth century (Meyer 1967, 70–78; Roth 1972, 7:177–179; Elon 2002, 73–74).

Mendelssohn remained an observant Jew throughout his life. He kept the dietary laws, celebrated the Sabbath and holidays, and heeded the commandments. He consistently defended the Jewish religion and the Jewish community in his writings, and he worked together with the rabbis of Berlin. In 1763, the community exempted him from taxes for life, and he was eventually appointed *parnas*—a community leader (Roth 1972, 11:1139). But the Haskalah was, both in the near and the long term, a threat to traditional Jewish practice. A religion measured against a standard of reason, with scientific and philosophic forms of knowledge and practice elevated to the same rank as revealed knowledge, is destabilized. If established means of social control are challenged—as Mendelssohn challenged the power of rabbis to employ the *ḥerem* (excommunication) on community miscreants—the ability of the community to maintain its cohesion is undermined. Unsurprisingly, many rabbis opposed Mendelssohn's thinking, opposed his Bible translation, and opposed all forms of secular learning. Even Mendelssohn came to sense that his views of Judaism might fall to a new Romanticism or fail even to survive the scrutiny of reason (Meyer 1967, 53–56; Roth 1972, 11:1341).

Mendelssohn did not envision Jewish emancipation as a program of assimilation (although that is how many Enlightenment thinkers conceived of Jewish emancipation [Hertzberg 1968, 335–336; Goldschmidt 2007, 58]). Mendelssohn imagined that Jews would achieve freedom as a people but remain rooted in their historical past (Goldschmidt 2007, 30–31). Nevertheless, some 200,000 Jews would convert in the latter decades of the eighteenth century and throughout the nineteenth century (Roth 1972, 8:712). By the mid-nineteenth century, only four of Mendelssohn's own fifty-six descendants remained Jews (Elon 2002, 208).

In the course of the eighteenth century, the condition of the Jews became a preoccupation of the state. Kings and princes recognized that the economic condition of their realms depended on the presence of Jews. Expulsions of Jews occasioned an overall decline in local economic conditions. Furthermore, court Jews proved to be indispensable to kings and princes for economic advice, the creation of credit, and the provisioning of armies. Rulers were also influenced by the Enlightenment, and Frederick II the Great of Prussia was considered a philosophe. He preferred French to German and composed literary works in French. He was a patron of the arts and invited artists and intellectuals, including Voltaire, to his court. He was also a gifted musician and composer. An absolute monarch, he nevertheless established a judicial code, eliminated torture as a means of judicial inquiry, eliminated press censorship, and proclaimed a tolerance for all religions. An astute political and military strategist as well as an intrepid battlefield commander, Frederick trained an army that was the most formidable in Europe, and he prosecuted a series of wars, more or less successfully, that greatly increased the size and geopolitical stability of the Prussian kingdom (Edith Simon 1974, 7:702–6).

While aware of the economic utility of Jews, Frederick was also wary of them and thought they were best confined to border regions where their commercial usefulness could best be realized (Stern-Taeubler 1949, 134–35). He endeavored to strictly control the Jewish population in Prussia in terms of its size and the occupations in which its members could engage so that Christian enterprises would not be disadvantaged. Consequently, in 1744 he allowed only twelve privileged Jewish families to remain in Breslau, which he acquired in the War of Austrian Succession (Dubnov 1971, 204). In 1750, he drafted a charter for the Prussian Jews (not promulgated until 1756) that strictly controlled the Jewish population of Berlin. It was this charter that distinguished between ordinary Jews, who could bequeath their rights of residence to one of their offspring, and extraordinary Jews, who could not. Manual trades were forbidden, and Jews could not deal in wool, hides, dyed leathers, or tobacco, although they were allowed to trade in certain luxury items like gold, jewels, and silver embroidery, for which there were no guilds. Jews could not peddle wares in cities except at times of a fair. Strict limits were placed on the interest that could be paid for loans. Foreign Jews were to be excluded from Prussia unless they could show a fortune of at least ten thousand reichsthalers and pay a fee. Jews were, however, permitted to maintain their schools, cemeteries, and synagogues, although communal prayer in private residences was prohibited and the *Aleinu* prayer was forbidden on penalty of death (Rogow 1961, 136–49).[8] Only after much persuasion was Frederick induced to grant Moses Mendelssohn protected status, and then only as an extraordinary Jew with no rights for his family (Roth 1972, 7:114).

Calls for toleration preceded and were not the same as calls for emancipation. Toleration had two meanings. There was the general meaning that individuals and groups had the right to hold different religious opinions. The term also had a more specific legal sense. Tolerated Jews had no right to permanently settle in a kingdom and could not engage in economic activity except as the employees of protected Jews. To be tolerated, in other words, did not bestow rights of citizenship.

Full rights depended on emancipation. There were some early calls for the emancipation of the Jews. Locke, who championed religious toleration, also called for emancipation: "Neither pagan, nor Mahometan, nor Jew, ought to be excluded from the civil rights of the commonwealth, because of his religion. . . . The commonwealth, which embraces indifferently all men that are honest, peaceable, and industrious, requires it not" (Locke 1824 [1689], 52). In 1714, Irishman John Toland (1670–1722) in *Reasons for Naturalising the Jews in Great Britain and Ireland on the Same Footing with all Other Nations* defended the Jews against many of the calumnies with which they had been slandered and argued that whatever deficits they might have would have obtained for any nation forced to live under like conditions. Toland made a case for the naturalization of Jews on practical, religious, and moral grounds (Toland 1715). A Jewish naturalization bill was introduced into Parliament in England in 1753, although public opposition to it was so virulent that it was quickly withdrawn (Roth 1972, 6:754).

The question of emancipation would not prove to be a pressing issue for most of the eighteenth century in France, Germany, or Austria. Rights were granted to Jews, rights were withheld, and rights previously granted were revoked. But the question of the role of Jews was becoming a more pressing concern, not so much for humanitarian reasons but for raison d'état—to make them serviceable to the state. It was believed, however, that Jews could not be given equal rights without their acquiring *Bildung* (personal and cultural maturation) and *Tugend* (virtue). For those who did not completely reject the possibility that Jews might one day become full and productive citizens—and there were many who believed Jews to be utterly alien and unassimilable—the question revolved around whether *Bildung* and *Tugend* were prerequisite for citizenship or whether *Bildung* and *Tugend* would only develop with the granting of civil rights and the full and equal participation of Jews in the institutions of society (Sorkin 1987, 16–17, 23). Mendelssohn believed that only the granting of full civil rights was likely to result in the intellectual and moral regeneration of the Jewish community. At the same time, he was leery of patents that lifted certain restrictions on Jews because he feared they were basically designed to convert Jews to Christianity (Hertzberg 1968, 185). This was his feeling about the *Toleranzpatent* (Edict of toleration) of 1781–82 ordained by Joseph II Habsburg for Lower Austria ("Edict of Toleration").

Nevertheless, Joseph II's *Toleranzpatent* did allow Jews to send their children to Christian elementary schools to learn reading, writing, and arithmetic, and it allowed Jews to fund, staff, and equip their own schools to the same ends. Jews were also admitted to the university, which had the effect of creating a real, if small, Jewish intellectual class. The edict also removed the humiliating *Leibzoll*, as well as the requirement to wear distinctive kinds of apparel, and eliminated the double fees that Jews had to pay for official transactions. It expanded the range of arts and trades in which Jews might engage, although they still could not become master craftsmen and they were prohibited from engaging in enterprises that competed with established Christian industries. The granting of these rights was attended by the reduction of the autonomy of the Jewish community under its own leaders. Left to stand, however, were limitations on population and residence, the restriction on the inheritance of protected status, and the protection fees and extra taxes paid to the government. Also, the validity of all documents and contracts written in Yiddish or Hebrew was declared to expire within two years of the issuance of the edict (Edict 1782; Roth 1972, 10:219).

Almost at the same time that the *Toleranzpatent* was proclaimed, Christian Wilhlem von Dohm published *Über die bürgerliche Verbesserung der Juden* (On the civil improvement of the Jews), a book that defended the Jews and argued for their political equality. It was immediately translated into French (*De la réform politique des Juifs*). The French edition also contained a summary of Joseph II's *Toleranzpatent* (Hertzberg 1968, 185). Moses Mendelssohn, who had been approached by the leaders of Alsatian Jewry to intercede on their behalf, urged von Dohm to write the book, believing that a defense from the pen of a Christian would be more persuasive than from his own. Von Dohm, who had already planned to write a defense of the Jews, agreed to write the essay.

Von Dohm's basic point was that there was nothing in their religion that prevented Jews from fulfilling their duties as citizens. Whatever negative characteristics might mark the Jews as a people—and these had been greatly exaggerated—had been brought about by the prejudices of the Christian community and the distortion of Jewish occupational life by edict, intimidation, and local prejudice. Any people subjected to the same conditions would have responded in the same way. The duty of an enlightened humanity is to see that the Jews are educated and given the same opportunities and responsibilities as other citizens of the state (Dohm 1957, 5–7, 9–22, 50–81).

It was in this social and political milieu that Lippmann Moses Büschenthal was born in 1784: two years after Joseph II of Austria issued his *Toleranzpatent* and Christian Wilhelm von Dohm published his defense of the Jews, two years before the deaths of Frederick the Great and Moses Mendelssohn, and five years before the event that was to most significantly affect the political status of Jews in Europe—the French Revolution.

Prior to the French Revolution, the Jews of Alsace were subject to royal decrees that both eased and exacerbated their condition. In 1784, the odious body tax (*péage*) was irrevocably rescinded. The crown declared that the tax was inhumane but that it also was a hindrance to commerce. At one point the king speaks of the Jews of Alsace as "*Our* subjects" only to revise the formulation to speak of conciliating "*their* interests with those of *Our* subjects" (Hertzberg 1968, 318–319; my emphasis). The king did affirm the position that once Jews were admitted to a district by a town or nobleman, their reception was irrevocable. At the same time, the king forbade Jewish marriages contracted without royal permission and ordered severe sanctions on rabbis who performed illegal marriages. Jews were allowed to rent and cultivate farms, but they could not live where rights of domicile had not been previously granted, and they were forbidden to employ non-Jewish labor. A census was ordered of the Jewish community with instructions to expel all from the province who could not prove their legal right to live there (319–21).[9] In 1787, Protestants were given the legal right to contract marriages, and since the term used in the edict was not "Protestant" but "non-Catholics," Jews hoped they too would benefit from the legislation. It was quickly decided that the act did not apply to Jews, although it indicated that citizenship in France did not ultimately depend on being Catholic (322–23).

The French Revolution proceeded in stages. The first stage was an attempt to refigure France as a constitutional monarchy. In May 1789, the king summoned the *États Généraux* (Estates General) in order to revise the tax system for a bankrupt France. The Estates General had not been summoned since 1614. The body represented the three estates: the clergy, the First Estate; the nobles, the Second Estate; and the Third Estate, the remainder of the population of France. The representatives of the Third Estate, which constituted half the members in this deliberative body, were largely lawyers, local officials, wealthy landowners, tradesmen, and industrialists. What was conceived as a body to reform the tax code was radically revised when the representatives of the Third Estate gained control of the process and reconfigured the body as a National Assembly, a body representing the people of France and not the feudal estates. When the king attempted to expel the assembly from meeting in royal apartments, the body reconvened on a tennis court and swore not to disband until they had given France a constitution ("French Revolution"). On August 4, 1789, the National Constituent Assembly completely dismantled the privileges of the First and Second Estates. It abolished the tithe, instituted equality in taxation, suspended and eventually abolished the judicial system rooted in the regional *parlements*,[10] and eliminated the manorial dues of the peasants.[11]

On August 27, the Assembly voted into law the *Déclaration des droits de l'homme et du citoyen* (*Declaration of the Rights of Man and of the Citizen*), which reflected the ideals of the Enlightenment. It formulated the notion of the natural rights of man, rights that were held to be universal and inalienable. These rights included freedom of assembly, freedom of opinion and speech, the right to property and security, the presumption of innocence, and the due process of law. It declared social distinctions to be obliterated except those based on skills and talent. It also declared the separation of legislative, executive, and judicial powers as basic to any constitutional society ("Declaration" 1789).[12] Despite the first article of the declaration, which asserted that "men are born free and remain equal in rights," the Jews did not thereby become citizens of France with equal rights.[13] It was decided in a long debate from December 21 to 24 that as some four thousand Sephardic Jews, largely living in Bordeaux, Bayonne, and Avignon (a papal city that came under the rule of the French crown in 1732), were already enjoying political rights as citizens—rights previously granted by the king—and were participating in the civil functions of their communities, the declaration should apply to them. There was considerable opposition even to this position, however.[14] The debate was unruly, and the measure passed on January 28 with 374 to 280 votes (Hertzberg 1968, 1, 339–43).[15]

The Jews of Alsace were another matter entirely. The arguments for and against emancipation were not new. Those in favor of emancipation maintained that the Jews were men first and Jews second and their degraded condition and deformed character were the result of centuries of oppression. Once they attained civil and political equality, they would become loyal and productive citizens. Furthermore, having given full citizenship to the Sephardim, who had long proved their worth, there was no basis for withholding the rights and duties of citizenship from the Jews of eastern France. It was against the articles of the *Declaration of the Rights of Man and of the Citizen* to regard them as alien and subject to special obligations and restrictions. Reason demanded that the Jews be made equal in order to complete the Revolution. The mission of the Revolution is "not to use men as you find them, but to make of them what you require them to be" (Hertzberg 1968, 363).

The arguments against emancipation—which came from both the extreme right and the extreme left—were that Judaism was not a confession but a nationality. Jews constituted a nation within a nation. It was not oppression but their superstitions, separateness, and character that made them utterly alien. Jews hated Christians and could never accept them as brothers and fellow citizens. What had happened to the Jews over the ages was their own fault. They were the "vilest people in the world." Furthermore, their usury and cheating—which had placed an extreme burden on the peasantry of Alsace—was innate both to their religion and character and could never be overcome. Even were they to give up their superstitions, their character had been so indelibly stamped as to make them unassimilable (Hertzberg 1968, 343–68 passim).[16] The municipalities of Alsace were strongly opposed to emancipation (Schwarzfuchs 1979, 11).

Although many Jews wanted to maintain the corporate character of their communities, Jewish leaders recognized that their special institutions would have to be abandoned if they were to gain civic and political equality. And they were willing to do so (Hertzberg 1968, 345). Those Frenchmen who were the chief supporters of the emancipation of all Jews—Abbé Grégoire (1750–1831) and Honoré Gabriel Riquetti, Comte de Mirabeau (1749–1791)—allowed the motion for the emancipation of the Jews of eastern France to be tabled in the Assembly because they knew they did not have the votes to pass it. Repeated attempts to reopen the motion failed, even on January 18, 1791, when Abbé Grégoire was in the chair as president of the Assembly (340). The emancipation of the Jews of France would eventually occur, but not until September 28, 1791, two years after the *Declaration of the Right of Man and of the Citizen* (Margolis and Marx 1927, 610; Hertzberg 1968, 339–40).

The immediate consequence of the emancipation of the Jews was their redistribution within the territory of France. Jews, theoretically, could now live in any city or region of the country. Following the emancipation, Strasbourg, which had prohibited residence to Jews, had a substantial Jewish population (Dubnov 1971, 6:540). The guilds were destroyed, and Jews were free to pursue any occupation, although they largely continued to pursue the ones they had traditionally practiced. Jews were eligible for public office, government employment, and army service. This is not to say that what the law permitted could be realized in fact. Local opposition often remained intense and there were efforts to maintain older discriminatory practices. But it was a milestone for change in the status of Jews in France. Beginning in 1792, the idea and the legislation of equality was carried into large parts of Europe by the revolutionary armies and the armies of Napoleon (Roth 1972, 7:156–58).

General A. P. de Custine, who conquered areas on the west bank of the Rhine, announced his intention to see to the equality of the Jews in the region (although the legal enactment did not occur until 1797). In 1796, French troops under Napoleon invaded northern and central Italy and declared the emancipation of the Jews. In 1798, they entered Rome, declared a republic, and carried off Pope Pius VI as a prisoner. The walls of the ghettos were torn down and Trees of Liberty planted, particularly in the Jewish quarters (Margolis and Marx 1927, 611; Roth 1972, 7:155–57; 12:823–24). The Jews of Holland were granted full rights, as were the Jews of the Cisalpine (1797) and the Helvetic republics (1798).

The expansion of French control of territory east of the Rhine under Napoleon, general, first consul, and eventual emperor, emancipated Jews and serfs in German lands. Guilds were abolished. The defeat of Austria and its Russian allies allowed Napoleon to redraw the map of Europe. He established kingdoms, duchies, grand duchies, and principalities under the reign of close relatives or client rulers. In 1806, Napoleon created the Confederation of the Rhine, consisting of

German states formerly part of the Holy Roman Empire under Francis II of Austria. The Holy Roman Empire was formally dissolved. With the defeat of Prussia, more states were added to the confederation.

Among the states of the confederation was the Grand Duchy of Berg—its capital at Düsseldrof—which included the town of Elberfeld (LeFebvre 1969, 231). Elberfeld had excluded Jews from residence in the town in 1794 (Roth 1972, 16:677). With French hegemony and the introduction of the Code Napoleon, Jews were permitted to reside anywhere. It was in Elberfeld that Lippmann Moses Büschenthal worked editing a newspaper and where his joke book was published in 1812 (Killy 1995–2003, 2:213).

Numerous odes were composed in praise of Napoleon, and Jews were not the least of these poets (Schechter 2003, 210). Büschenthal wrote such odes (Goedeke 1938, 63). But Napoleon was a somewhat ambiguous figure in Jewish history. Having heard many complaints about the Jews when he rode through Strasbourg in January 1806, and particularly sensitive to the practice of usury, Napoleon convened an Assembly of Jewish Notables to answer twelve questions concerning Jewish communal organization and practice, polygamy and divorce, Jewish-Christian intermarriage, relations with non-Jews, obedience to the laws of the sovereign nation, rabbinic jurisdiction, and usury (Roth 1972, 3:671–675; Schwarzfuchs 1979, 68–77).[17] Following that assembly, Napoleon proceeded to explore the ways in which the Jews could be made part of the French nation. He called for a Grand Sanhedrin, with seventy-one Jewish representatives—rabbis and laymen—from the French Empire and the Kingdom of Italy. They met in Paris in February and March 1807. They affirmed that polygamy was prohibited; religious divorce could only follow a civil divorce; mixed marriage was civilly, if not religiously, binding; Jews must treat their country of birth as their fatherland and treat their fellow citizens as brothers; they must engage in useful professions; and the lending of money at interest, whether to Jew or Gentile, would be subject to French law (Roth 1972, 14:840–841). But Napoleon, in his zeal to incorporate Jews into the body of France, promulgated three other decrees on March 17, 1808. The first two decrees established a "consistorial system"—similar to that of Protestants—so that every department with more than two thousand Jews would be represented by a committee of two rabbis and three laymen. There would be a central consistory in Paris. It would be the job of the consistories to ensure that the resolutions affirmed by the Sanhedrin were adhered to as well as to represent the Jewish communities to the administration. No provision was made for the payment of rabbis, although Catholic and Protestant clergy were paid by the state. Jewish taxes, in other words, served to pay for the support of all clergy but their own (Schwarzfuchs 1979, 121).[18] Rabbis' salaries in France were not paid by the state until 1831 (181).

The third decree—which was known as *Le décret infâme* (The infamous decree)—basically undermined the economy of the Jewish communities of Alsace. While Napoleon lifted a one-year suspension of repayments of loans to Jews proclaimed in May 1806, he decreed that all loans made to minors without the authorization of their guardians, widows without the permission of their husbands, and soldiers without the permission of their officers were null and void. The amount of money lent to a Gentile by a Jew had to be confirmed by witnesses when the loan was contracted. Interest on debts higher than 5 percent would be reduced. A debt higher than 10 percent was deemed usurious and would be nullified. Repayment of legitimate, non-usurious debts could be extended as well. These directives also applied retroactively to debts incurred prior to the decree's proclamation. In most cases, however, it was not possible to prove that the full amount of money had actually been lent, which resulted in the economic ruin of Jewish creditors. It is estimated that one-half to three-fourths of the loans made by Jews were never paid back (Schwarzfuchs 1979, 125, 128). These restrictions, however, were not imposed on Gentile creditors.[19]

Furthermore, Jews could not change their residency unless they acquired property and moved into agriculture. They could not move into new areas and open businesses. All Jewish businesses required a license that had to be renewed annually. All businesses entered into without such a license were null and void. In some municipalities, the licenses were granted easily; in others, they were delayed (Schwarzfuchs 1979, 129). Jewish draftees, unlike other citizens, could not provide substitutes for their military service ("Décret infâme"; Schwarzfuchs 1979, 126). A final decree was added on July 20 that stipulated that all Jews must assume fixed family names, which could not be biblical names or names of towns, so that their movements could be monitored by the consistories and central government (Schwarzfuchs 1979, 127–28). The decrees of 1808 were to last for ten years, and they could be extended if there was no evidence of improvement in the moral status of the Jewish community—although Napoleon's empire did not last that long.

It is evident that Napoleon did not know all that much about Jews or the Jewish communities in France or in his expanding empire. What is clear is that Napoleon was willing to contravene the *Declaration of the Rights of Man and of the Citizen*, the French Constitution, and his own civil code by abrogating Jewish rights.

Napoleon's infamous decree was, at times, ignored, however. His brother Jerome, who was given the newly created Kingdom of Westphalia to rule, quickly introduced the consistorial system, received a Jewish delegation, and made Jews equal citizens of the kingdom (Schwarzfuchs 1979, 149–50). Baden had granted Jews civil equality in its new constitution of 1807 (Sorokin 1987, 29–30). Karl Theodor Anton Maria von Dalberg, whom Napoleon elevated to prince primate of the Confederation of the Rhine and Grand Duke of Frankfurt, promised a liberal constitution but delivered one in 1807 that allowed the Lutheran consistory to select rabbis, proposed Lutheran inspectors for Jewish schools, and maintained restrictions on Jewish marriages. While the constitution eliminated special taxes on Jews, those taxes were eliminated only when the recipients of those taxes were dead. When the Grand Duchy of Frankfurt was created in 1810, Dalberg granted equal political and civil rights to Jews and eliminated the ghetto, but only upon a payment of 440,000 gulden (approximately $28 million today) by the Jewish community (Schwarzfuchs 1979, 156–57; Elon 2002, 64).

In Prussia, there was also movement toward reform. After their defeat at Jena in 1806, Prussia made *Bildung* the basis of a reorganized educational system and the regeneration of the state. Ministers Karl August von Hardenberg (1750–1822) and Wilhelm von Humboldt (1767–1835) pushed to free the serfs and emancipate the Jews. In 1808, Jews were permitted to stand in municipal elections but were otherwise restricted in residence, marriage, education, and employment. In 1812, Prussia issued an act of emancipation declaring Jews with legal residence to be full citizens and opening occupations, including academic positions, to them. State offices remained closed, however, and the oath *more Judaico*, a special oath administered only to Jews in judicial proceedings, remained in force, as it did in France, until 1846 (Roth 1972, 13:1290–91; Schwarzfuchs 1979, 172–73).

The introduction of the Code Napoleon to the Duchy of Warsaw, which was created out of parts of Prussia in 1807 and enlarged by territory seized from Austria in 1809, had little effect on the rights of Jews. The duchy had negotiated with the French and justified the refusal to emancipate the Jews on the basis of Napoleon's infamous decree. Jewish rights to reside in the capital were rescinded, Jews were forbidden to buy patrimonial estates, and prohibited from selling liquor. Full political and civil rights were never established (Schwarzfuchs 1979, 161–63).

The retreat of Napoleon from Russia in the final months of 1812 triggered the War of the Sixth Coalition—Russia, Prussia, Austria, Spain, Portugal, Sweden, England—against Napoleon. In 1813, a greatly diminished Grande Armée was decisively defeated at Leipzig, and Napoleon was forced to retreat to France. France was invaded, and in 1814, Napoleon was made to abdicate and go into exile. With his exile (excepting his hundred-day return in 1815, after which he was defeated at the Battle of Waterloo), a quarter century of almost continuous warfare in Europe came to an end.

With the defeat of Napoleon, Jewish rights in Europe suffered as well. The walls of the ghettos in the Papal States that had been torn down by the French armies were resurrected. At the Congress of Vienna in 1815, at which the new balance of power in Europe was negotiated, the question of the status of Jews in the German states came up for discussion. The old laws against the Jews had been repealed under the French. Although von Hardenberg and von Humboldt proposed complete equality for the Jews, when the proposition was first introduced, the Bavarian representative initiated an infectious laughter that spread to the rest of the delegates (King 2008, 273).

An article about the protection of the Jews was finally inserted into the German constitution by Prussian chancellor von Hardenberg, diplomat von Humboldt, and Austrian foreign minister Prince Klemens von Metternich, but a later change of a preposition inserted by the representative from Bremen into the final document—from all the rights "granted *in* the several states" to "*by* the several states"—was to have outsized consequences. The German states were later able to argue that the rights bestowed by the French were not rights granted *by* the German states. Consequently, in many areas where the French had established equality, Jewish rights were rolled back. Former Hanseatic towns like Bremen and Lübeck again expelled their Jewish populations. The 1812 constitution in Prussia, which von Hardenburg and von Humboldt worked so hard to see enacted, but to which King Frederick Wilhelm III had never been committed, was allowed to lapse (Elon 2002, 95; King 2008, 272–74). The Jews of Frankfurt had their civil rights revoked and the 440,000 gulden paid for those rights were declared forfeit (Elon 2002, 108). After Napoleon's *décret infâme* had ended in France with the Bourbon restoration, it was instituted by Prussia in the Rhineland (Roth 1972, 13:1291).

In the wake of Napoleon's defeat, considerable hostility arose in many German states and cities toward the idea of Jewish civil and political rights. There was the reflexive reaction against anything that Napoleon had instituted. Although Jews had enlisted in the Prussian army in the fight against Napoleon, their patriotism did not necessarily redound to their benefit. The widows of Jewish soldiers killed in battle could not collect pensions, and those soldiers who did survive the war were not eligible for government positions (Elon 2002, 96).

Furthermore, by the end of the Napoleonic era, the Romantic reaction against the Enlightenment was firmly established. Emotion and sensibility came to supplant reason as the more authentic and more profound response to art and the world. While Romanticism began as a literary and artistic movement—indeed, Büschenthal himself was a Romantic poet—and although there was nothing essentially anti-liberal about the movement, the romantic-nationalistic program formulated by Johann Gottfried von Herder (1744–1803) had significant political effects. Herder argued that each people was distinct and the product of their own particular history and environment. There could be no set of universal laws, beliefs, or customs congenial to societies with different origins and territories.

Herder was no racist, but his notions fed into conceptions of national distinctiveness and consequently to the stigmatization of peoples who, by virtue of their history and geography, could not be participants in the spirit of the nation. In the past, the problem of the Jews had been thought soluble by conversion. The perfidy of the Jews was that they had not accepted Christ. With such acceptance, so it was believed, the Jews could be redeemed and assimilated. By the nineteenth century, however, the Jews were regarded as essentially irredeemable. They constituted a separate "race" with ideas and a character antagonistic to that of the nation (Elon 2002, 97–98). While the Jews in Europe had, for centuries, been charged with embodying all society's evils, Romantic Nationalism introduced a new theory and provided a new justification for regarding the Jews as alien, even those who had dwelled in the German lands for centuries. *Bildung* and *Tugend* could not change the Jews. *Humanism* and *cosmopolitanism*—core values of the Enlightenment—became terms of abuse, and these values were attributed particularly to Jews (Elon 2002, 104). Conversion would no longer suffice. As the poet Heinrich Heine said in 1825 after he converted: "No sooner have I been christened than I am cried down as a Jew" (Heine 1893, 145). The stain of Judaism had become ineradicable.

Lippmann Moses Büschenthal died in his mid-thirties on December 27, 1818. Some seven months later, the "Hep! Hep!" riots broke out in the German states. The riots began in Würzburg in Bavaria and spread throughout the Confederation of the Rhine as far north as Bremen, Hamburg, and Lübeck (Elon 2002, 102). They also spread to Odense, Copenhagen, Danzig, Königsberg, Riga, Cracow, and Prague and erupted in the countryside as well as in the cities (Roth 1972, 8:330–32).[20] The riots were named for the cry of the rioters, *Hep! Hep! Die Jude verreck* (Hep! Hep! Kill the Jews!).[21] Persons, homes, and property were attacked, and troops had to be called out—in some instances, in time, and in others, far too late. These were not strictly peasant or lower-class uprisings since professors and students seem to have been among the instigators (Elon 2002, 103). Except for Danzig, there were no riots in Prussia, and there were few in Austria (Roth 1972, 8:330). Philosopher and poet Friedrich Schlegel (1772–1829), one of the early Romantics and a witness to one of the riots, wrote to his wife that they were a return to the "wrong end" of the Middle Ages (Elon 2002, 102).[22] Riots against Jews would continue to break out in Europe throughout the nineteenth century, but overall, the position of the Jews in western and central Europe would improve. After fifty years, Jews would be completely emancipated in a unified Germany. Some sixty years after that, however, the spirit of the Middle Ages would return with a vengeance.

Notes

1. In some cases, the Jewish community was literally regarded as the property of the treasury. In 1349, Charles IV of Bavaria mortgaged his community of Jews to the city of Frankfurt (Elon 2002, 24).

2. Before the Revolution, the Jews of France never constituted an organized community. Each local population constituted a community unto itself. There were no supralocal Jewish institutions. The rights of the Jews in each community varied. Even in the province of Guyenne, where the Jews enjoyed the most extensive rights, these rights were not necessarily

identical. The Jews of Bordeaux, for example, had rights of residence in Bordeaux, but the Jews of Bayonne were confined to the suburb of Saint-Esprit. Avignon was in a papal state where the Jews were subject to all kinds of prohibitions and restrictions. The Jews of Nancy in Lorraine could live anywhere although the majority lived on one particular street. The various communities were often in competition, and the Portuguese Jews of Guyenne often tried to differentiate themselves from the Jews of Alsace (Posener 1945, 199–204).

3. *Conversos* were Jews of the Iberian Peninsula who had converted to Christianity under threat to their lives or of expulsion. If it was believed they had, in secret, continued or reverted to their Jewish practices, they could be tried as heretics by the Inquisition and turned over to the secular authorities for execution.

4. In some ways it was easier to tolerate Jews and Muslims—those who had never known or found their way to Christ—than to tolerate those who had known the truth and had become "heretics" and "schismatics" (Marshall 2006, 8).

5. The world was French but the concept was international.

6. The character of Nathan was modeled on Moses Mendelssohn, whom Lessing had befriended in 1754.

7. There are those who believe that the greater part of Voltaire's antipathy to Judaism was based on his antipathy to the church and that he used Judaism as a way to attack the church (Posener 1945, 198); others thought Voltaire was an anti-Semite *avant le mot*. When philosophes sought to defend the Jews, they cited Montesquieu's *De l'esprit des lois* (*The Spirit of the Laws* [1748]), never Voltaire. Those who attacked the Jews, however, invariably quoted Voltaire (Hertzberg 1968, 287–90).

8. The *Aleinu* prayer was believed to contain an insult to Jesus. The idea was promulgated by Jewish apostates in different centuries (see Roth 1972, 2:557–58).

9. The census showed a total population of near twenty thousand individuals while in reality there were probably more than twenty-five thousand. In 1786, the expulsion order was suspended until 1788. It was issued by the Sovereign Council of Alsace at the end of 1788, but it was further delayed in 1789 to avoid expelling the Jews in the middle of winter. By the end of that year, the issue was moot since the Revolution was by then in progress (Hertzberg 1968, 321–22).

10. There were thirteen *parlements* under the *ancien régime*. These were not local legislative bodies but appellate courts composed of judges. Official edicts did not become law until a *parlement* consented to publish them ("Parlement").

11. Originally the peasants were supposed to compensate the nobles for the loss of their land, but in 1793, that obligation was voided so that a quarter of the agricultural lands of France had passed into peasant hands without indemnification ("French Revolution").

12. The *Declaration of the Rights of Man and of the Citizen* drew heavily on the constitutions of the American states, particularly Massachusetts, Virginia, Maryland, North Carolina, Vermont, and New Hampshire (Declaration 1789).

13. To participate in political rights, one had to be a French male over twenty-five years of age who paid at least three days' labor in taxes and was not a servant. Rights were granted only to "active" citizens and excluded women, slaves, children, and foreigners. Jews were considered foreigners—"passive" citizens. Even Protestants had not been given full political rights by the declaration (Hertzberg 1968, 341).

14. Although the "Portuguese Jews" of southern France have often been depicted as integrated into French society, expulsion orders against them had been issued in 1734, 1740, 1760, and 1772 (Shechter 2003, 28).

15. Violence against Jews broke out in Alsace as the *Declaration of the Rights of Man* was being debated in the Assembly in 1789, and there was a near riot in Bordeaux when the

emancipation of the Sephardic Jews was announced. The national guard had to intervene to stop it (Hertzberg 1968, 340–41, 343; Schechter 2003, 28).

16. The clergy felt that only after Jews converted to Catholicism might they merit civic equality (Hertzberg 1968, 351).

17. While Napoleon did not seem to know much about Jewish marriage practices in Europe, his question about polygamy may have reflected a broader concern about Jewish population increase. When in exile on Elba, he outlined a proposal to secure French colonies in America by promoting polygamy (Roberts 2014, 725).

18. After the Revolution, the state would assume the corporate debts of the Catholic and Protestant churches, but it did not assume the debts of the Jewish community. Consequently, the Jews were required to continue to pay off these debts, although community leaders no longer had the same power to command the necessary revenue.

19. A similar assault on Jewish moneylending occurred during the *ancien régime*. In 1777, François Hell, the bailiff of Landser, organized a counterfeit ring to flood Alsace with receipts showing that loans made by Jews had been paid. The royal government became involved and was concerned that if Jewish creditors were ruined, they would not be able to pay their taxes. They also discovered that most of the Jewish lenders were as poor as those to whom they lent. A government decree reduced the amount owed to the Jews and extended the time of repayment (Hertzberg 1968, 120–21).

20. For a map of the areas of the riots see Roth (1972, 8:331).

21. There are a number of folk etymologies for the word *hep*. Some believe that it was an acronym of *Hierosolyma est perdita* (Jerusalem is lost), a cry purportedly shouted by the crusaders. Apparently, a newspaper account of 1819 mentions this acronym, but it seems an unlikely derivation. Jacob Grimm lists the word in his dictionary as a cry made by goat herders. There are other etymological theories as well (Jacobs 1906).

22. This movement included the Schlegel brothers, Novalis, Friedrich Wilhelm Schelling, and others, including Johann Gottlieb Fichte, who nevertheless regarded the nation as a "mystical experience of the soul" and who stated that the only way for Jews to gain civil rights was to "cut their heads off one night and plant new ones on their shoulders that contain not a single Jewish idea" (quoted in Elon 2002, 98–99). Although his reference to cutting off heads was figurative, there were those for whom such an idea was literal.

Part II
THE TEXTS

CHAPTER 3

Collection of Witty Notions from Jews as a Contribution to the Characterization of the Jewish Nation

Recorded by L. M. Büschenthal.
Published by H. Büschler by commission, Elberfeld, 1812.

Foreword

Jokes and quick-wittedness have long been recognized as an attribute of the people of Israel. Therefore many have tried to describe these traits in their conspicuousness. But because one was for and the other against this nation, the result was a moralistic depiction instead of an intellectual one. The description always missed the mark because it had either too much light or too much shadow.

The editor of these pages believes that the selection in the current collection has been compiled with total impartiality, in that [iv] it includes what the Jewish nation has characterized as its mental nimbleness, regardless of whether the anecdote brings honor to the subject or not.

This collection of jokes will also confirm what we have often experienced, which is that understanding and wit are two very different things. There can be one without the other.

That Jews on the whole are as funny as they are, we believe, is due to their centuries-long oppression.

Necessity and weakness, as the feminine sex shows, gave rise to cunning. Cunning is the mother of wit since you find it more frequently among the oppressed and poor of the country Jews as opposed to among the rich and well-to-do.

∼

1. [5] One Jew calls another a rascal. He is called before the judge to recant. This he did saying the following: "I have maintained that this man is a rascal, which is true. But I also have to say he is an honest man."

NOTE: Landmann 1962, 150–51; Landmann 1972, 113; some resemblance to Sadan 1953, 150, joke #241.

∽

2. A young Jewish girl sat in a box in B—— Theater. A young, well-known libertine entered and was very familiar and pushy with her.

"Young man," said the young lady, "I think you have probably made a mistake."

"God forbid," he said, "I see you are a young lady," all the while becoming more impetuous and finally shameless.

The young lady, very outraged, used her tongue as only young lasses do. "Now, now," exclaimed the young man, "Don't devour me."

"Don't worry, young man," [6] she replied quickly, "I am a young Jewish lady, and we don't eat pork."

NOTE: Mendelsohn 1935, 39; Teitelbaum 1945, 281; Sadan 1950, 397, joke #753; Rawnitzki 1950, 1:24, joke #46; Druyanow 1963, 2:310, joke #1966; Spalding 1969, 200. In Mendelsohn the statement is attributed to Israel Zangwill. Druyanow states that the joke appears in a Russian joke book of 1809. For a similar scenario, but with a less chaste retort on the part of the woman, see *Joe Miller's Jests* 1963 [1739], 2–3.

∽

3. On the yearly anniversary of the death of his parent, a Jew must fast. A Jew visited another on the normal fast day, and found him—eating.

"How can you be eating; it's a fast day."

"Excuse me but I have a special memorial day for my father."

"That just means you especially can't eat!"

"Ha, ha, as if one could observe two fast days at once."

NOTE: Teitelbaum (1945, 287) told about a *ba'al ta'anit*, a man paid to fast for others; Druyanow 1963, 1:167, joke #534; 1:264–65, joke #822. There are a number of jokes on fasting—actually, failing to fast—in the joke literature. See Olsvanger 1931, 182–83; Mendelsohn 1935, 154–55, 159; Teitelbaum 1945, 284–85; Mendelsohn 1951, 62, 106; Mendelsohn 1952, 6, 48–49; Richman 1952, 130, 142–43, 169; Learsi 1961, 183–84, 294–95; Spalding 1969, 68, 231, 232, 233–34; Landmann 1972, 30. See Büschenthal joke #53.

∽

4. A Jew visited another, who loved to boast of his new magnificent home that he had just built. Hungry for applause, he showed the visitor around but couldn't get more than a nod out of him. Finally he takes him into the garden and asks, "Even here you have nothing to admire?" "Oh, yeah," he answers coldly. "The height"

NOTE: Ernst 1933, 134; Landmann 1962, 149.

5. [7] A Polish Jew came into the post office thirty miles from N—— and asked how far it would be to N—— if he took the mail. "That depends on the number of horses," said the postman. "With four you are faster than with two, with six faster than four." "Oh, my," said the Jew, "Let me take a hundred; then I don't have to leave!"

NOTE: Teitelbaum 1945, 287; Ausubel 1948, 336–37; Spalding 1969, 121. See Büschenthal joke #82.

6. A Catholic priest came to a Jew, who was building a thatched hut. "What are you doing, Hebrew?" "I am building a thatched hut, Mr. Pastor." "What for?" "In confidence, Mr. Pastor. We have a tradition that God gives his daughter in marriage at this time. And so each pious Jew believes that this ceremony will take place in his hut." "Ha, ha, what a simpleton Jew! God has a daughter? God has a daughter?" "Ha, ha, ha! At the clever Mr. Pastor! God has a son! God has a son!"

NOTE: The Jew is building a hut, a *sukkah*, for the celebration of the festival of *Sukkot* (the Festival of Tabernacles), which occurs on the fifth day after Yom Kippur, the Day of Atonement. One is enjoined during the holiday to sleep and eat in the sukkah. The last day of the festival is known as *Simchas Torah* (Rejoicing in the law) when the ritual reading of the final portion of the Torah is completed and the reading of the new portion in Genesis is begun again. In the rabbinical literature, the Torah is likened to the daughter of God and is betrothed to man (Freedman and Simon 1977, 2:352, 414, 423). The one who reads the final portion of the Torah in the synagogue is called the *ḥattan torah* (bridegroom of the Torah) and the one who reads the first portion in Genesis, the *ḥattan bereshit* (the bridegroom of Genesis). This may account for the idea that God gives his daughter in marriage on this holiday. It is not clear, however, why the joke states that the ceremony of marriage will take place in the sukkah, although the booth, in some respects, resembles a bridal canopy.

7. A Jew stood on a balcony with an iron railing. A Christian joker passed and called, "Hey, what's the difference between a Jew and an ass?" "No more than an iron railing," was the answer.

NOTE: This is an old joke that is sometimes attributed to the medieval Scottish philosopher Duns Scotus where the question put to the philosopher is: "What is the difference between a *Scot* and a *Sot*?" See *Joe Miller's Jests* 1963, 5, joke #18. *Znamenityj evrejskij shut Haskel' iz Berdicheva* 1902, 16–17; *Znamenityj evrejskij shut Gershko iz Ostropolya* 1902, 10–11; Shmerka i Shlemka 1906, 5–6; Teitelbaum

1945, 92. It is also a standard joke in the routine known as "The Arkansas Traveler"; see Bluestein 1962, 154. Vkontakte 2011.

~

8. The archduke of Mainz ran into one of the court Jews in his garden. "Haimann!" he called out, "if you can now tell me an impromptu lie, you'll get a wonderful fish for your holiday tomorrow." "Your eminence," said Haimann, "You had promised me two!"

NOTE: Mendelsohn 1935, 16; Ausubel 1948, 314; Richman 1952, 397; Druyanow 1963, 2:97, joke #1305; Spalding 1969, 69; lying contest in Landmann 1962, 230–31.

~

9. The Prince of D—— once met the Rabbi of B——, who was a very moody man, at a post office where the latter wanted to change his horses. The prince asked how the rabbi was doing, and started a very friendly conversation with him. "Tell me, dear Rabbi, does your job earn so much money that you can travel with the mail coach?" "My job?" the rabbi responded surprised. "With your permission, your honor, I have more to order [to give more orders] than you, your eminence." "How's that?" [9] the latter asked with a smile. "In the most natural way. Your honor gives an order with one word, a glance. I however, have to give orders all day long until something is done the way I want."

~

10. A Christian hypocrite, who was also an arch usurer, always wanted to convert a Jew. The latter was enlightened and was convinced that in principle all religions were the same. Once the former let drop a word that led the latter to assume he wanted to convert him. He called out enthusiastically, "I am convinced that you will finally become a Christian."

　Jew: "Perhaps I already am one more than you believe."
　Christian: "Really, how is that possible?"
　Jew: "Why not? I am already convinced that you are Jewish!"

~

11. On his way to market, a Jew passed a woman who was offering eggs for sale. He wanted to make fun of her and asked [10] how much an egg was. "One kreuzer," was the answer. "I'll give you two, if you allow me to choose the eggs." The woman was happy and went to let him choose. To keep the rejected eggs from being mixed up with the rest, the good woman had to cross her arms so the rejects could be piled there as high as her chin. He put twelve eggs into his bag and left. If she didn't want to drop all the piled up eggs in her arms, the woman couldn't

move, and she stood helpless in the face of the robbery. She screamed but the passersby just laughed instead of pitying her. An hour later the Jew, who only wanted to pull a trick, came back [and] gave her the eggs and a little compensation for the fright he had given her.

NOTE: The first part of this story is in Learsi (1961, 181–83), although the trick is played on a peasant who was known for his "arrogance and greed." While the peasant is holding the eggs, the protagonist, Hershele Ostropolyer, either slaps him or undoes the peasant's belt so that his pants fall. The tale continues as in Büschenthal joke #17. Slight similarity to Uther (2011) Type 1592B*: *The Deceiving Merchant*, where a merchant asks a buyer questions about ages of people and adds those numbers to the count of eggs.

⁓

12. During the time of the Republic, in a French border town a country Jew came to the passport office and wanted a passport to go to Germany. [11] Since he couldn't prove that he wasn't a conscript, he was denied. He became insistent and yelled when he was denied the passport, "I will do something —— [take a shit] in your Republic." "What, you scoundrel," said a zealous police officer, "You're going to do what —— in this Republic?" "Oh, God forbid," said the country Jew. "I don't have to? Then give me the passport, and I'll carry it over the border."

⁓

13. The common Jews do not call a man a man until he is married. Before that he is a youth or a bachelor. Once an old bachelor, who was rich and sixty years old, decided to marry. At the nuptials another said, "Tomorrow he will be an old man."

⁓

14. "You Jews are all damned," said a Christian to a Jew. "Why?" asked the Jew. "Because you crucified our Lord." "Tell you what," said the Jew, "When you find ours, crucify him too."

⁓

15. [12] Someone said in jest to a Jew, "How come you don't believe in the Son of God? Don't you always like to offer credit to the sons of rich parents!"

The Jew responded. "How can we give credit to the son when his father will live eternally!"

NOTE: Told about Mendelssohn in Sadan (1950, 409–11, joke #764); Rawnitzki 1950 1:28, joke #57; Landmann 1962, 535; Druyanow 1963, 1:xi; 2:319, joke #2003. For a Jew who learns to only take orders from the father but not the son see Gross (1955, 374–75) and Schwarzbaum (1968, 335–36).

16. A devious Jew came into the passport office in W—— where a distinguished, brutal man passed out the passports. "What's up," he brusquely asked the Jew.

"I'd like to get a passport." "When did *we* arrive?" [indirect address]. "Huh? Did your Excellency also sit in the car? I thought for sure I was there alone." "Does he know that he is an ass?" "Forgive me, your Excellence, but in our educated German language one no longer says, 'He is an ass.' Now it is, 'You are an ass!'"

~

17. A student in Prague met a fairly poor Jew and, without much ado, slapped him. The Jew quickly goes into his pocket and pulls out a little money [13] to give to the student. "What are you doing, Jew?" asks the student. "You are rewarding me for slapping you?" "Oh, dear sir, if you knew what a favor you did me, you would be surprised. We Jews live with the firm belief that he who gets slapped today by proxy loses all his sins and becomes a child of the eternal life. So you can imagine my surprise at your slap. Oh, I only wish I were a rich man, so I could reward you for the magnitude of your favor. A thousand thanks in the meantime." And with that he was gone.

Amazed, the student stopped, not knowing what to think. Suddenly he sees the most important among Prague's Jews coming out of the synagogue. And quickly he's made a financial plan. He goes to the head man, and without the man being able to stop him, he slaps him with all his might. Stunned, the man stops for a moment, with the student next to him, waiting for his large tip from the rich man. Barely the former comes to his senses, [14] he picks up the now equally surprised opponent, yells for help, and hands him over to the rapidly approaching guard. The next day the student is condemned to twenty-five on the backside and significant monetary damages. This is how the poor Jew avenged himself with his quick wit, albeit at the expense of a fellow believer.

NOTE: Richman 1954, 350–51; Mendelsohn 1952, 7; Learsi 1961, 181–83; Landmann 1962, 488; Spalding 1969, 53–54; Landmann 1972, 183.

~

18. A Jew found himself in the company of ladies and some elegant dandies of his faith. They were courting the ladies and made fun of him because of his shyness. So he stood up and spoke pathetically,

> To spend time with ladies,
> Does a man of honor do this?
> May they all go to the devil
> and I—should be the devil!

~

19. An elegant gentleman said to a Jew, "Do you know that Spain issued a decree that condemns to death all Jews and all asses that are on Spanish soil?" "Oh, no," said the Jew. [15] "We are truly lucky that we are both not there."

NOTE: Mendelsohn 1935, 44; Ausubel 1948, 436; Rawnitzki 1950, 1:25, joke #47, 1:57 joke #112, 1:76–77, joke #152; Learsi 1961, 304; Spalding 1969, 182. See also Landmann 1972, 195–96, and Büschenthal joke #28.

∽

20. The Jews generally complain about their oppression but don't want to give up the most ridiculous customs, which have largely caused them, and continue to cause them, this oppression. A funny Jew compared this behavior with the following story:

A country man drives his cow to water. But the cow spooked and wanted to get into the river. The countryman grabbed her by the tail and wants to hold her back, which of course doesn't work. Suddenly he is in danger of drowning and—still holding on to the tail—calls out for help. "Hey," another countryman, coming by quickly to help, yells, "Why are you screaming? Drop the dumb cow tail!"

NOTE: See Learsi 1961, 102. This is one of the jokes in the collection that relates to the *maskilic* (the Enlightenment) perspective that advocates abandoning superstitious, meaningless, or outmoded customs. The tale itself may be related to Uther (2011) Type 1849*: *The Clergyman on the Cow's Tail*, in which a clergyman ties the tail of the cow to his jacket while it is being milked. The cow runs away, dragging the clergyman behind. Büschenthal joke #20 is also one of the few examples of a story in the collection that is employed as a parable—a form very common in eastern European Jewish jokes and anecdotes.

∽

21. This same Jew said of another who worked to improve mankind, and who was impatient about the results of his useful suggestions, "This man is fattening a goose and at the same time feels her to see if she's getting fat."

∽

22. [16] A simple Jew was wondering how his young wife of four and a half months gave birth to a healthy baby boy. He mentioned his doubts to his rabbi. "Aside from that, do you really like each other?" asked the rabbi. "Oh, yeah, really. We live like we are in heaven." "So, be happy. The whole thing is only an error in calculation. See, you have your wife four and half months and your wife has had you the same number of months, which makes it exactly nine months." "Oh, I see," says the Jew joyfully. "Now I get it."

NOTE: Uther 2011, Type 1362A*: *The Three Months' Child*; Ausubel 1948, 331; Spalding 1969, 115–16. See a fifteenth-century analogue in Poggio (1968, 110–11) about a twelve-month child. Jokes in Ernst (1933, 111) and Druyanow (1963, 3:8, joke #2098) turn on the speediness of the groom rather than the calculation. See Büschenthal joke #58. Also Vysokovskiy 2004.

∼

23. A Jew was summoned to be a witness. As he stuttered, the judge said, "I think he is a rogue!" "But not nearly as much as you i—i—i— imagine," stuttered the Jew.

∼

24. A Jew, who stopped at an army camp and was brought to the general, revealed that he was afraid of the number of guns surrounding him. "Are you so afraid [17] of shooting?" the general asked. "Oh, no, only the hitting!"

∼

25. Between M—— and F—— was once a customs office where each passing Jew had to pay duty on his person [*Leibzoll*]. Once a Jew coming from M—— going to F—— stopped by this customs office but pretended he was coming from F—— and going to M——. He begged that due to his great poverty, he be allowed to pass without a tax. The customs officer, a very rough man, denied him very harshly and ordered another customs official to take him to the barrier from F——. As the Jew arrived there, no longer coming from the other direction, he called after his escort, "Please convey my most sincere thanks to the customs official for your company to accompany me to F—— where I wanted to go, as I really came from M——."

∼

26. It is well known that Jews cannot eat everything offered in a Christian restaurant [18] because they have to stick with certain dishes such as butter and eggs. Once a Jew came to a restaurant and since it was lunch time, ordered some eggs and a pint of beer. In the same room were some officers who made fun of the Jew's customs.

The next morning the Jew asked for his bill in the presence of the officers, which was so high that no officer had paid more. While the Jew complained to the innkeeper about the exorbitant amount of the bill, the innkeeper's wife comes in screaming that the rats had gnawed and bitten a beautiful cloth to bits. She said to the assembled crowd she'd give the world for a means to rid herself of this trash. "Dear lady," says the Jew, "I will give you the means, which, if you apply it immediately, is really the best." "And what is it?" said the woman eagerly. "Give each rat a bill like you gave me; then none will ever cross you threshold again."

NOTE: *Znamenityj evrejskij shut Haskel' iz Berdicheva* 1902, 14–15; Mendelsohn 1935, 55–56; Teitelbaum 1945, 261; Rawnitzki 1950, 1:106, joke #217; Richman 1954, 174–75.

~

27. [19] In —— lived a rich Jew who was a merchant. In his neighborhood there was a goldsmith and a clockmaker who all lived very comfortably with each other.

The Jew had a large quantity of valuable merchandise packed to send to the forthcoming fair.

The goldsmith and the clockmaker discovered this and made a plan to appropriate the merchandise for themselves. They came up with the following plan. They had a box made that was large enough for a human being to be comfortably locked up in. Then they went to the Jew and told him that they also had the intention of going to the next fair. But since it wasn't possible for them to keep their wares in their limited quarters, they asked him if he would be so kind that they might store a box in his house until it could be brought to the fair with his wares. They would gladly pay the transportation costs, and the box contained a number of different kinds of clocks.

[20] The Jew agreed to the proposition and told his people to accept the box when it was delivered. In the evening, the clockmaker had himself locked in the box, which was then delivered to the Jew and stowed in a convenient place. Late at night when everyone was asleep, the clockmaker opened the box from the inside. But a small dog was with the merchandise. He started to growl and finally to bark, so the clockmaker had to close the lid. When the dog was calm again, the clockmaker tried his luck once more, but at the slightest movement, the dog started to bark anew. On the third try, the maid also woke up from the repeated barking of the dog, and the clockmaker thought he'd been discovered and felt lost. He pulled back into his hiding place. In the meantime the maid got up, started the fire and lit a lamp. When the dog saw the maid, he ran around the box, growling and barking.

[21] With all of this commotion, the Jew also finally awoke. He jumped out of bed and asked the maid what the barking of the dog and her getting up meant. The maid said, "I don't know what is up with the dog, but he is barking constantly and sniffing the box that came last night. Heaven only knows what's in that box." As the clockmaker heard this he made a quick decision, worthy of his presence of mind. He made a noise with an instrument at hand, as if clocks were ticking. The Jew scolds the maid, "Are you crazy? Haven't you ever heard clocks tick? I even think that they will ring soon."

This explanation was very convenient for the clockmaker. He made his instrument strike twelve times. The Jew counted the rings, found they were right, ordered the maid to go back to bed and to lock the dog in the kitchen. All of which happened. The maid was soon asleep, the Jew also, and the clockmaker could now in all comfort, [22] and uninterrupted, climb out of his box. He then gave his partner in crime the agreed-on sign, for which the latter had long been waiting. Both now removed the best and most valuable wares of the Jew and left in the dark of night. The next morning, the Jew, to his horror, discovered the theft and then had to suffer the insult of his maid who said sneeringly. "You always know best what the bell has rung!" ["*Sie wissen immer am besten, was die Glocke geschlagen hat*"]

NOTE: The final statement is a proverb that means something like "You know which way the wind is blowing," or "You always know how the matter stands." On imitating an inanimate object while in hiding see Büschenthal joke #71.

～

28. At the occasion of a story about the Turks, who in their processions slaughtered Jews and asses, someone asked a Jew if he didn't want to go there soon, since Jews were probably in short supply there. "No, Jews are not in short supply, but asses are. Don't you want to go?"

NOTE: Learsi, 1961, 304; Rawnitzki 1950, 1:25, joke #47, 1:57, joke #112, 1:76–77, joke #152. For a tale of a rabbi and a freethinker with a similar reversal, see Richman (1952, 157). Also see Büschenthal joke #19 and Ascher joke #280.

～

29. It is well known that the town of Meseritz in south Prussia is the home to a large number of very poor Jewish families, who can almost all be counted as functional beggars.

[23] One of these beggar Jews moved to B—— and went to one of the richest Jewish bankers to ask for charity. He gave him one groschen. "Oh, my God, what can I possibly do with this in such an expensive town?"

"Be happy," replied the banker, "If every one of your fellow believers gave you this much, you will have enough."

"My, I should run around to all. I'm a stranger here, and you are the richest man. Have mercy and give me enough so I can survive today."

All his entreaties were for naught. The rich skinflint didn't want to understand anything. Finally the begging Jew made a move to leave. Leaving, he turned around once more to the Croesus and said, "If you give me twelve groschen, I will tell you a secret, a big secret! One about how you can become really, really old." The miser stopped. A long life! What a wonderful thought for him, who thought only with horror [24] that soon the time would come to leave all his money, jewels, banknotes, maritime trades, and earthly possessions. He was a bit wary, but the desire to live long triumphed over his doubt. He opened his wallet, counted the twelve groschen, and asked urgently, "And the secret?"

The beggar Jew quickly put the money in his pocket and said laconically, "Move to Meseritz. No rich Jew has ever died there."

NOTE: Mendelsohn 1935, 109–10; Ausubel 1948, 282; Richman 1954, 129–30; Learsi 1961, 191–92; Landmann 1962, 274; Druyanow 1963, 1:74, joke #229; Spalding 1969, 36.

∼

30. A Jew had an important legal suit in St. Petersburg that had already gone on for a long time. A minister, whom he had often asked to help accelerate the matter, once took the opportunity to question him about how things were going.

The Jew answered, "I wish the Lord Jesus had been tried in St. Petersburg and not in Jerusalem."

"Why?"

"Then he'd still be alive."

"How's that?"

"In Jerusalem, your excellency, they only [25] had one Pilate and one Herod. But here you never get through all the Pilates and Herods!"

∼

31. A Jew had repeatedly written an officer to remind him and warn him to pay his debt. Once more the Jew reminded him urgently to return the money. Thereafter he received the following:

"My dear Levy Freibisch!

You demand an answer and money from me. One always deducts half for a Jew. Herewith my answer: Money you will not get, and with this I remain

    The constant intercessor

    for your damned Jewish soul."

      N. N.

∼

32. At the beginning of his reign, the successor to Frederick the Great undertook some changes in the appearance of the army. Among other things, he eliminated the three-cornered hat and adopted the two-cornered one. Right after this change an officer asked a Jew [26] who was the supply agent for the officer's regiment what he thought of the new hat.

"Oh, my, what can I say? Only that the army has lost one corner of its support."

∼

33. The famous actress-directrix Mme. Neuberin was in a miserable situation in Hamburg, so much so, that at one point she was considering declaring bankruptcy. But even in her misfortune, perhaps out of her theater pride, she couldn't

let go of her joking mood. That is why, when she welcomed a rich Jew, whom she had asked to come to her, she met him fairly puffed up.

"Listen, Mayer," she said to him, "the great Neuberin will let herself get so low as to borrow a thousand thalers from you."

"Listen, Madame," answered the Jew, "the little Mayer doesn't want to reach so high as to give you one shilling."

NOTE: Druyanow 1963, 1:25–26, joke #75. Friedrike Caroline Neuber, née Weissenborn (1697–1760), known as *Die Neuberin*, was a famous actress and director influential in the development of German theater. She stimulated Gotthold Ephraim Lessing to become a playwright.

∽

34. At the play "The Resignation of Officers," [27] a Frenchman said to a Jew, "There are two mistakes in the piece. The Jew and the innkeeper are honest folk."

"But," said the Jew, when the character Pointraison came on stage, "the Frenchman is well described; he is impertinent and boring."

NOTE: The play is *Die abgedankten Offiziere: Ein Lustspiel von fünf Aufzügen* (The resignation of officers: A comedy in five acts) by Johann Gottlieb Stephanie the Younger (1741–1800) published in 1778. Pointraison is the valet of the character Count Reichenthal. The play is also referred to in Ascher joke #210.

∽

35. A Jew had a ring with a fake stone that he wanted to sell for a lot. He went to a place where a great gentleman exercised his horse, because there were a lot of people gathered there.

As the gentleman rode off, he pretended to find the ring and said to the crowd, "Looks like the gentleman lost his ring and will pay a large reward to the finder. Who wants to buy the reward from me?"

One offered one ducat, the other two. The Jew took the greatest amount and crept away.

∽

36. In the newly established Jewish regiments in Austria, an Israelite armored cavalryman strapped his armor on his back.

[28] "What's with the armor on your back," an officer asked him.

"Well, since we are retreating," was the answer he got.

NOTE: Richman 1954, 214–15; Clements 1973, Type I, 1.6, 38.

∽

37. Abraham Moses, a well-to-do Jew, was sued by one of his fellow believers because of an outstanding debt of a thousand gold coins. In front of the judge,

Abraham denied having received the amount, and he denied that the note was given by him. His opponent pointed out not only the similarity of his signature with other signatures of Abraham Moses but also the testimony of witnesses who were present at the making of the loan. The judges of the city where the witnesses lived were asked to examine them and both said unanimously that Abraham Moses received the thousand gold pieces and signed the note in their presence. The credibility of the witnesses had great weight as both [29] were known as honorable and honest men who could not have conspired to agree over every small detail as they lived far apart. Abraham Moses had to pay.

Sometime later he, out of the blue, went into a coffeehouse where he found a strange Jew sitting. He talked to him and to his great surprise, he learned that he was one of the witnesses against him in the dispute over the loan. He asked the stranger if he knew him and got a no for an answer.

"How can you swear under oath that I borrowed money in your presence when you don't even know me," he asked heatedly.

The stranger was as surprised by this question as Abraham Moses was by his discovery.

"Heaven forbid!" he said. "I didn't bear witness against you, only against Abraham Moses, whom I know well."

"I am Abraham Moses and had to pay the [30] loan because you are an ——."

After a long exchange of words, the whole affair was brought before the judge. After a short examination, he found that the reported creditor was a fraud who in the presence of two honest Jews presented an evil villain as Abraham Moses, whose signature he could fake, and paid him the money. Both fraudsters were handed over for investigation and punished as impostors.

~

38. One afternoon a Jew came to a gatekeeper and put two French gold coins in his hand, saying: "Tomorrow morning I'm going to come with two wagons full of beans. Check me out but don't hold me up too long, because I have to get somewhere on time."

The investigator took the money, but he went right to his superior to lodge a complaint. They were all convinced that the Jew wanted to bribe the official.

[31] So they sent another official to the gate through which the Jew had to come, so that they could thoroughly check out everything he was bringing. The Jew finally came. Immediately the wagon was unloaded, each sack was emptied and, after a long search, nothing was found—except beans instead of the coffee that they had hoped to find.

The Jew finally showed his displeasure at the extraordinary rigorousness with which his wares had been examined, since he had no contraband.

"But," said the gatekeeper, "if you hadn't been willing to bring in contraband, why did you give me the two French gold coins?"

"What?" said the Jew. "What did you say I gave you? Two French gold coins?"

"Yes," answered the gatekeeper. "Here they still are." With those words he pulled them out of his pocket.

"Oy vay," called the Jew. "I made a mistake." He quickly took the gold coins and gave him two groschen pieces instead.

[32] Then they accused him of trying to test the gatekeeper if he'd take the money to let him pass the next time with forbidden wares. But he insisted he had made a mistake and peacefully left with his wagon.

∼

39. A strange Jew, who traded in valuables, was in Mainz and found himself called to the archduke. The archduke asked him, among a number of things, how he liked Mainz.

"Very much," said the Jew, "except for four things, which don't seem to be present in a significant number here."

The archduke was quite surprised when, in answer to his "What could those things be," he had to hear, "priests, loose women, bars and beggars," especially when he believed that the town was most richly endowed with those four things. The Jew had to explain himself, and he did it as follows: "You can't have enough priests because they each have two benefices. [33] There aren't enough loose women because there are complaints that the honest women aren't safe from the priests. There aren't enough bars because if there were, the Dominicans wouldn't be pouring wine in their cloisters. And there can't be enough beggars because otherwise wouldn't you see begging monks everywhere?"

Just as satirical heads aren't readily suffered easily, neither was this Jew in Mainz. Especially the religious folks wanted to get him. They decided that religion was the best way to embarrass him. They wanted to see him punished as a Christian or as a heretic. One of them held a crucifix in front of him and demanded that he should declare what he thinks of it.

"My," said the Jew, "which one of us goes first? First let him say, what he thinks of me. Then I will say, what I think of him."

NOTE: For failure of the image of Jesus on the cross to acknowledge the Jew, see Teitelbaum (1945, 344–45), Gross (1955, 246), Schwarzbaum (1968, 230–31), and Druyanow (1963, 2:318, joke #1997). For a variant on the requirement of the groom to kiss the bride before the bride kisses the groom, see Teitelbaum (1945, 309) and Rawnitzki (1950, 1:43, joke #82).

∼

40. [34] A poor Polish farmer came to a Jew and asked him to lend him two Polish guilders (eight groschen) until his harvest time. The Jew was willing on one condition: the farmer should leave him a token for security, pay six pfennigs interest per week, and pay all the interest in advance.

The farmer was content with the conditions. Now the accounts were made. Since there were eighteen weeks to the harvest, the interest was nine groschen. Since these had to be paid in advance and the loan amount was only eight groschen, the farmer had to add another groschen. Since he had no other item for security, he took off his fur coat and left it with the Jew.

The transaction was concluded in a few minutes to the satisfaction of all concerned. Only on his way back, the farmer asked himself: "It's a bit unusual. I have no money and no fur coat. Had to pay a groschen and now owe eight. But the man did add it up correctly."

NOTE: Landmann 2006, 278.

~

41. [35] It is well known that some Jews, starting at an early age, dedicate themselves exclusively to the study of the Talmud. Their only occupation is to meditate constantly over each part and, when they get together, to debate over it. Such people, who are separated from the rest of the world, are unconcerned by worldly things that are important to the rest of mankind. Following old oriental tradition, they are always in deep meditation, which is why all Jews have a deep respect for them and consider them as almost holy. Living completely separate from their surroundings, they are very ignorant of and consider all things unimportant that have nothing to do with the Talmud.

In Berlin one of these students, completely immersed in the Talmud, incurred a legal suit. He had convinced a Christian girl to convert to Judaism. A complaint was filed, and an examiner was appointed, who summoned him to accept his responsibility.

A messenger brought the citation and gave [36] it to the rabbi's wife, because the rabbi, always obligated to think deeply, was rarely seen.

The woman would never have disturbed her husband in his deep meditations and, like him, had little knowledge outside of her circle of acquaintances. So, she didn't understand what the messenger wanted and put the paper down in a corner, without any further thought.

In this way the summons to appear at the given date was repeated, and finally the sheriff came for the implementation. The Jewess was very surprised at his demand for monetary penalty. Pointing to the written orders, which were still lying there, she answered, "I did not know what to do with them."

The sheriff responded, "You should have given them to your husband so he could present himself."

"Oh," she cried, "my husband is a scholar; he can't read or write!"

NOTE: The implication is that the rabbi is unworldly and cannot read or write German. It is said that unworldly rabbis do not know *tzurat matbeya* (the shape of a coin), that they cannot even tell one coin from another. See Richman (1952,

159) and Mendelsohn (1951, 41). For a poet who translated Shakespeare but didn't know English see Oring (1981, 264).

∽

42. [37] A rabbi brought his commentary on the Lamentations of Jeremiah to another one, so he could look them over for him. After a few days, he received his commentary back, and he asked the rabbi for the same favor for a small work of his that he would bring him shortly. "Gladly," said the rabbi, "And what will it be?"

"A lamentation over your commentary," was the answer.

NOTE: Ernst 1933, 85; Sadan 1950, 46, joke #76; Landmann 1962, 202; Druyanow 1963, 1:178, joke #577. Also see Teitelbaum (1945, 353).

∽

43. A Jewish merchant had a son, whom he and the doting mother held very dear. A certain and quiet phlegmatic nature and an aversion to every commercial transaction by their son led the parents to believe that a great Talmudic or philosophical genius was behind his expressions. They decided to dispense completely with him in their shop and to promote him into the sphere of Mendelssohn or Ben-David.

The father gave him his own room in the rear apartment and left him to his own devices. [38] Since he had been prepared by a Polish sage, everyone believed that, given his predisposition, only the Talmud was required, out of which an active spirit would draw sustenance and enlarge the domain of wisdom. Four years passed and young Isaac rarely left his study, and when he did, he did not say much and was withdrawn. The father respected this deeply and in no way disturbed him. He did share his great hopes with his friends.

One day one of the Christian intelligentsia came into the shop. The father had heard of him and started a learned discourse with him, in which he highly praised his son. Yes, he bade the man to come to the son's room so that he could be in awe of the wisdom cultivated these last four years. With some curiosity the man followed, and the smiling mother and all the members of the household behind them, to witness the first test of her darling's erudition.

The door was opened quietly. Little Isaac sat at his study, deeply occupied by the Talmud and did not allow himself to be disturbed by the rustling of the [39] entrants. The father pointed out delightedly the diligence of his son. Now everyone came closer. The father spoke, "Isaac, this gentleman would like to hear about your scholarship. Tell us, what have you studied over the last four years, what occupied you? Tell us, my dear son, tell us!"

Now one saw that Isaac had the title page of the Talmud in front of him. It was an edition that had a picture of Moses on the border, who was wearing the customary outfit of the Israelites.

After repeated questions, the son finally answered keeping his eyes fastened on Moses: "For four years I've been sitting and pondering, is it summer? Is it winter? If it's summer, why is he wearing fur? If it's winter, why is he going barefoot?"

That was the reward of four years of studying.

NOTE: Sadan 1950, 367–69, joke #720d; Learsi 1961, 146; Spalding 1969, 24; Landmann 1972, 25.

~

44. A Jew who had studied the Talmud saw that many of his neighbors, whom he [40] knew to be ignorant, had earned a sizable income from trading their wares each time they came back from the fair in Frankfurt.

"If you," he thought, "would only start to trade, with your scholarship how large would your profit be!" He opened again all of the places in the Talmud that spoke of trading. He thought them over and went to the fair with this treasure of wisdom. Among the wisdom he memorized, "Get wares that you can't find elsewhere because then you can be certain of your sale. Accordingly he stood under different arches and watched what his countrymen were buying. In one of these he noticed black stockings with a red gusset and gloves embroidered with gold. Since both appealed to his taste, he watched carefully if anyone was buying them. Nobody seemed to notice them, so following the Talmud, he bought the whole supply of both. But in his fatherland no one that he offered them to wanted to buy even one pair.

[41] Tired of constant failed efforts, he stopped his trading and studied again, as always, the Talmud. But in order to get at least something for his wares, he decided to send them to market and let them go for any price. His only concern was that he didn't want to confide in even one of his neighbors, partially because he didn't want to reveal that he had traded two such poor articles and partly that he didn't want to give the rest of his fortune into the hands of one person without being assured of their honesty.

He first asked a Jew by the name of Simson and then one named Hirsch. He gave the former the black stockings with the red gusset and the other the gold embroidered gloves. He gave them both the authority to let them go at any price they could get or to trade them against other wares.

Upon returning from the market, Simson said, "I could not get any money for the stockings and had to trade them for these wares." [42] He opened a package and there were the old embroidered gloves. Soon Hirsch came and also said, he could not monetize his wares and had to trade them, which were for nothing else than the red stockings with the red gusset.

So the poor scholar had both his bad articles back, and the most painful thing for him was that both of his subcontractors maintained they had to make the trade.

NOTE: Teitelbaum 1945, 227–28; Mendelsohn 1947, 234–35; Spalding 1969, 1–2; Landmann 1972, 77–78.

∽

45. Two stagecoach men complained to each other that they had to drive some Jews to the fair with the extra mail, and that they left a very poor tip.

"Oh," said the one, "those two shall pay. When we leave, drive into my wheel. Let me handle the rest."

As said, so done. The one almost broke the other's axle. A big fight ensued between the two coachmen.

Finally one of the Jews jumped off the wagon and tried to calm the brawlers. [43] But he had barely spoken the first words of peace before the coachman, who had driven into the other, yelled back, enraged. "What business is it of yours what we are doing?" As the Jew made a few more attempts, the coachman took his whip and made him black and blue.

"What are you doing?" says the other coachman, apparently furious. "What? You dare to beat my Jew? That won't go over well. If you beat my Jew, I will beat yours," and with those words he went after the other passenger, whom he also beat down.

After the double execution, both punished victims sat back down and reached their next station.

Both Jews had been badly beaten. They found it advisable to order half a quart of spirits so that they could wash each other with it.

After washing each other, the one Jew said to the other one. "Listen! What do you think? We can't use these spirits anymore. [44] What do you think about giving them to the coachmen?"

"What, those impertinent louts who beat us?"

"Yeah, sure!" says the other one. "It shows a good will!"

NOTE: Spalding 1969, 9–10. Another joke in Learsi (1961, 302–3) reveals a similar idea. A Russian captain dislikes the orderly of the Russian major, and the Russian major dislikes the orderly of the Russian captain. They beat each other's orderly in turn, and the orderlies remark that they are "not without friends and protectors." A similar joke is found in Richman (1952, 321–22), about two Jewish manufacturers who each have a worker who is despised by the other manufacturer.

∽

46. It was long ago decided that among Jewish character traits, not the least is the artful ingenuity and talent for getting out of embarrassing situations quickly and which often enough gives them courage and honor. Examples prove this over and over because these talents seem to be innate to them.

At a fair in Frankfurt, a Jew went into the store of a Christian merchant of remnants and demanded to buy junk wares. (Merchandise that has faults in the color, printing, or finishing, called rejects.)

Getting the response that nothing of the sort was available, he did not calm down. Instead he continued his line of inquiry.

His persistence angered the merchant, who suffered from a severe toothache, [45] and he told the Jew to leave. But he who didn't leave was the Jew. On the contrary he intruded more fervently in his questioning the merchant.

The latter lost his patience and said to the Jew: "If you take away my toothache, you can have the remnants.

"Great," said the Jew. "First give me the junk and, being an honest man, I will also take away your toothache afterward."

The wares were brought, the transaction completed, and as the payment had been made, the Jew put one groschen on the table with the words, "Here is one groschen down payment on the toothache. Keep it for me until the next fair, and I will exchange it then."

NOTE: Druyanow 1963, 2:307, joke #1952.

47. It is well known that at fairs strange merchants customarily put up a wax cloth with the name of their company written in oil paint.

A Jew by the name of Moses, who traveled to the fair in Braunschweig, ordered his helper to do the same in that he said to [46] him: "Dear David, go into the attic and bring the company sign down."

"Oy vay, where is the banner? The mice have eaten it almost completely."

Initially the Jew was very concerned, but after thinking about it, he caught himself.

"Tell you what, dear David. Run to the fair and scream at the top of your lungs, 'Where there is nothing, there is Moses!'"

48. A Jew in B——, a very repulsive man, in his appearance as in behavior, had the idea to establish a snuff factory.

"He couldn't have started a worse enterprise," said M——. "Who is going to buy tobacco from him when he is already such a disgusting pinch [*Prise*]."

NOTE: For not being worth a pinch of snuff, see Teitelbaum (1945, 265).

49. A rich Israelite had a stroke and therefore lost control over his face. [47] When he started to improve, his doctor held his hand in front of his eyes to watch if he could see anything.

"What is that?" he asked the patient.

"As much as I can see, a hand; but that is very unusual. My own hand I cannot see when I hold it in front of my eyes."

"That's natural," responded the doctor, "You were always used to watching the hands of others."

~

50. A Jew had a fever and complained to his doctor of such a serious thirst that he almost couldn't quench it.

The doctor asked what he liked most to drink.

"Beer," responded the patient.

"Good. Get someone to bring you city beer. That won't be too strong."

In the evening the doctor visited his patient and found his fever had seriously increased. After posing many questions as to the diet of the patient, the patient finally confessed that he had drunk two bottle of Mannheimer beer.

"Heaven forbid," the doctor said sternly. [48] "Didn't I say clearly that you should drink only city beer?"

"Well," responded the patient, "how can that hurt? Just imagine I'm ill in Mannheim."

NOTE: For a similar anecdote based on time rather than place see Spalding (1969, 356).

~

51. At a ball in winter a young Jewish dandy was caught up in a brawl caused by his arrogance. His opponent, very upset, said: "Sir, I do not want to create a scene here because of the company, otherwise I would show you how you deserve to be treated. But step outside, and I will give some blows to your head."

"Oh, no!" yelled the Jew. "You want me to step outside. No way will I do that. It's cold out there, and even if you gave me twenty, I still wouldn't want to."

NOTE: Landmann 1972, 234.

~

52. A crowd mistreated a Jew in the street. To save him, one of his relatives said to the bystanders, "Have pity on him because this poor man is mad."

[49] This actually saved him but then the victim lodged a complaint against the rescuer because now the public believed he was mad, and this deprived him of all social contact. The elders informed him that they wanted to levy a two-thaler fine against the defendant. "That's not what I want," said the plaintiff, "because he is a poor man and he will have to let his wife and children starve if he has to pay this amount." "So," the elders say, "we will throw him in jail for a day." The plaintiff objected to that, saying that the defendant wouldn't be able to earn any

money in jail and that his family would still suffer. "OK," said the elders, "What shall we do to compensate you?"

"I do not ask for compensation," said the plaintiff, "What better proof that I am not crazy than that the elders have to ask me what they should do?"

∽

53. [50] One morning a young Jew visited a Christian merchant to work out a trade. When this was concluded, the merchant invited his young guest to breakfast.

"No, thank you," replied the Jew. "It's no bother," responded the merchant. "Everything is here."

"No, dear sir, I cannot accept," answered the Jew. "First of all it is a fast day for us, and second, I've already had breakfast."

NOTE: See Büschenthal joke #3. For a similar structure see Rawnitzki (1950, 2:180, joke #792).

∽

54. Coming from court in Prague, a Jew said: "Charming people, like milk and blood! May God keep you from chicken pox."

∽

55. A Jew visited a bureaucrat so often to further his suit that the latter, being unwilling, finally yelled: "You dog! I have told you often enough that your file is awaiting a verdict."

"God forbid," answered the Jew. [51] "What shall I do with that? I wish the verdict were awaiting the file."

∽

56. The son of a reputable Jewish commercial enterprise in Silesia traveled to L——, and a banker, to whom he had been recommended, invited him to dinner.

The young man arrived in the evening, and since the master of the house was still occupied, he was brought into the chamber of the lady of the home where he met her and her company.

The company was just starting a small concert, and the lady of the house asked the stranger if he was musical.

He answered: "Yes, Madam."

"Do you play the piano?"

"No, Madam."

"Or the violin?"

"Also not"

"But you are musical?"

"Yes, certainly."

"Well then, you play the flute?"

"Begging your pardon?"

So he was asked every instrument, [52] but the young man didn't play one, always asserting that he was musical. The company wasn't sure what to think of him and looked at each other.

Finally the master of the house entered and greeted all present, including the stranger, "How are you, Monsieur Kalish?" Now the mystery was solved. His name was Kalish, and he was used to always being called Musie Kalish. That's why he answered the repeated questions if he was musical [*musikalisch*] without hesitation with a yes.

NOTE: Landmann 1962, 438.

∼

57. "Now tell me," said a doctor to a Jew who had called him because of an insignificant complaint. "Why is it that Jews are more afraid of death than the Christians?"

"Well, where should it come from?" replied the Jew. "Christians have someone who died for them on the cross. We Jews have to carry our own skin to market."

∼

58. The wife of a Jew gave her husband, contrary to all his expectations [53] and five months after the wedding ceremony and its completion, a young son.

He poured out his aching heart over this to a Jew of his acquaintance.

"What's bothering you," he said, "Your son will one day become a good courier."

NOTE: See Büschenthal joke #22. There is a different version in Druyanow (1963, 1:323, joke #1014) that depends on the idea that a seven-month baby can still come two months early.

∼

59. Two Jews, Ruben and Simon, were both considered to be the best chess players in B——. One day Ruben played in a coffeehouse with a stranger. During the play, Simon also came to the coffeehouse and stood quietly behind the chair of his competitor. At a move of his opponent, Ruben saw no saving move and wanted to gather the pieces with the words, "Checkmate," when he received a slap to his head that made his wig fly off. Naturally, he quickly turned around, to find where the blow came from. Since he only saw Simon, he said no more than, "Well, what move can I make?" Without one word, Simon made the move, and Ruben [54] didn't say one more word about the blow to his head. Instead he

said, with a quick glance at the chessboard, fixing his wig, "As long as I live, you are right!"

⁓

60. A traveling Jew went to a German theater in Berlin and afterward to dinner with one of the richest Jewish bankers, who had invited him.
"Why are you so late?" asked the banker.
"I went to the theater first."
"How did you like it?"
"Not at all. I was horribly bored."
"Why didn't you leave so you'd be here earlier?"
"Yeah, that's easy for you to say. You are a rich man, but one of us cannot throw away half a thaler so easily."

⁓

61. Moses Mendelssohn was an accountant in a business in Berlin, and that for a Jewish merchant of limited abilities.
[55] "Fate is really unfair," said Mr. —— to him. "You, such a clever man, have to serve so limited a head."
"I find that fate easy to understand," replied Mendelssohn. "Because if I were the boss, I couldn't use him."

NOTE: "Anekdoten" 1812, 354; Teitelbaum 1945, 298–99; Richman 1952, 175; Mendelsohn, 1952, 7–8; Landmann 1962, 535. For other anecdotes about Mendelssohn, see Mendelsohn (1935, 41, 111, 149), Teitelbaum (1945, 356), Mendelsohn (1952, 37), Richman (1952, 174–175), Landmann (1962, 535), Spalding (1969, 14, 296), and Landmann (1972, 185).

⁓

62. A bureaucrat was ranting at a Jew standing in front of the judicial bench, and said, among other things: "You are a disreputable fellow. The rascal looks out of your face."
"No, Mr. Bailiff." he answered, "If that is so, then my face must be a mirror."

⁓

63. A very miserly Jewish banker heaped empty praises on his pleasant stay in the country in spring. He especially praised the lovely concert of the birds, the lark's early morning song and the melodic plaint of the nightingale.
"Do you know why the bird song is so inspiring?" asked Mr. —— [56] of one of the others in his company. "Afterward they don't go around with their written notes."

⁓

64. Once in Berlin Moses Mendelssohn was insulted in the street by a common soldier.

His companion, a young scholar, expressed his displeasure.

"No big deal," said Mendelssohn. "What remains to such a being when he can't even insult a Jew?"

NOTE: "Anekdoten" 1812, 354.

~

65. Some rich Jewish families in Vienna raised, at their expense, the son of a very poor fellow believer, who showed very early a gift for science, and they let him study medicine.

To complete his training, the donors sent him to Berlin, to stay there for a couple of years, attend the medical college, and mainly listen to the lectures of the famous anatomy professor Walter.

[57] He undertook his journey and had a number of recommendations to well-to-do Jews in Berlin. Among those was the now deceased but renowned Jewish doctor Marcus Herz, to whom he was urgently recommended for active support.

The young man delivered his letters but was coldly rebuffed by Dr. Herz. In the beginning, he attempted repeatedly to contact him, but he remained unsuccessful as he was never received.

In the meantime he did find enough help from other friendly families, which allowed him to achieve his intention of staying in Berlin for two years to complete his studies.

At the end of this time, he prepared his return trip and said goodbye to those who had helped him. He even went to Dr. Herz to say good-bye and to ask him if he wanted to send a message to Vienna.

At this departing visit, Dr. Herz was very friendly and engaged [58] the young doctor in a wide-ranging conversation about his metier and the progress he had made during his stay in Berlin.

The conversation naturally came to the subject of anatomy.

"I learned a lot here," said the young man, "especially in the classes of Dr. Walter where I saw many strange specimens. But a couple of days ago, at a friend's, I saw something very unusual that seemed most peculiar to me."

"What was it?" asked Professor [*Geheimrat*] Herz.

"A child preserved in spirits that was born without a heart and had lived for eight months."

"That's not possible!" exclaimed Herz. "Somebody pulled your leg."

"Why do you say that?" replied the departing man. "I don't see that as impossible. I know two people who've lived two years without a heart. That's you and me."

Collection of Witty Notions from Jews | 75

With these words he stood up and left the room.

NOTE: Landmann 1972, 189–190. Markus Herz (1747–1803) was a Jewish physician, philosopher, and author who settled in Berlin. He was a friend of Moses Mendelssohn and corresponded with Immanuel Kant on philosophical matters.

∿

66. A young and very poor Jew had been treated [59] in a very stepmotherly way by Mother Nature in endowing him with mental capacity. He had the peculiar idea to dedicate himself to veterinary medicine. As he was lacking completely in the means to fulfill his intention, he wrote to all the benefactors, especially his fellow believers, to support his efforts with small contributions.

This invitation began with the following words: "As I want to become an animal doctor [*Vieharzt*] etc."

When this note was presented to the famous Jewish Dr. Markus Herz, he said drily: "Too bad, there is a grammatical error here. I have to correct it." And from the word animal doctor [*Vieharzt*] he made two [animal, doctor].

∿

67. In a public gathering, two young and brave men approached a Jew, and to amuse the bystanders, they tried to tell him some silly stories to convince him that the stories were true, in order to tease him.

[60] He seemed to listen with patience and resignation.

Finally they brought the conversation to hunting and told him unbelievable stories of their expertise in shooting and hitting.

"That's all fine and good," he said, without losing his composure, "but I have a cousin who is even better. You see, gentlemen, he goes daily to the stock exchange and asks the exchange rate for gold against currency. And when finally someone holds a friederich d'or between his fingers, he shoots the premium down to the rate from twenty feet away."

∿

68. Moses Mendelssohn had a large hump, and additionally he stuttered. Once he found himself in the company of scholars in Berlin, such as the Sulzers, Ramlers, [and] Lessings, among others. Everyone was having a lot of fun, and finally someone had the idea that everyone should improvise a satirical poem. Mendelssohn didn't have to think very long before reciting the following verse:

[61] "You call Demosthenes great,
Who is the stuttering orator of Athens.
Aesop, the hunchback, you call wise.
Triumph! In your circle I will be

doubly grand and wise,
Because in me I combine
What separately one saw and heard
in Aesop and Demosthenes

NOTE: There are a number of jokes that depend on the idea of praising a person by comparing his attributes to a number of distinguished individuals. Only later is it discovered that those qualities are the negative qualities of those individuals. Mendelsohn 1935, 168–70, 175–76; Ausubel 1948, 392; Gross 1955, 329; Landmann 1962, 271; Schwarzbaum 1968, 312–13; Spalding 1969, 38, 85. For a similar idea of the recommendation by biblical allusion see Learsi (1961, 256–57); on the negative traits of a beautiful statue see Heine in Freud (1960, 70).

69. A young officer was guarding the gate to Berlin when he saw an ugly, crippled Jew coming out whom he didn't know. He decided to make a joke at his expense. Among the things he asked him, he wanted to know what he traded.

The unknown Jew was the learned Moses Mendelssohn. He had a right to his answer, which was, "What I trade in, you'd never buy!"

Officer: "Well, what is it?"

Mendelssohn: "Intelligence."

NOTE: "Anekdoten" 1812, 1, 354; Adler 1893, 457; Teitelbaum 1945, 319–20; Landmann 1972, 185.

70. A Jew called Hirsch had a [62] very wicked wife under whose thumb he suffered greatly.

It was not only quarreling and abuse; she physically attacked him quite frequently. Since she was a large, robust person and he a misshapen and small man, resistance was futile, and he had to lose.

Once she let him feel the true strength of her arm, so that he, full of fear, crawled under the table to get away from her blows.

He had barely hidden when the front doorbell rang.

"Hirsch," his wife said, "the doorbell rang. Open the door."

"No," he said. "You open the door." The doorbell rang again.

"Go, open the door, Hirsch!" the woman screamed again.

"No! No!" answered the refugee. "You go open the door. For once I want to show that I am the master of the house."

NOTE: Uther 2011, Type 1366: *The Cowering Husband*; Ausubel 1948, 345; Learsi 1961, 123; Druyanow 1963, 2:211, joke #1653; Spalding 1969, 151, 152–53; Landmann 1972, 64–65. Lolanekdot n.d. There are a number of jokes about who should be considered the master of the house; see Anek-dot. n.d.; Anekdotitut n.d.; Anekdotov n.d.; Lolanekdot n.d.; https://www.anekdot.ru/id/10890/; Smeshok. n.d.

∼

71. [63] During the last war in Poland, a Russian was in pursuit of a Jew.

He hid in a farmer's hut and implored the owner to hide him.

For fear of the Russian, the farmer didn't want to agree initially, but finally he relented, when the Jew promised him a handsome reward for his good deed. He had the Jew crawl into a sack that he then hid behind the stove.

Barely had the runaway been secured in this way than the Russian opened the door and asked about the escaped Jew.

The farmer denied that he was with him.

But the Russian insisted that he had to be in the house and threatened the farmer with severe punishment if he lied to him.

The farmer repeated his first assertion, but while he was saying with a quavering voice, "No, no, definitely no Jew hidden here," he pointed with his finger to the sack behind the stove.

[64] The Russian who understood the sign, asked, "Well, what's in that sack there?"

"Old glass, broken bottles and other things like that," he got for an answer.

The Russian now pulled out his saber and with the flat side gave the sack a few hard strokes.

The Jew was overcome by pain. He couldn't refrain from screaming for very long, but so as not to contradict the farmer, he screamed, "Clink, clink, clink, clink!"

NOTE: See Uther 2011, Type 161: *The Farmer Betrays the Fox by Pointing*; Poggio 1968, 139–40. Druyanow (1963, 2:25, joke #1073) recounts an incident on a train. Examples in Sadan (1950, 369, joke #721b) and Oring (1981, 260–61) involve pretending to be something that can't talk.

∼

72. A Jewish banker wanted to appear as a man of knowledge and taste even though he had a very limited horizon and was just an ordinary, haggling Jew.

That is why he frequently received famous scholars and artists in his home who loved his good food and wine but didn't much concern themselves with their simple host.

Once a scholar visited him and unfortunately found him alone. Out of politeness he had to engage in a conversation with him.

[65] They both sat by a window that looked out on a pedestrian path.

Suddenly the banker, to show his wit, began to say something clever.

"How unusual, dear Professor! The preferences of human beings are really very different in all things. For example, here from this window we see some driving around, others are riding, and others are taking a walk, and you and I—we are going for a walk sitting here."

~

73. A Jew and a Christian became partners in a cigarette stand. It happened that they had the place open continuously throughout the day. On Saturday the Jew observed his Sabbath and the Christian waited on his customers. [On] Sunday the Jew took over the business. When someone scoffed at this, the Jew said, "When the laws were made, tricks were also developed."

~

74. [66] In Catholic countries Easter is celebrated by giving eggs. The giver of the eggs usually says, "Today Christ is risen," and the recipient of the eggs has to say, "He is truly risen."

The General von —— also gave the court Jew ——, who came to him on Easter, an egg with the words: "Today Christ is risen." The Jew took it, bowed, and answered: "As your majesty orders!"

"Rascal!" exclaimed the general, "Can't you say, 'He is truly risen!'"

"Oh, my," responded the Jew. "How can I? Haven't I heard all my life long that you can't report anything to a dreaded general what you don't know for sure."

~

75. A Jew by the name of Herz Aron Heiman had himself baptized.

During the baptism he received the name Heinrich August. At the end of the ceremony he said to one of the invited witnesses, "Do you know why I took the name Heinrich August? [67] Now I can use my old seal initials H. A. H."

NOTE: This anecdote using the same name Herz Aron Heimann reappears in *Beiwagen zum Volkboten* 1851, 108; Ausubel 1948, 437; Rawnitzki 1950, 1:45, joke #86; Mendelsohn 1951, 41; Mendelsohn 1952, 37; Richman 1954, 343; Landmann 1962, 504–5; Spalding 1969, 59. It is told about Markus Herz in Landmann (1972, 190). Heinrich Heine makes use of this witticism in *Pictures of Travel*, 1856, 331).

~

76. A baptized Jewess was asked, while learning the catechism, what did Christ do for you?

"He never did anything for me," she answered. "I was always pious."

NOTE: Other jokes suggest that converts to Christianity still continue to think of themselves as Jews. See Mendelsohn 1935, 120, 121, 128; Teitelbaum 1945, 47; Learsi 1961, 297–98, 299; Landmann 1962, 494–510 passim; Landmann 1972, 32, 149–54 passim; Spalding 1969, xviii, 67; Novak and Waldoks 1981, 94.

~

77. It is well known that poorer Jews from the former kingdom of Poland must do their trading with borrowed capital. If they borrow this from their richer fellow believers, they have to pay incredibly high interest rates, 30, 40, up to 50 percent.

At a fair in Frankfurt such a Polish Jew came to a merchant of his faith and wanted some goods from him.

The merchant showed him what he had and then asked him if he wanted to pay cash or to take credit, because if the former it was going to cost a little less.

"Pay cash?" said the Jew. "I'm not a crook!"

∼

78. [68] A small, Polish, Jewish trader at the fair came to a merchant of his nation and asked him.

"Tell me in confidence, is the banker —— (he named a well-known commercial enterprise) a good man I can count on."

"Why do you ask?" asked the man, surprised at the question. "Do you have something to demand of him?"

"My, how could I!" replied the former. "I want to borrow from him. If he is not a secure man, what will I do if he is not solid and goes bankrupt? If I then have to pay him at a future fair, I have no more credit with him. But if everything is good with him, I will pay him at the future fair, and then I have new credit."

∼

79. A Jew reminded an officer about the money he had advanced him. The debtor was annoyed by this. He paid, but with a dagger in his hand, he forced the Jew, no matter how much he objected, to eat the note.

A little while later the officer had the Jew called on him and asked for an advance of money.

[69] The Jew said he'd be willing, "But under one condition," he added. "That your Honor write the note on a Nürenberger gingerbread."

NOTE: Vejnberg 1870, 109–14; Vejnberg 1874, 145–49. A Polish nobleman is asked to write his next note on matzah in Richman 1952, 356. Also Druyanow 1963, 1:24–25, joke #71.

∼

80. A Jew was involved in a legal proceeding in which he had to swear an oath in order to resolve the complaint. He took the demanded oath and leaving the chambers, an acquaintance, who perhaps knew the proceedings better than the judge, said to him: "Well, you took a false oath."

"What are false oaths for?" replied the Jew and went, smiling complacently, onward.

∼

81. During a very cold winter, a Jew bought himself a coat of wolf fur. An acquaintance met him wearing this coat and asked him derisively, "Why are you wearing the fur on the outside?"

"Why are you asking me," he answered. "Better you should ask the wolf."

NOTE: "Don't ask me, ask the horse" in Freud (1954, 258).

∼

82. [70] A Jew wanted to send his servant to a village four miles away to collect a debt. He ordered him to rent a horse for the purpose.

The servant, who had never been on a horse, went to the man lending horses and asked to borrow one.

Like all men who rent horses, this man praised all of his animals and pointed out a white one, saying: "Take this one. He rides seven miles in one trip."

"My, what shall I do with him," responded the Jew. "I can't use him. I only have to ride four miles, and he will run three miles too far."

NOTE: *Bez zaglavija radi potehi* 1880b, 103–4; Druyanow 1963, 1:320, joke #1002; Landmann 1962, 151. For variants on the matter of time and distance in travel see Ausubel (1948, 336–37), Mendelsohn (1952, 87), Spalding (1969, 121), and Freud (1960, 54). Also see Büschenthal joke #5; *Best Jewish Jokes* 2014.

∼

83. A civil servant wanted to screw with a Jew with whom he had had a number of dealings. So, he said to him: "What is that I hear about you? People are saying that you practice witchcraft."

"My, oh, my, people talk a lot," replied the Jew. "That doesn't mean it's true. It's a miracle, how curious. Me they berate as a [71] sorcerer; they say a bureaucrat isn't one."

∼

84. A Jew of significant body mass demanded at a mail coach office to be marked down as half a passenger because he had just seen that a small, crippled person had been entered as a half upon his urgent entreaties.

The manager of the stagecoach denied the Jew his unfair request by letting him know that between him, a large, broad-shouldered man, and a small, dwarf-like man there was a huge difference.

"Yes," said the Jew, "the difference is very tangible. But this small person sits completely enclosed in the coach, and I am half out of it."

NOTE: There is some similarity to the Jew who will pay only half his hotel bill because he has to be awakened in the middle of the night because of a fire. Landmann 1962, 296.

∼

85. A Jew who had just lost a lawsuit stopped on the floor of the court chamber and contemplated the picture of justice that hung there.

"Tell me then [*eppes*]," [72] he said to a man standing next to him, "who is this woman with a scale and a sword?"

"Don't you know her? She is Justice."

"Well," countered the Jew, "What is she doing here?"

NOTE: Anekdoty.ru. n.d.

⁓

86. A Jew named Moses frequented the house of a rich fellow believer where he was appreciated because of his funny stories.

Finally his coat became so shabby that the rich man was embarrassed each time a stranger met the Jew in his house.

"Buy yourself a new coat," he said one day. "Now," answered Moses, "Do you think I only have one coat?"

"Well then, put on the other one."

"Yeah, that is even worse!"

NOTE: *Znamenityj evrejskij shut Gershko iz Ostropolya* 1902, 11–12; Mendelsohn 1952, 6; Landmann 2006, 207.

⁓

87. The Baron of P——, who reached a good old age despite his dissolute lifestyle, was taking a walk with a number of good friends. [73] He met a Jew with whom he had interacted more than thirty years before in foreign lands.

The baron spoke to him, and since he was giving some funny responses, the company jumped into the conversation. Among the questions the baron posed, he asked the Jew if he was surprised to still find him alive.

"Why should I be surprised?" asked the Israelite, "I know that the baron never rushed to pay his debts."

⁓

88. A young officer wanted to borrow money from a Jew. But the latter declined because he knew him as a poor risk.

The officer, annoyed by this, said in parting to the Jew, "You are a bum [*Lump*]"

"Oh, my," responded the Jew. "You, sir, are also no paper [*Papier*]."

NOTE: There is something similar in Landmann (1962, 204; 1972, 26).

⁓

89. A Jew sold another one a horse and swore in the contract that the animal was not flawed.

A few days later, the buyer came back and said, "Dear friend, the transaction is not valid. [74] The horse has a big flaw; it is blind in one eye."

"Oy," said the seller, "how can you call that a flaw? That is a misfortune."

NOTE: Vejnberg 1880, 69–70. Druyanow (1963, 2:100, joke #1314) has a dispute about the sale of a blind horse with a different punchline. For a man who is supposed not to be alive but is discovered to be in jail, it is claimed "You call that living?" See Freud (1960, 55).

∼

90. A young Jew in B——, where he was studying medicine, went to the professor Doctor Z—— and begged him to let him listen to his illustrious lecture without paying.

The professor declined, saying that young people who had little money should not be studying medicine because that entailed a lot of costs and would always keep someone who was needy a bungler.

The Jew discovered that the professor was the private doctor to rich Jewish bankers, M—— and L——. He turned to them, imploring them to put in a good word for him with the professor.

And they did. Professor Z—— declared to both that, due to their friendship, he would reduce the fees by half.

Both bankers announced this to their protégé, [75] and he attended the lectures of Professor Z——.

When these lectures were over, the young man went to the professor and asked for a report card

"I'd be happy to," said the professor. "But first you'll have to pay me the half of the fees you still owe."

"How is that? I still owe you the fees?"

"Definitely."

"Oh, my, I don't understand. Didn't you promise the banker M—— that you will forgive half of the fees? And didn't you say the same to Banker L——? Two halves are a whole! So you forgave me the whole."

∼

91. During the time of the former French colonial justice system in Berlin, it was customary that all judicial proceedings were written up in in French, even when one of the parties didn't speak French at all. [76] A complaint was filed against a Jew by one of the citizens subject to this judicial system. He had to present himself at the appointed time to be interrogated regarding the circumstances of the suit.

After his explanation, made in German, had been taken down in French, he was read the record and asked to verify it with his signature.

The Jew declined because he didn't understand one word of the record read to him. But it was pointed out to him that he had to meet this demand unconditionally.

"All right," he said. "If I have to, then give me the pen."

Then he wrote for quite a while. Finally one of the present court employees took a look at the record and noticed rows of unknown letters.

"What is that?" he asked the Jew. "He only needs to write his name. Nobody can read this!"

"It's Chaldean," replied the Jew. [77] "If it doesn't make any difference if I sign a transcript I do not understand, no one will mind if I write something under it that no judge will understand."

NOTE: Landmann 2006, 462.

∽

92. A baby with six fingers on his right hand was born to a Jew. The father, as well as the mother and the rest of the relatives, was very brokenhearted.

An acquaintance visited the family, and when the mother complained about her bad luck, their Jewish friend responded, "Hey, what's there to fear? I congratulate you. Your son is a born piano player."

∽

93. A soldier's wife, whose husband was lost in the war, hired herself out to a young Jewish merchant who had an ugly wife whom he had married only for her money.

The Israelite had a store, in which his wife offered her wares during the day. He himself took care of his business at home.

[78] The soldier's wife was not ugly, and the son of Israel found her pleasant. He made a few tender advances, and since he furthered those with not insignificant money presents, it didn't take long before he was lucky enough to see his wishes fulfilled.

The natural consequence thereof was pregnancy.

One morning the soldier's wife brought the Jewess her breakfast in the store. She was already close to her due date and showed it in her appearance.

"God forbid," said the Jewess, who was also getting close to her due date, "God forbid, you are pregnant!"

"You are also."

"Well, why shouldn't I be? I'm with child from my dear husband."

"Me, too," said the soldier's wife.

∽

94. On the boardwalk under the linden trees of Berlin, a Jew ran after a pedestrian whom he thought to be an actor in the national theater.

[79] "Sir," he yelled loudly after him, "sir, hear me out."

The stroller calmly continued his walking without turning around.

Finally the Jew caught up with him and, putting his hand on his shoulder, said to him: "So, stop already, Mr. ——"

The stroller turned around, and to his horror, the Jew discovered that he had mistaken the person.

"Excuse me," he said immediately, without losing his composure. "I thought you were the actor ——, but I have to confess that close up you have definitely won."

NOTE: There are a number of examples in which the setup of this joke appears but with different punchlines: Ausubel 1948, 423–24; Herschfield 1932, joke #16; Teitelbaum 1945, 356; Richman 1952, 49–50, 189; Gross 1955, 216; Schwarzbaum 1968, 189; Spalding 1969, 433.

∼

95. In a social circle there were a few daughters of Israel with their mothers.

A Christian young lady played the aria of the Danube nymph: "In my castle it is very nice," etc. on the piano.

After the completion of this piece a Jewish mother said: [80] "My Soorche also plays this, but with her a few of the pauses are different."

NOTE: "In meinem Schlosse ist's gar fein" (In my castle it is very nice) is a song about a woman waiting for a knight to come and claim her as his bride. It is from Karl Friedrich Hensler's (1759–1825) *Das Donauweibschen* (The Danube mermaid) staged in Vienna in 1798. The music was composed by Ferdinand Kauer (1751–1831). It is still to be found in German songbooks.

∼

96. A rich Jewish widow, who still followed the old ways, had an only daughter whom she adored with an exaggerated love.

Everything that the daughter desired, she granted, and she left nothing undone to give her as complete an education as possible.

The dear daughter was educated in all the elegant feminine arts, which gave her a touch of aestheticism and aesthetic sensibilities that were often manifested in ridiculous affectation.

The tender girl of eighteen years was therefore also sickly and suffered from neurasthenia. That is why an understanding doctor was consulted, who then also prescribed some different things.

Once he visited his patient and she complained, with many melodious tirades, that her nervous collapses had not improved [81] and even the smallest thing had a serious effect on her mood.

"Yes," said the doctor, "no medications will help that, Mademoiselle, if you do not want to help yourself. Don't let yourself go like that, and try to master your sensitivities."

"Ach," sighed the sensitive Jewess, "how can I help it. It comes from my temperament."

"Now look here," called the mother, "What are you asking for? Don't you have everything that your heart desires? Why do you also want a temperament?"

∽

97. "What are you reading?" asked a Jewish maid of her Jewish employer, as she entered her room and looked into her book.

"Heaven forbid, Wieland? And on top of that *Agathon*! —— Dear God, how can anyone read *Agathon*? He's the one! After completing all his trials, at the end he'll become a freemason. —— Heaven forfend, how could I read that?"

NOTE: Poet, novelist, and literary editor Christoph Martin Wieland (1733–1813) translated Shakespeare into German and wrote *Geschichte des Agathon* (The story of Agathon) in 1767, which some regard as the first coming-of-age novel.

∽

98. [82] A young Jewess, a fashion plate, who was devoted to the latest aesthetic school and who only spoke of feelings, artistry, natural beauty, idealism, and such, was visited by an apostle of art while she was rocking her one-year-old daughter on her lap.

The gallant dandy told her many pleasantries and also praised the young being that she bounced on her knees.

"Yes," said the mother, "there is nothing better than such a child. Do you see how friendly her smile is and how she wiggles her legs, how sweetly she raises her arms, how openly she looks at the world through her big, black eyes. Don't you think that this is pure nature speaking?"

With these words she handed the child to the young man, and while he was holding her up high, the child disposed of one of its needs onto the visitor's vest. Startled, he handed her back to the mother and said, "Oh, yes, nature has expressed itself purely here."

∽

99. [83] A rich Jew was admitted to a closed society whose statutes demanded that each new member give a speech to the assembly.

This he did in the following manner:

"Gentlemen!" he began. "You want me to give a speech, but first I want to tell you a fable. One time the moon called for the tailor so that he should measure him for a dress. Since the tailor didn't come, the moon had guards come to get him. 'Why didn't you come to measure my dress?' the moon let fly at him.

"'Now,' the tailor answered, 'what shall I do with that? How can I measure you for a dress! Sometimes you are a quarter, then a half, soon you are full, and soon you are nothing. What shall I do that a dress will fit you?' I feel the same way. You want me to give a speech. Here you have young people, old people. There are dumb ones and clever ones. How shall I [84] give a speech so that everyone will like it? I'll gladly pay double the fees, as long as I don't have to give a speech."

~

100. A Jew in H——, even though he was not educated, had his children raised by current standards.

Among his children was a daughter who loved geography.

The father could not understand that kind of love, and so he asked his daughter one day: "But, my dear child, what are you doing with geography? You can't become a coachman."

~

101. After the war of 1806 to 1807, when the exchange in state treasury notes brought bad luck to many speculators in Prussia, a Jewish merchant also went bankrupt.

Since he had no other means of support, he sat down to write a book. Someone who heard of this noted: "Paper brought him ruin; now he wants to ruin paper."

NOTE: Teitelbaum 1945, 104; Mendelsohn 1947, 130; Ausubel 1948, 358–59; Druyanow 1963, 1:179, joke #582; Landmann 1962, 204. A similar idea is formulated in Mendelsohn (1935, 216–17) and Spalding (1969, 372–73).

~

102. [85] An old Jew, a confirmed bachelor, had a Christian housekeeper. Once he gave her a piece of Hamburger beefsteak weighing eleven pounds that he had gotten as a present from a fellow believer at the completion of a small transaction. The housekeeper found it advisable to sell the meat on the sly and to use the money for her own needs. A few days later the old Hebrew asked for the meat and ordered something to be prepared with it for lunch.

"Oh, just imagine my bad luck," yelled the housekeeper. "The cursed cat just ate it."

Without a word the Israelite went into the kitchen, grabbed the cat, and put her on the scale. The cat weighed exactly eleven pounds.

"Yes," he said to the housekeeper, "here are exactly eleven pounds. But where now is the cat?"

NOTE: Uther 2011, Type 1373: *The Weighed Cat*; Rawnitzki 1950, 2:101, joke #590; Mendelsohn 1952, 100–101; Druyanow 1963, 2:33, joke #1103; Schwarzbaum 1968, 55; Spalding 1969, 130–31. Meatprikol n.d. In some versions: "If this is the cat, then where is the meat? If this is the meat, then where is the cat?" as in the Hodja Nasreddin story in Downing (1965, 10).

~

103. A Jew was riding a fairly wild horse, and since he didn't possess the art of taming it, it reared up and threatened to throw him.

[86] The Jew pulled with all his might in his effort to stay in the saddle, all the while making hideous grimaces as well as uttering involuntarily cries of fear when the horse jumped to one side. All of this attracted spectators, who enjoyed the spectacle of the shaking Israelite.

Finally all of his efforts were in vain, and the brave steed threw his rider down to earth. The fall was accompanied by the general laughter of the spectators.

"Oh, my!" said the Jew, angrily picking himself up from the ground. "What is there to laugh at? The smartest one gives in."

∽

104. When Moses Mendelssohn first came into the world of scholars, it was common usage in Berlin among scholars to play chess during the evening gatherings.

Moses Mendelssohn never wanted to understand this game, and when he was invited, he said: "Chess is too much play [*Spiel*] for the brain, and the game [*Spiel*] demands too much thought."

NOTE: "Anekdoten" 1812, 354.

∽

105. [87] A Jew named Lazarus N——s had a very lucrative trade in contraband.

For a long time he did this without any challenge; finally, though, somebody snitched on him.

Very early one morning a few tax collectors appeared at his doorstep. They came into his bedroom very unexpectedly while he was still in bed. "Does a certain Lazarus N——s live here?" one of these officials asked.

"Yes," said the surprised man, without losing his composure, even though he noticed right away with what intention his morning visitors came. "But he has moved out," he added.

With this assurance the unwelcome guests removed themselves. The Jew jumped quickly out of his bed, got dressed, and hid the available contraband.

In the meantime the tax collectors questioned the landlord about Lazarus N——s and learned, to their amazement, that they had just been in his quarters and had spoken to him.

So they returned to him and [88] accused him of lying by saying he had moved.

"My, I only spoke the truth," replied the confronted man. "You asked if Lazarus N——s lived here. And I answered, 'Yes! But he's moved out [*ausgezogen* = undressed, moved out]. Since I was lying in bed I was undressed, and it would have been inappropriate to receive such distinguished gentlemen while I was undressed."

106. Two Jews, Nathan and Levi, traveled a few stations on the common stagecoach.

There were more passengers in the coach, and Nathan, who was a well-traveled merchant, ceaselessly entertained his companions with what he had seen. He came to the latest news and recounted many interesting anecdotes.

His fellow believer, who got bored in the end because none of the other passengers or he himself ever got a word in, [89] finally interrupted with a derisive remark.

"Is it true, Nathan, that you are a great politician?"

"Don't complain," he responded.

"How is it complaining when I call you a politician?"

"Of course it's complaining. Do you know what a politician is?"

"Well, a politician is—well, what is he going to be? A politician."

"Don't you see that you don't know? Pay attention, I'm going to tell you. A politician is a good sheath around a crook."

~

The Jew by the name of Nehemie [Nehemiah] Jehuda Leib or Löbel was born in 1759 in Streikow in Poland, where his father was a hatmaker. Starting with his earliest youth until he was twenty years old, his parents let him study with the rabbis. Then he needed to earn the fruits of his labors; he had to leave the school and became a teacher himself. For six to seven years, he was occupied with [90] teaching the children of his fellow believers in his area, but from this he could only barely feed himself.

The wish to improve his fate and the hope that he would find his luck elsewhere gave him the idea to move to Prozetvorsk in the Austrian part of Poland. But he couldn't find employment anywhere until finally a fellow believer, who was conductor and supplier to the imperial court, took him in as stable boy.

He stayed with this supplier for two years. During this time, he became acquainted with a clergyman who frequently talked to him from his window as he brought the horses to the monastery's drinking trough, often but unsuccessfully trying to convert him to Christianity.

In the beginning he was content with his fate. But when, after a year had gone by, his master reduced his pay from the promised eight Polish thalers and Polish twelve guilders in [91] money, deducting his costs, and as he no longer was fed from the table of his master, he wanted to leave his employ. Only at the urging of his master's brother did he drop his intention and return. Now he was promised that he would be better cared for, but this promise was not kept. And nothing changed in his circumstances. Since, due to increasing inflation, his allowance did not suffice to procure the basic necessities, he decided a year later for the second time to leave quietly.

He scarcely escaped when the imperial soldiers caught him, and as punishment for escaping, he was to receive two hundred strokes of flogging.

When he had received the first half, the Catholic clergyman appeared whose acquaintance he had made before and promised the forgiveness of the rest on condition that he would become a Christian.

[92] What the most articulate persuasions of the clergyman could not achieve before was now achieved by fear of the beating. The unlucky and helpless Jew decided to convert to Christianity. The clergyman kept his promise, and he was relieved of his punishment. He was brought to the cloister in Michev, where he was baptized and set free.

Here he stayed for two years, and even though he lacked nothing (according to his own account) in the cloister, he did feel pangs of guilt about the apostasy against his father's faith. Therefore he sought to flee to a place where he could, without danger and fear of maltreatment, return to his old religion. In the cloister of Michev, where he was, there was also a baptized Jewess who also felt the urge to return to her paternal religion. With her he went on his way to Breslau, where he pretended she was his wife and that her one-year-old son was also his. From Breslau they continued their trip to Frankfurt on the Oder. There he left [93] his travel companion and went alone to Berlin, to try finding work there. He hired himself out to the Jewish merchant Moses Aaron, again as stable boy. With him he traveled to Schwerin in Mecklenburg. In Grewitz, two miles from Schwerin, Moses Aaron sold his horses and wagon, took Nehemie Jehuda Leib's few things with him, and got into the stagecoach to return to Berlin. The latter had to walk all the way back.

The poor Nehemie Jehuda Leib actually came back to Berlin and met his master, who left him in a very secretive, underhanded way, didn't even pay his outstanding salary entirely, and didn't even return the few articles of his clothing and shirts.

Deprived of everything, he decided to follow his master, who'd gone to Hanover. He got on his way, and during his trip, he met [94] another poor eighty-six-year-old Jew from West Prussia, known by the name of Salomon Nathan.

Nehemie Jehuda Leib again met his former boss, Moses Aron, in Hanover and finally received from him, after a lot of difficulty and unpleasantness and through a compromise, instead of his total outstanding salary of twenty thalers, not more than three.

Since he didn't get his clothing back from Moses Aaron, he had to spend almost all of his money on retrieving his jacket pawned in his greatest extremity, a jacket to cover his naked body. After he had paid for his stay, he had only three groschen of the three thalers he had received to leave Hanover. With this little money he wanted to go to Strykow in Poland, and with this purpose he started on his way through Saxony and Brandenburgia.

On his way he again met the Jew Salomon Nathan, [95] whom he had met before, and in whose company he continued on his way back.

In the following pages written by Nehemie Jehuda Leib himself, he tells in detail how miserable he was on his wanderings alone and in the company of Salomon Nathan. Often he had to pay a tax on his person twice in one day, often he found himself between two bridges where he could neither advance nor go back without having to pay a tax on his person [*Leibzoll*]. Often he had to sell the few articles of clothing he had left to the first person he met just to get ahead.

Both Jews made their way through Coswig and Treuenbrietzen to Berlin. During their journey the old Salomon Nathan behaved very badly, which Nehemie Jehuda Leib complained to him about. The old man excused himself due to his poverty and his bad luck and added: "The little that I have I want to bring to my wife and my children."

To which Nehemie Jehuda Leib [96] answered: "If you don't eat or drink, then the devil will come for the money."

Only once did the old Jew show his companion his silver money: when he sold his cane in Treuenbrietzen for one thaler and nine groschen and put it with the rest of his money that he had in his handkerchief, tied in a knot, and carried in his pouch. In passing he told him that he also had ducats in addition to his silver money.

On the night on February 23 to 24, 1790, both travelers stopped in the village Elsholz, one mile from Belitz. In Belitz a young tailor noticed that Salomon Nathan had bugs. Nehemie Jehuda Leib had noticed it also. The following day, when they passed a bush, the latter therefore made the suggestion to his companion that they go into the bushes to rid themselves of the bugs. They both went into a not-so-thick bush, and Salomon Nathan took off his leggings so that he could more readily take care of this business.

[97] The certain calculation regarding Salomon Nathan's helplessness and the upcoming body taxes, from which he was exempt being a West Prussian protected Jew, awakened in the unlucky Nehemie Jehuda Leib the thought to take his money and thereby eliminate once and for all the hardship he experienced from the demand of this tax. Therefore he grabbed the man from the back, threw him down, and with both hands in his left pants pocket, said with these words: "Give me the money." The old Salomon Nathan held onto his pocket with both hands and since he [Leib] didn't stop pulling on it, told him with tears in his eyes how horrible and unjust his actions were.

This description was not without its effect. Filled with pity, the robber (as described by Salomon Nathan himself) really let go with one hand and wanted to desist from his horrible deed. Unfortunately his good intention didn't last long. The thought of the body taxes [98] stifled all other compassion. He tried again to tear the pocket, and since this remained unsuccessful, he took his bread knife and actually cut the pocket and ran away. Salomon Nathan maintained that the robber came at him with the following words, "Give me the money or I get the knife!" Only the latter isn't completely sure of the words and assures at the same time that when he used the knife, he had no other intention than to cut the pocket.

After he cut off the pocket, he took flight. Soon three hussars, who were detailed to this area and had heard the screaming, caught up with him. The hussars asked him why he was running like that and who was screaming in the bushes. "It's my father!" answered the fugitive. "He owes me money and didn't want to give it to me, so I took it myself." The hussars took him with them into the bush where they had heard the screams and found the Jew, naked except for the trousers, [99] leaning against one of the few trees in the bushes. There they discovered the circumstances of what had transpired. They found the kerchief on Nehemie Jehuda Leib in which the stolen money was wrapped, which consisted of four thalers and five groschen Prussian, Courant, two Mary groschen, and fourteen pieces Bohemian. They gave it back to the owner and gave the robber thirty strokes and let him go. However, an officer coming from Treuenbrietzen learned of the incident and ordered them to stop the robber and to deliver him to Belitz.

The investigation was undertaken by the authorities in Saarmund, in whose jurisdiction that deed took place, and on the sixteenth of August 1790, the court, confirmed by the imperial Prussian circuit court, condemned Nehemie Jehuda Leib to a flogging and lifelong hard labor.

∼

[100] The personal history of Nehemie Jehuda Leib (composed by himself)

May the almighty God have mercy on me, wretch that I am, I will transpose my life from my Jewish writing to German, so that the court may better understand it. So help me God in my need as I want to speak truth to the court and in writing. I have nothing to say about my life. I have to die. I have to have my thoughts, of the other world and this one. I only want to write about my life, how I came to my thought, up to the time I was arrested in Saarmund. The court shall hear that I am Nehimmie [sic] born in Strückhoff. I am thirty-one years old. Don't know how old my mother and father were; my father died, that is in the month of April it will be six years and my [101] mother died on the ninth day of the month of May, and was twenty-five years old. My father was a hatmaker. They spent their life in Strückhoff, and there they died. I have a sister in Klomnau called Irninnet. She is older than me, she is three years older than me, she is thirty-four years old.

Her husband's a tailor and is called Beisey. I had two sisters and one brother; they died in Strückhoff. I don't know how old they were. My father, when he lived, wrote his name Jude Leib. I call myself Nehimmie. I went to school in Strückhoff and studied for twenty years, which cost my father and mother a lot of money. They said that I should have good thoughts for them. I had good thoughts, which I learned with [teaching] the children from the villages around Strückhoff whom I taught for six to seven years. Then I thought that I could make more with people and went away, to Schaffortz, in the imperial lands. There I couldn't get work teaching the children. There I connected with a Jew, [102] who was a minister of the emperor. He was never home; instead, he was always with the emperor in Wittna. I never saw him only when he hired me to work with the horses in Schafforz. He had a brother called Kumpel, who knew me. What the Jew was called, who took me on, I do not know. He promised me wages of eight Polish thalers a year and for food per day twelve Polish groschen, which is one groschen and six German pfennigs. I was two years with the Jew. The first year was good because then I still got the food money. The second year I had to give six dreier [three-pfennig piece] and that was too expensive at the time. I couldn't live from the six dreier, so I left the employ. But then the brother Kumpel promised that he would make it better, so I came back. But he didn't keep his promise, so I left the second time. During this time, while I worked for the Jew, I sometimes took my horses to the fountain close to the monastery, where [103] there was always a Catholic priest at the window who called to me asking if I didn't want to be baptized. I never had thoughts about getting baptized because I knew what our Jewish law said. You shall know from where you come and your thoughts shall be that you will go to such a place. That worms will eat you in the earth, that God will judge you when you will die, such thoughts I had at the time when the priest called to me. Since I was born a Jew I also have to die in my Jewish religion, even today as I go locked in chains, I prefer that I am in my Jewish religion. When I left the second time my master complained to the general, who ordered my arrest. Then I was beaten and arrested. The soldiers said I should also be beaten on the third day. I fell ill from the first strokes. At this time it happened that the Catholic priest came to my jail [104] and said to me that I should count on him and should not be beaten anymore and would get off jail. So I had enough. I promised I would let myself be baptized. But my thoughts were that I could soon return to my religion. But it would have been better if I had lost my life at that time. That I denied my religion, my thoughts are, that it will be hard and bitter to pray in my faith. I see that in front of me. At this time I take all from God. So I was freed. The priest took me to Müllhoff, and I was baptized on the third day. After the baptism they gave me the keys to the dining hall, and I could eat and drink in the cloister. But I always thought that I could return to my religion. In my heart I always had my faith. For two years I prayed to my God that I could die in my faith. Had I been very rich, I would have run away and would have left my things, as I [105] also did. Through this I became acquainted with the woman with whom I left, because we had one faith. I didn't say a word to the woman that I wanted to leave because I was afraid that she would betray me. But then she said that she would like to leave. So I left with her. She also had a child with her. So we went three miles to the water and bought two horses and a wagon. If a Christian asked if she was my wife, I said yes; if a Jew asked, I spoke the truth. I had saved money in the monastery from which I bought my clothes. As we could we went from small Poland to great Poland to Ludemirks, where we sold the wagon and horses for four ducats minus six Polish guilders. With that we went to Breslau. At the gate I was asked where I came from and if I had a passport. Since I didn't need one in Poland, I was brought to the magistrate. There I said that I was a baptized Jew. The magistrate laughed [106] at that. They gave us the passport. We said everything in front of the magistrate and stayed five days in Breslau. After that we went by water until half a mile before Frankfurt, where there was a fair every day. The Jews gave me a letter that all Jews should help me. The woman stayed in Frankfurt, and I went with a good friend to Berlin. As I arrived in Berlin, I met a merchant from Prott, Mosis Arend [sic], to whom I hired out as a farm laborer for the horses. As wages he promised two and a half ducats until Easter, and for food one thaler weekly. For a few weeks I traveled with the Jew all the way to Mecklenburgia to the town of Schwerin. At the hostel the Jew threw one ducat in a bag into the room to test me if I was honest. Since I found it, I gave it back to him. The innkeeper can attest to that because I had no need. From Schwerin we drove to Crewitz. Here my boss sold the wagon and the horses. He put his things on top of my sack and sent them by post. But I learned that he did not [107] send them. He sat down in the stagecoach and went to Berlin. I had to walk to Berlin. When he came to Berlin, he left during the night and left me all alone in Berlin. Now I was a stranger in Berlin and didn't know where to go. I went to his landlord Leimbecker, who told me that he had left at night. I went to the post to ask where he had gone and heard he had gone to Potsdam. I went to the rich Moiss, that is the man where he always left his things, and cried. He gave me six groschen but no further counsel as to what I should do. The Jews said I should follow him. So I went out of the gate and immediately had to pay two groschen tax and went to Potsdam. As I left, I again had to pay two groschen tax. I went to Brandenburg and again had to pay two groschen. I went to Magdeburg, where they kept me a whole day before the bridge because I should give the gatekeeper four groschen, and I only had two groschen. When I had more than two I had to use the rest for my sustenance. So I had to leave my shirt with the gatekeeper and [108] again had to pay money to cross the bridge. I went to the Jews and collected four groschen and got the shirt back from the bridge keeper. So I thought I was free. I went to the gate to Holberrstadt and in town I met a soldier who asked me where I was going. I explained my circumstances to him. He gave me one groschen. As I left the city, the gatekeeper asked me for my tax papers. I showed him my tax papers, but he said that wasn't my tax paper. "You have to go back to town, where you have to pay duty, without that you can't leave." But I didn't want to go, so he wanted to beat me. So I went back to the gatekeeper and asked him if I had the correct paper that he gave me. He said, I had to go to town in a house over the bridge where I had to give another four groschen. They made it so difficult for me with the taxes that I wanted to jump from the bridge into the water. When I got to the house, I asked if I had to pay taxes one more time. The man said, "Yes, you have to pay taxes again." I [109] had nothing more than the groschen that the soldier gave me. After that I wanted to sell my pipe at the customs, but the soldier wouldn't pay more than one groschen six pfennigs for it so I didn't sell it. I wanted to leave my shirt for the second time. He didn't want to take it, so I cried in front of him and begged him saying I didn't have more than a groschen. But that didn't help. A Christian came into the room and paid my toll for me. I can't begin to tell you how badly I fared in Madgeburg because of the toll. From Magdeburg I went to Halberstadt. There they didn't even let me into the town. It hit me that I had to pay toll four times in one day. In Saxony is a village called Lobido, where the gatekeeper wanted eight groschen toll. But through my crying and begging he took only five groschen six pfennigs from me and saying he'd have to add the rest. I could write a lot of what I suffered with the tolls. Then [110] I spent more than six thalers in taxes. My path became very difficult, as a Jew to follow my boss. One mile before Braunschweig in a village I met the old Jew for the first time, where we spent the night. In the morning I went toward Hanover, and the old man stayed in the tavern. I did meet the merchant, my boss, in Hanover. I had nothing left to live on in Hanover. I had to take my clothing off my body to pawn it with the innkeeper. I didn't have to pay toll for two groschen only for the night paper. I asked my boss and went with him to court. In court he said he didn't even know me. He was asked to swear that he didn't know me. All of this took three days, but it was taking too long for me to wait there because I had no money. The Jews advised me that I should go to the magistrate and lodge a complaint that I had a contract with him. But I was afraid because I heard say that I had tried to murder the Jew and in court [111] I had to take off my jacket. I thought I would be beaten again. I made some points, out of fear. I had to pawn my clothes to pay fifteen groschen of that to the magistrate. But I couldn't understand anything in court. When they spoke German I could understand, so I was told to go to Berlin and bring the record from the clerk. Since I had nothing on my person because I had pawned the jacket, I went to the Jew and asked him for one thaler. My boss said he would give me three thalers. I had to take the three thalers even though I was owed twenty, so I could get back my jacket from the innkeeper. After paying for my lodging and redeeming my jacket I had only three groschen. In my whole life

I never took anything from anyone. The thing with the old Jew I did out of necessity, because of the tolls. When I went back and came into a village I asked the sheriff for a piece of bread because I was hungry. But the sheriff wanted to beat me and said, "We [112] have to give to the Christians, not the Jews." I went from Hanover to Berlin and wanted to go again to my sister in Poland which is eighty miles. In the area between Oranienbaum and Werlitz I met the old Jew again. We shook hands. At first I didn't recognize him because in Braunschweig he was wearing a black jacket and now he had a white one. But he said right away that he knew me because we had met in Braunschweig. He said he couldn't walk very well because of his feet. I pointed to my feet and said I had also walked my feet raw. So we went together from Coswig to Schawitz. The old man told me we want to go to the other Schawitz to go to Berlin. So we went from Coswig to Treuenbrietzen. At the gate the Jews gave us one groschen each. I wanted to go into the town. The gatekeeper wanted two groschen. Because of these tolls I was frequently cash-strapped. The old man sold his cane to the Jews for one thaler and nine groschen. Afterward we came to a village, whose name [113] I do not know. The old man went begging in the village, and I went into the tavern. When he came to me he said that in Belitz was a fair. I told him I had also heard that. The old man said we should have been in Belitz today because he wanted to buy a pair of shoes. I told him we should go but it was already four hours after noon and day was short. He had told me his life's history. I had no thought to do anything bad to him. I ask God to be my witness that I was always good to the old man. In Coswig I went with him to buy a pair of shoes. The old man asked me what I was called. I told him my name was Nehimmie. I asked him for his name. He said his name was Leib and tomorrow he wanted to buy a pair of shoes. At night the people from Belitz came from the fair, and the old man asked if he could still get a pair of shoes. Two Jews, one Pole, one tailor, one Christian, came to Treuenbrietzen into the tavern where we were. When I saw the old Jew take off his pants at night, I saw that [114] lice were falling off him. The tailor said that the old man had to have had lice because he was always scratching, and I said, "Yes, he has lice." I said to the old man, if he wants to, we can leave early, a little before dawn, and buy a pair of shoes. At night the old man couldn't sleep. But he answered me saying he was too cold; he couldn't sleep. I would have liked to cover him with my fur, but he was unclean. He didn't leave early for Belitz. Instead after we Jews had prayed, we had our breakfast. The two Jews went to Belitz, and the tailor left. I told the old man that the two Jews were almost in Belitz, and we had still not left. The day before, we had deloused ourselves between Treuenbrietzen and the village where we spent the night. As the people were going to get wood, they laughed at us as we deloused ourselves. If you want to delouse yourself you have to get off the beaten path, not where people pass. That's what I told the old man. During the delousing the old man said to [115] me, "I don't know where [sic] I have so many lice." I told him he didn't want to buy a shirt. Each Sabbath you have to put on a shirt. You're waiting until someone gives you a shirt. You don't eat and don't drink and the devil will get the money, why is that an old saying. We're going to Belitz to the mill, where the old man went to beg. I waited for him. Then we went another quarter mile on our path. We talked about going to Hamburg over Easter holidays. The old man said that when we get to Belitz, let's spend the night. This was around 11:00 a.m. As if we still had time to make it to Belitz. So I said to the old man, "Let's delouse but not on the path, but on the side." We went to the right about forty steps, but my God knows I had no intention to harm him. But the old man said to keep walking. That was about fifteen to twenty steps from the place, we went under a tree. There was [116] no bush, only a meadow. I stood on the right side of the tree to delouse myself, and the old man stood on the left side of the tree, dropped his pants, and deloused. This took a quarter of an hour. I should die, that under that tree I had the thought of how I would get to Poland if I don't have any money. I need money to pay tolls, permits, and lodging. That's when the thought came, and I threw the old man down and tore his pants and said to him, "Give me the money right away or I'll have to use the knife." But my thoughts were not to harm him, only to take his money because of the tolls. I don't know if that is what I did. I am said to have said, "Give me the money or I'll get the knife." That his pants are torn, I don't know. I promised him that when I get out of jail, I will give him my jacket. He told me when I took his money that he had to run around a whole year [117] to get this money together. "And you want to take it." At that point my hands dropped from the pants, and it came to me that I should leave the old man his money. But then I thought again about the tolls, which began the deed. It wasn't even a real knife. Then in how many towns did they ask me for my passport and right away for the toll. When I took the money from the Jew, I ran away. On the right was the village where I wanted to go. Then the three hussars came, who heard the old man yell. They came to me and asked what was going on. I told them that it was my father who owed me money and didn't want to pay me. I had always called him father as he was old. Because we came from Werlitz on the way to Coswig, we had to cross the water. For the crossing I had to pay one groschen for him. I asked him often to pay me back. He always said he was going to give it back but he never did. We drank beer together but he never contributed. But my thoughts weren't [118] to take his money because of the groschen and six pfennigs, only the tolls. Then the hussars took me to the old Jew, who took the money right off my chest. The hussars took eight groschen. Since I said it was my money, they gave it back to me, the money that I took from the old man. It was about four or three thalers. When I didn't have it, the old man said to me if he had money left after the shoes, he would trade it for one ducat. When the old man took the money from me, the hussars gave me thirty strokes. I felt them for eight days. Then they let me go. A man drove by in his wagon, who ordered the hussars to catch me. Now I came to Belitz before the magistrate. The mayor relieved me of my identification papers and the eight groschen he gave to the messenger of the guards. The identification papers I got back, and we were sent with one of the hussars to Saarmund.

Of my writing that I wrote, God, who created me, [119] knows that it is all true. If not, then I can swear in my Jewish faith of the shul, that it is all true, so help me God in the hour of my need.

Saarmund, July 6, 1790.

Jewish signature

CHAPTER 4

Texts from The Friend of the Jews or Selected Anecdotes, Pranks, and Notions of the Children of Israel

Published by Judas Ascher
Leipzig, from Baumgärtner
Bookseller 1810

Foreword

A few years ago a small brochure appeared called "Anecdotes of Good Jews" with an appendix of Jewish wisdom-teachings.

While the aim of this publication was very praiseworthy, it did not have the expected impact. The zeitgeist is more for the huge instead of the good, and the brain is prized higher than the heart.

The publisher has therefore considered the taste of the readership in the collection of the following anecdotes, pranks, and notions and has preferred to choose those that illustrate presence of mind, quick-wittedness, cunning, perspicacity, and humor. No impartial observer will deny that his fellow believer has excelled in the above qualities in all aspects of life. And if they do not shine very numerous as authors in the academic world, then that is entirely due to the correct calculation that it is a thousand times more lucrative to have someone write them a check than to write books themselves.

J. A. [iii–iv]

201. To a Jew, who administered the everyday activities of a company of actors, and who was not unfamiliar with dramatic literature, an actor, who wanted to enhance the prospects of his ambitions, said, "Have you read 'Nathan der Weise' by Lessing?"

(The piece had just been published.)
The Jew: "By Lessing? That has to be good."
The actor: "Read it. You will like it. It praises Jews highly."
The Jew: "Praised?—What?—I get six cuffs and get criticized." [5]

202. When in the fourteenth century the people's emperor Nikolaus Gabrici Rienzi was murdered in Rome and hanged after his death, the mob tore him from the gallows and delivered him to his enemies the Jews, whom he had often subjected to his strictness.

They now roasted the sad remains of his mangled corpse on a slow fire, in order to prolong their barbaric delight to satisfy their need for revenge. [5–6]

NOTE: Cola de Rienzi (1313–1354) was born in Rome of humble origins. He aspired to return the city to its ancient greatness and to reestablish a united Italy. He led a revolt that chased the nobles out of the city and assumed the title of tribune. His career had ups and downs, but he eventually alienated the church and the populace that had initially supported him and was murdered by a mob.

203. In the year 1493 at the time of the Archbishop Ernesti, a Jew called Salomon fell into a ditch outside the town of Magdeburg. So as not to desecrate the Sabbath, he remained lying there the whole day.

When the bishop heard this, he forbade all Jews and everyone else from helping the Jew out of the ditch the following Sunday, so that this day also not be desecrated. Thus the Jew had to remain in the ditch two days before he could be rescued from his painful situation. [6]

204. Two Jews were traveling from Venice to Bologna. While on the way one of them fell sick and died. The other one wanted to take the body of his friend back to Venice. Since it was forbidden to do so publicly, he cut him into small pieces and put him into a barrel, added different herbs and honey so a very pleasing smell came out of the barrel. This barrel he gave to another Jew so that he could take it to Venice. The barrel was loaded onto a ship and when it was on the canal by Ferrara, it happened that a man from Florence sat on it. When night fell, he was tempted by the delicious smell from the barrel, and he opened it without being observed and began to taste it. It tasted so good that through the night he emptied almost half of the barrel and imagined he was tasting something very delicious.

When the Jew wanted to disembark in Ferrara and lifted the barrel, he noticed that it had become significantly lighter. 'Oh!" he screamed, "What bad luck, the dead Jew left the barrel!!!"

You can imagine how the Florentine felt when he thus learned what he had really consumed. [6–7]

205. A Jesuit student in Lemberg purposely threw a stone at a Jew. The Jew bent over, and the stone went through a window on the other side.

As a result, the owner of the house filed a complaint. The judge wanted to know the sequence of events and found the Jew guilty and fined him, but not the Jesuit scholar.

The religious prejudice and the contempt against the Jewish nation were so common that anyone could beat them and mistreat them without any consequences to the miscreant. Finally that was stopped; only the right to still throw things was expressly granted.

And this gave the judge the cause to say, "Not by the student throwing did the window break, but because the Jew bent forward. And because of the law he should not have bent forward because the right to throw is on the side of the Jesuit student and gave the Jew the obligation to let someone throw things at him." [7–8]

∽

206. In the town of Halle in 1735 the medical doctor Christian Heinrich Immanuel Frommann [= pious man], who had previously been Jewish and later converted to Christianity, died.

The manner of his conversion and the story of it prove that he did not take his pious name without any rhyme or reason, and it is a rare example of conscientiousness. Because at his conversion to Christianity, he sent 240 thalers to Professor Caltenberg as the amount for which he as a Jew had taken advantage of others and had cheated them. He added a list naming the persons he had taken advantage of and asked that they be reimbursed. The rest should go to the orphanage. He also added forty useful books for Jews. [8–9]

∽

208. The son of a Jew in England was about to marry a Christian. The father of the Jew had nothing against the religion of the girl, but her fortune was too small for him; he therefore asked him to look to the future and advised him to take a richer one, with the threat that if he persisted in his intention, he would not leave him more than a shilling.

The son declared that regardless of whether he agreed, he would not be dissuaded from the object of his desire, and if the father refused his consent, the son would be baptized and then, according to English law, could be entitled to a half of the father's fortune.

At this answer the parent became quite alarmed, and inquired hastily of a lawyer if there really was such a law.

"Of course," assured the lawyer, "but if you give me ten guineas, I will tell you the means to upset his calculation so that the disobedient one would not get a shilling."

The Jew was very happy, took out his purse, and counted the money.
The lawyer calmly collected it and then said:
"You also have to let yourself be baptized." [13–14]

~

209. The king of Prussia, Friedrich Wilhelm I, did not want to see shyness and fear of him from his subjects.

Once he rode with his groom through the zoo in Berlin.

He barely rode a few feet when he thought he saw two people who had been coming toward him disappear into the thicket as they caught sight of him.

He ordered his groom to search for these people and bring them to him. Shortly he brought these two beggar Jews to the monarch.

"Why did you hide yourselves?" asked the king.

"We were 'fraid!" replied the Jews.

Angry, the king took his Spanish cane and beat the two fugitives black and blue, saying:

"Love, you should love me, not fear me!" [14–15]

~

210. In Gotha the famous actor Grossmann played the role of the Jew Pinkus in "The Retired Officers."

When the play was over, someone asked the Jew how he liked it.

"Predy gud!" answered the Hebrew. "Only the change he shouldna gi'en. No Jew does that." [15]

NOTE: Gustav Friedrich Wilhelm Grossmann (1743–1796), actor, theater director, and dramatist, was an acquaintance of Gotthold Ephraim Lessing and Friedrich Nicolai. He had his first big acting success in Gotha. The play *Die abgedankten Offiziere* is also referred to in Büschenthal joke #34. The Pinkus character is a Jew from Holland. Grossman's plays were about middle-class family life.

~

212. One day, Professor Engel and his friend Nicolai, a bookseller, were in Stralau, a pleasant fishing village near Berlin where the late Dr. Bloch, of the Jewish nation, had once spent a few weeks to improve the state of his health and on hot days delighted in the play of fish before his window, and so accidentally found the impetus for his famous work on fish (ichthyology).

"If this small, poor, and insignificant village," Nicolai said, "didn't have such a romantic situation on the Spree, it would always remain noteworthy, because Bloch sailed from here into larger rivers and finally into distant seas and returned with so precious a cargo."

"And even more remarkable," said Engel, "that this Jew had so much heart not to have fear of the water but an *accursed greed for gold* [Latin: *auri sacra fames*]." [16]

NOTE: Marcus Elieser Bloch (1723–1799) was a doctor and was Moses Mendelssohn's physician. He was also a famous naturalist who published a brilliantly illustrated, twelve-volume encyclopedia on fish between 1782 and 1795. It went through several editions in both German and French. Christoph Friedrich Nicolai (1733–1811) was an important publisher and editor and a friend of Gotthold Ephraim Lessing and Moses Mendelssohn. He published Mendelssohn's first work *Philosophische Gespräche* (Philosophical dialogues) in 1755.

∼

217. A Jew by the name of Wahl Bamberger gave good service for twenty-five to thirty years in Königsberg in Prussia and again in Berlin in a Jewish business. His ability, good heartedness, and exemplary behavior had earned him praise as a good man with everyone, as well as enabling him to save a good fortune. After he had the bad luck of breaking his leg, he decided to live out his days in his father's city of Meinderheim in Franconia.

Here lived his brother, Samuel Bamberger, who, with his wife and children, long found himself in the direst of circumstances. For twenty-five years he had already benefitted from the support of his brother with twelve ducats a year, not to mention as well the most extraordinary presents.

Wahl Bamberger came to his brother with the noble intention to share his wealth with him and his family. This also came to pass and in the beginning there reigned between the brothers a friendly harmony.

Wahl Bamberger belonged to the number of enlightened Jews and he therefore did not adhere strictly to Mosaic Law and even declared himself free of some of the Talmudic rules. This incurred the wrath of the orthodox Jews, especially that of his own brother, who tried to insult him with pharisaic hypocrisy.

Wahl Bamberger spent three years with many disappointments, which also caused him to become unwell. Still he almost always recovered. After the passage of three years, he was attacked in the middle of the night by a stroke, and in the morning, they found him dead in his bed. His brother, Samuel, was his only heir, because the departed had expressly named him as that in his testament.

But this did not keep his brother from crudely slandering him upon his death. Nor did he agree to allow his benefactor, as a heretic, to be buried next to the bones of his parents and relatives. Finally, he was shabbily buried in the Jewish cemetery. He was stuck in the earth far from his relatives. Out of pure hate against his dead brother, he also hung an inherited portrait onto the secret chamber. [20–22]

∼

219. In Amsterdam a Jew came to a merchant and offered him jewels, which he showed him, and against which he wanted to borrow 12,000 guilders.

The merchant asked other experts, and they agreed that the jewels were worth at least 20,000 guilders. The Jew was given the money, and in exchange, he gave the little box with the jewels (which with all speed he exchanged with another one). He sealed it with his seal and went off.

The time for the redemption had already passed a while back. The merchant was concerned, and he ordered the notary to come and opened the box in his presence and found sand. The merchant did not know the Jew. The name he had given was certainly made up. He was probably long gone from Holland. What could be done to make him come back and make himself known?

The merchant went to a legal scholar who gave him the following advice, which the merchant faithfully followed. In the evening, he did not have the windows of his shop shuttered, and at night he had the windows broken into. And the next day the following news was published: "A major burglary occurred at the merchant N—— N—— last night. A break-in occurred because the windows were negligently left open and the following items were taken, etc. Above all he is most concerned about a small box of jewelry which did not belong to him but which was only left to him as pawn, and which includes the following pieces, etc."

The deception worked. The Jew, who had received the news about it, soon came back thereafter and said: "Since you secure your house so poorly and didn't even close the shutters, the loss of the pawned items is not mine as owner, but yours as pawnshop keeper. You either return the jewels to me or at least give me the 8,000 guilders, since the box was valued at 20,000 guilders."

No one wanted more than that the Jew reappear. The notary document proved sufficient and the lawsuit was quickly decided. [22–24]

NOTE: Mendelsohn 1935, 128–29. In using the lure of greater rewards to catch a thief see Richman (1954, 329–30).

---

221. A rich Jew in B—— had a brother-in-law in L—— who also had a respectable amount of wealth.

Since the real names of the people are not important, but you can't tell a good story without names, we will call the first one Moses and the other one Isaac. One day Isaac received a letter that, according to the main content, stated: "A while back I advanced the bishop of K—— a bond of 40,000 thaler. Since I did not have the whole amount in cash, I had a local Jew named Schmai Moses give me 13,000 thaler, and I promised him a part of the profit that the deal would bring me as a percentage of our combined money. Little by little I paid him a total of 8,000 as a rebate on his demand against the bond so that his principal amount was still 1,000 louis d'or. Some days ago he came to me and told me a lot about an advantageous deal that he could pull together if I could give him the capital. We agreed on the split of the profit and since we always were used to do deals together, I gave him without consideration the bond of the bishop, since I had no cash. To my great dismay, I received yesterday the news that Schmai Moses had filed for bankruptcy and is absolved. He has taken my bond, and I am afraid he will either give it back to the bishop or sell it to someone else at a discount. Just now I learned that he is on his way to L——, and I don't want to have him arrested since he knows all about my business and could harm me. So can you do me a big favor and try in every way to find where he is in L——. So that you can't miss him, I will describe him exactly. He is small, thin, has a red beard, wears a black wig, etc. If you find him, I will do everything to get the bond from him. Offer him his 1,000 louis d'or, and try to come to terms with him for the interest. If he is not willing, then threaten that you will have him arrested and handed over to his creditors. I will not ask for your effort for nothing and will immediately pay you your advanced money through a money courier."

The writing, the signature, and the seal of his brother-in-law were well-known to the honest Isaac. The matter was so important and urgent that he did not suspect any deception nor take the time to be suspicious of the considerations. He started immediately to make inquiries regarding Schmai Moses, and two days after the receipt of the letter, he had the pleasure of finding him. In the beginning the swindler denied the whole thing. But when Isaac started to press him, especially when he threatened him with arrest and turning him in, then he gave up the bond and as his part of the same 1,000 louis d'or, for which interest was due, he took 100 ducats. The former willingly paid this as he had so happily ended this miserable affair. Without hesitation the bond, the money order for 5,300 thaler and a brief summary of the whole story were packed up and sent off to B——.

Moses received the whole packet from his brother-in-law, read and reread, and could not believe his eyes. He called his wife, had her read, and she also could not believe what he believed he had read. At first they both believed the brother-in-law was joking, but since the courier cost thirty thaler, that was too expensive for a joke. Then they assumed that the man had lost his mind, but the letter was in order and written coherently, the bond was well sealed, and everything was as it should be. Finally they wrote to Isaac and reassured him that not even a bishop of K—— in the whole world nor the letter he referred to had been written by Moses in B——.

After a long back-and-forth written exchange, it was figured out that Schmai Moses was probably the false name of a swindler, who had copied Moses's handwriting, described himself, and in this way had stolen 5,300 thaler from the helpful Isaac.

They tried everything to find the cheat, but in vain, and the brothers-in-law finally ended up in court because Isaac didn't want to carry the damage, or at least not all of it, entirely by himself. [25–29]

222. A Mohammedan had accidentally and unintentionally put out the eye of a Jew. The Jew lodged a complaint for revenge.

The Kadi decided according to the long pages in the books of law.

"For this case there is nothing determined in the laws, but what it does say is that if a Mohammedan takes out both eyes of a Jew, then the authority shall allow him [the Jew] to take one eye."

"So, do you want," the Kadi continued to the Jew, "that I should let the defendant take one eye, then let him first tear out your second eye."

Since the Jew didn't want to exact his revenge at such a price, the defendant was set free. [29–30]

NOTE: There is something similar in Richman (1954, 72–74), but it is combined with Uther 2011, Type 1534A*: *Barber Substituted for Smith at Execution.*

∼

223. The poet Saintfoix owed a Jew 100 ducats, which he could not pay.

His creditor met him by chance at the barber's, who had just washed his beard.

The Jew reminded him instantly. Saintfoix asked him if he didn't at least want to wait until this man had removed his beard.

"Oh, yes," answered the Israelite, "be delighted."

"Now you are witness, my man!" Saintfoix then said to the barber, and stood up, wiped off the soap, paid, and left with his beard unshaved. [30]

NOTE: The reverse trick of shaving a beard for financial gain is in Rawnitski 1950 (2:158, joke #733).

∼

224. The son of a very rich merchant came to a Jew from whom he had often borrowed small amounts of money and begged him to lend him 2,000 thaler guaranteed by a note. They made an appointment to meet, so that the note would be made for only one year, but the Jew would be obligated to extend it for one more year. The money was paid in the house of the Jew and in the presence of a notary so that the exchange would be legally binding and not the smallest objection could be made against it.

The notary had barely closed the door behind him when the Jew said it should only be for one year when the payoff would be due. He could not agree to the extension and wanted to be paid at the end of the year. His intention was to make the young man miserable, and this he so well accomplished, according to his plan, that the latter, after a long exchange of words, said: "You rascal, I don't want your money if you will not keep our agreement."

"Good'" answered the Hebrew putting the ducats in his pocket. "Then the money is mine and here is the note."

With those last words he pulled the note out of his pocket, tore it into pieces and threw them into the chimney fire, which, not unintentionally, burned in the room.

After a year had passed, the Jew came and demanded his 2,000 thaler. The young man wanted to throw him down the stairs, but the Jew referred to the note, which he also showed him. It didn't occur to the former that the Jew could have thrown a similarly folded paper into the fire at that time. He let himself be sued and was condemned to pay the debt since the notary was an unsuspecting witness to the receipt of the money. [30–32]

∼

225. During the insurrection in south Prussia, King Friedrich Wilhelm II traveled in the province for the first time since its acquisition in the fall of 1794, and when the news of his arrival sounded in Posen, many festivities for his arrival were organized.

Among those, about fifty Jews decided to ride out one mile to ceremonially welcome the new Mailach [Yiddish: *meylekh* = king], as they called him.

Toward this end, they dressed very outlandishly. Their pants were very wide and long, part black and part red, and on the outside along the seam, they were decorated by a colorful zigzag like the Hussars. The doublets were out of all possible colors, very short, and with wide half-sleeves, so that the underarms, without the trace of a shirt, were completely bare. Everyone had a Turkish turban on his head, in his right hand a wooden pole with a small white flag with the black Prussian eagle on it, and on the left side, a broad curved sword. A few ringleaders in the front and in the back didn't have lances but held similar shining swords in their fists. The horses and their decorations were largely poor and bare and the riders rode noticeably short. Imagine in addition to this, the grim faces of a strongly pronounced Jewish physiognomy with long curly red or black beards, and you get a truly frightening cavalcade. Despite this, they elicited widespread laughter at their departure. From afar they looked like Cossacks or even Turks.

As this Hebraic cavalry saw the coach of the king about one mile out of Posen, they approached in a headlong rush.

The king, whom they had forgotten to inform of the plan of the Jews, and who couldn't quite explain to himself what this adventurous troop wanted, watched them with intense curiosity.

The swarm instantly surrounded the coach, some pulled back their panting horses in the strangest caricature, and when the ringleader saw that the advance guard and the coachman were looking at him suspiciously, he yelled with a happy, smiling face:

"Don't be 'fraid, your majesty, we're no Turks; we're your majesty's Jews from Posen."

Whereupon the voyage continued on to the town to the great amusement of the monarch. [32–34]

∼

226. When the Marshal de la Ferté made his entry into Metz, he was greeted by several business groups as well as a deputation of the Jewish community who appeared in the antechamber to greet him.

When they were announced, he said, quite disdainfully, "I do not want to see the local thieves; they have crucified Christ, let them go to the devil."

When they were told that the marshal could not and would not speak to them, they replied, "We are sorry for we have a present of 4,000 louis d'or from local Jewry to present to His Excellency."

This was immediately conveyed to the marshal, who said:

"Let them come in. These poor devils can't help it. Had they known the savior as we know him, they would not, out of honor, have crucified him." [34–35]

NOTE: The marshal is probably Henri François, duc de La Ferté-Senneterre (1657–1703) who, in the reign of Louis XIV, participated in the conquest of Holland. He was made governor of Metz in 1674.

∼

227. A Turkish sultan ordered a mass call-up [*Insurrektion*] of Jews in Antioch.

Eight thousand should move armed through the forest.

They then asked the sultan for a small escort because of robbers. [35]

NOTE: Richman 1952, 284.

∼

228. A Jew from —— went to a merchant every month and borrowed six guilders. With this small capital he traded the whole week, brought a fourth of his capital back every Friday evening and still had saved so much that he could live Saturday and Sunday without working. He continued this frugal life style over twenty years. [35–36]

∼

230. In Cologne lived a famous painter, who lived very comfortably, was profligate and a great lover of wine.

He painted a lot of images of Christ, which he gave as security to those innkeepers where he entertained himself. Folks asked why he didn't sell them.

"Because!" he said, "I do not want to be a Jew." [36–37]

∼

231. Under Emperor Joseph II an attempt was made to use Jews in the Austrian states for military service.

So a Jewish regiment was organized. But as soon as the officer in command issued an order, it ran through the ranks like wildfire:

"Attention, he said, he said."

Finally, annoyed, he said: "Shut up." And the ranks echoed: "Shut up, he said, he said." [37]

∼

236. A Jew borrowed the amount of 6,000 thaler from a banker. He knew, however, to quickly exchange the note made out for this amount with another one which was made out for 1,000 thaler, without the trustee noticing.

After the due date, the banker demanded the repayment, and the Jew also declared himself ready, upon the return of his note. When this was presented to him, he paid the written amount of 1,000 thaler.

Naturally this resulted in an intense altercation, since the Jew supported by his note, didn't want to hear anything else. So it resulted in a lawsuit, in which the banker provided so much evidence that the Jew was found guilty of fraud. Out of fear he offered the following excuse:

"Damned habit that I always write in abbreviations." [43–44]

∼

238. Three Jews were sentenced to death on the gallows because of breaking, entering, and theft.

As the day of the execution came closer, they were taken to the place of execution in the company of a multitude of people.

As the three criminals stood under the gallows, and the executioner was ready to do his duty, an urgent message arrived granting one of them a pardon.

He was immediately informed of his reprieve and was given permission to leave unharmed.

To the astonishment of the public, he remained in his place and appeared to be waiting for the execution of his robber comrades.

"Why are you still here?" asked the executioner. "He was pardoned. He needs to go."

"Mr. Executioner," replied the Jew, "I would like to wait until the others have been hanged. Perhaps I could bargain for sumptin' [*eppes*] of their clothes." [45–46]

∼

243. According to the Talmud, every scholarly and pious rabbi will receive 362 worlds to rule. A Jewish merchant once asked a rabbi why it was exactly 362 worlds?

After considering this for a while, the rabbi confessed finally that he couldn't say why.

"Well," said the merchant, "so I will tell you. The dear God loves peace and in order not to have any argument, he puts you scholarly windbags pretty far apart." [53–54]

NOTE: There is similarity with Rawnitzki (1950, 2:196, joke #47).

∼

245. A few years ago in H——schen, five Jews were arrested because of breaking, entering, and robbery, and after the required investigation, sentenced to hanging.

A very rich Jew in H—— went to the local administration and asked for permission to take the five criminals on the evening of the hanging, after the execution of the judgement, and cut them down from the gallows and bury them in the Jewish cemetery. For this he offered to bring the sum of 100 friedrich d'or pieces to the poorhouse himself.

His request was granted and he paid the offered amount for the issuance of the permit to cut down the five delinquents from the gallows on the day of the execution.

In the meantime, one of these Jewish miscreants had the idea that he could perhaps get a reduction of the sentence if he converted to Christianity. He asked for a priest and quickly let himself be baptized while in jail. To his horror, this was all in vain because without further ado, he was also hanged with his four comrades.

The Jew, who had concluded the previously mentioned deal about the bodies of the delinquents, also learned of the conversion of the hanged man from the Jewish to the Christian religion. Since he now abhorred him as an apostate, he went to the administration of H—— and asked to get 20 pieces of the paid 100 friedrich d'or back, because now he only wanted to take down four of the hanged Jews. The apostate was to be left to his own fate since it wasn't allowed to inter him in the Jewish cemetery.

As a consequence the administration in H—— made then the following pronouncement:

"Once made, the deal had to adhere to the terms. But the supplicant is free to cut down all five or he could let the baptized one hang there, in which latter case he should keep the first one as credit." [55–58]

∼

247. A poor tailor lived with a Jewish family consisting of nine persons, namely the grandmother, both parents, and six children, all in one house together and on the same floor.

The son of the tailor, a boy of almost five years, had put a three-pfennig coin [*Dreier*] in his mouth, which was given to him as a toy, and it was stuck in his throat. The child was seriously choking and in danger of suffocating. The concerned father hurried quickly to the neighboring surgeon to get help.

In the meantime the coin slid down the boy's throat; and the neighboring Jewish family had taken the boy with them to their rooms since they noticed what had happened. Now the tailor came back with the surgeon. He looked everywhere for his son but in vain. Finally he opened the door of his Jewish neighbors, and look, what did he see? His son in the middle of the room sitting on a high chair and the whole Jewish family squatting in a circle around the stool groaning "Ah a! My child, ah a!" [59–60]

NOTE: It seems they are encouraging the child to pass the coin in order to retrieve the money. Also see Milburn (1926, 14).

～

249. At the fair in Frankfurt on the Oder, a Polish Jew was caught as an accomplice in a theft and brought before the judge. The stolen goods were returned, and he couldn't be accused of anything more than that he was in close contact with the thieves. One of the witnesses said casually that he had already seen this Jew arrested in other places but that he always knew how to get out of it. He swore he was innocent and cried over and over again, "I am an honest man, I am an honest man!"

After a consideration of all the circumstances, he was sentenced to receive twenty strokes on the bare back.

He screamed about the horrible unfairness and repeated constantly that he is an honest man. Nothing helped. His clothes were removed and a brand was discovered on his back.

"Boy!" said the judge: "How can you say you are an honest man? You have a brand on your back!

"So," cried the Jew, "how can I help that? They gave it to me against my will." [61–62]

～

250. At a trade fair in —— a poor Jew had hawked and offered his yard goods all day long in all the streets, but without any success.

Ill-humored, he went to return to his hostel in the evening, when someone under the eaves of a five-story building waved to him.

In delighted anticipation of still making a bit of money, he hurried up the steps until under the roof.

He wanted to knock on the door, but as it opened, a man with a screaming boy in his arms came out, threatening the child in a harsh voice:

"See if you don't stop immediately, the Jew is already here to take you."

Surprised, the boy fell quiet, and the man said very kindly to the Jew: "It's all good, my friend. I thank him," and returned to his room leaving the deceived man standing there. [62–63]

NOTE: Milburn 1926, 55.

251. During a voyage of the king of —— through a newly acquired province, in a small little town, the Jewish school director with his charges, among others, came to him to welcome him.

Principals like these occasionally still have one teacher as a helper, called the assistant [*Beihelfer*], as was the case here.

The monarch addressed the principal very courteously and asked him about his domestic situation.

"Dear God," said the latter, "I have very meager bread and have to work like a slave."

"Does he have a wife and children?" the monarch asked further.

The principal, however, understood, does he have many children, namely pupils to teach.

"Oh, yes, thirty-seven!'

"That's a lot!"

"I also have a competent assistant," replied the principal.

"Yes, if you have a helper, then I'll let it go," he got as a smiling answer. [63–64]

252. In —— lived a Jew called Hirsch Aron. A court musician asked him to lend him ten thaler for eight days.

He received it immediately with the following comment: "You know, I love to serve."

On the third day, the musician gave him a double louis d'or and said, "Mr. Aron, I thank you and what do I owe you for your goodness?"

Aron put the money in his pocket and replied, "Well, it's already so right." [64]

253. An aged Jew lost his wife. He complained to his relatives about his fate and that he would now have to exist in helpless loneliness.

"Ay, then marry again," said one of his brothers to him.

"Man, how can that help me?" responded the widower. "Should I take a young one, I am an old man. She will not be faithful to me. If I take an old one, she didn't become old with me." [64–65]

254. A Jew who didn't really come to trade at the trade fair in Leipzig, stole a watch from a student and was caught in the process.

The victim wanted to turn him over to the courts. Due to the many entreaties of the thief, he finally came to an arrangement with him—namely, that he could count forty strokes on him.

As he finished counting the first twenty cane strokes, he stopped to pause, which took too long for the Jew, and he begged, now humbly.

"Dear sir, give me the small remainder quickly, or I shall miss too much [time for stealing]." [65]

∼

260. A rich Jewish banker in B——n called Markus Kuh had an only son, Isaac, on whose upbringing he spared nothing, even though he was no less than a profligate.

The rich heir was therefore sent on long trips to get to know the world. He visited the most refined cities of Germany, and as his father died during his absence, he had himself baptized in W—— and took instead of the name Isaac the name Johann.

From W——, he now went farther to Switzerland and France, where he in a short while made such progress that he became completely French and a complete *Fat* [sic]. He pretended not to understand German anymore and only French.

So metamorphosed, he returned to his paternal city B——, but despite all his efforts not to be recognized, some did remember him.

As he passed through the gate, the officer on duty recognized him immediately by his looks.

"What's your name, sir?" he asked him.

The Frenchified one lisped; "Jean Cu."

"Oh, I understand already," replied the officer. "In German: Hans A——" [French *Cu* = German *Arsch* = ass]. [68–69]

∼

263. An official in his office scolded a Jew as a scoundrel.

The Jew replied, "Mr. Official, be careful; don't scold or I will tell him something that no one has ever told him."

"Well, what is that? Say it now you rascal," yelled the official.

"Well, he is an honest man, sir officer!" replied the Jew. [70–71]

∼

264. A Jew in B—— was brought under judicial investigation because of gross fraud. According to the criteria for the average crime, he was sentenced to two years in prison with thirty cane blows and after completing the sentence, he was to be housed in a correctional facility until he had satisfactorily proven his future honest occupation.

As this sentence became public, his defense attorney, Justice Commissioner K——, came to his side and asked him: did he want to use the means of an appeal in the sense that he wanted to achieve an easing of the judgment.

"Man," said the Jew, "we can try it, dear Mr. Justice Commissioner. The prison I will agree to, and the whipping I will gladly accept, but the improvement I want to be free of." [71]

~

265. To a famous doctor in wound care there came a rich Jew to be healed of damage to his leg. He did not have all three of his fellow nationals in the coach with him since a few of his various friends and acquaintances followed on foot, so they could hear the diagnosis of the wound specialist. He examined the leg. Whenever he probed the leg, the pain forced the patient to scream, and every time the entire escort joined in the screaming.

The wound specialist was put off by this peculiar screaming.

"Why are you all screaming?" he finally asked impatiently.

Drily the Jew, who held the patient's leg, answered:

"Man, don't you know that when one grunts, then they all grunt?" [72]

~

268. Two Jewish merchants, one of which was called Simon Cow and the other Abraham Ox, were traveling together to the Frankfurter fair.

When they went through the little Prussian town D——, the coachman stopped at the gate, and the officer on duty stepped toward the coach to check the passengers' names, profession, etc.

Officer: "What's your name?"

"Cow."

Officer: "And you?"

"Ox."

The officer, who was irritated by the answers because he thought they were an inappropriate joke, said: "Good, coachman, the cattle can pass!" [74–75]

~

269. Some gay students at the university of K—— finally brought it about that one of their Jewish compatriots had to duel with another student.

Shaking he took the blade in his hand and, during the first round, received an insignificant cut on his arm.

"Oy vay," he screamed, throwing the blade away. "That's what happens if one takes shiny metal in hand." [75]

~

271. The captain in —— had arranged a trade with a Jewish merchant. Soon thereafter the Jew was on the parade ground and saw the recruits drilling their maneuvers. The captain noticed him and asked:

"Do you know how to shoot, Jew?"

"Oh, yeah," he replied, "but in advance [*vor*]" [*schiessen* = shoot, *vorschiessen* = advance money]

An officer nearby who knew the relationship between the captain and the Israelite said smiling: "He shot well."

"And struck," the Jew quickly added. [76]

∼

279. In a café, a Jew displayed a ring with a genuine stone and praised it in a highly exaggerated manner, probably with the intention to advantageously dispose of it.

A painter, who was also present, examined the ring closely and had a lot to criticize.

Indignantly the Jew took it back and said: "What do you have to say, you only know how to handle a paintbrush."

"Now, yes, but otherwise with reasonable people!" answered the painter. [80]

∼

280. The count of N—— had a Jew come to him to sell him a few old pieces of clothing. After the transaction was completed, he said to the Jew:

"You do know that now in England they hang a Jew together with an ass?"

"Oh, then it's really good that both of us aren't there now," responded the Jew.

NOTE: Similar to Büschenthal joke #19 and joke #22.

∼

282. On a Saturday someone passed a hospital. Here he heard a Jew scream:

"Don't cut it! Don't cut it! Today is the Sabbath!" [83]

NOTE: In Jewish law, cutting things on the Sabbath is forbidden.

∼

283. A young, very poor Jew, whom nature had blessed very much like a stepmother with mental capacity, had the strange idea to dedicate himself to becoming a veterinarian. And since he was too broke to fulfill his intention, he wrote to well-off philanthropists, especially his fellow Jews, asking them to support his undertaking with small amounts.

This request began with the following words:

"As I want to become a veterinarian [*Vieharzt*], etc. "

When this was presented to a well-known Jewish doctor, Markus Herz, he said drily,

"There is a punctuation error there that I have to correct."

And then he inserted between the two syllables in the word "veterinarian," a comma [i.e., *Vieh, Arzt = Animal, Doctor*)]. [83–84]

NOTE: This text also is also used by Büschenthal joke #66 with somewhat different wording.

∼

284. A Jewish trading woman who had lots of slow-selling merchandise wanted to exchange these. She convinced one of her fellow believers, who was on his way to the trade fair in Leipzig, to take some of these and authorized him to exchange them against other goods when he could make an advantageous trade.

She gave similar instructions to a second acquaintance on his way to the fair, to whom she gave a job lot of cotton hats.

Both commissioned agents promised to do their best, and each fulfilled their instruction honestly. Unfortunately, since neither had the smallest idea of the orders of the other, they traded goods with each other and the Jewess received both articles back but had to carry the shipping costs. [84–85]

NOTE: This story is basically the same as Ascher joke #242, 51–53, which is also reproduced in Büschenthal joke #44.

∼

288. An Israelite who understood notes, those that are valid with banks, and who had heard much about General Leases but not much about General Bass, checked out the beautiful concert hall in the German theater in Berlin.

It's well known that the names of some of the greatest musicians are incorporated into the decorations. Handel and Gluck were the first to strike his eyes.

"Yes," he said, "They have, God knows, decorated this with insight and good taste, Handel [trade] and Glück [luck]." [87]

∼

289. Some time ago in the old theater in Berlin, joygirls and their chaperones were seated in special loges because they couldn't just sit anywhere. Only young good-for-nothings with no sense of honor had themselves seated in such a loge next to these courtesans.

Once the well-known copper engraver J. W. Meil was on the ground floor and noticed in one of these loges the Jewish dandy next to one of these made-up ladies of the night.

"Look up there to the loge," he said to an acquaintance standing next to him, "The young Jews are all being Christian, they are so debauched like the devil." [87–88]

NOTE: Johann Wilhelm Meil (1733–1805) was an illustrator, engraver, and director of the Academy of Arts in Berlin.

291. A man, who had the reputation of always needing money, and also really took out loans where he knew and he could, once let some gold coins be seen in a public place.

A Jew saw these.

"Don't you want to trade with me," he said.

"Why not!" was the answer.

"I will," said the Jew, "come to you and when you have a small money negotiation, I ask you not to forget me. I am as cheap as anyone else."

"Can easily happen," replied Mr. ——.

Afterward the Jew came and offered him goods. He took some for a few friedrichs d'or and then approached for a loan for 100 gold thaler, which he was asking for eight days.

"Could well happen," said the Jew, "but first I need the few friedrichs d'or for the goods. Then I will come again this afternoon at two o'clock on the dot, and you will write me the note, and I will bring you the money."

Everything happened as the Jew suggested except that he never came to bring the money. [89–90]

292. In the morning, a Jew stole into an inn and into the room of a registered traveler, quietly opened the door, and approached the table on which his watch lay, and wanted to get out without being noticed.

Only the traveler was not asleep; he had only pretended to be. As the Jew approached the door, he jumped quickly out of his bed, grabbed the uninvited visitor by his arm, and called for help.

A man in the inn came immediately. The Jew was detained, and his pockets were searched, the watch found, and he was sent to jail.

Here the whole incident was heard. He could not deny the deed. He answered the following questions in the following way.

Was he in the room of the traveler?

"Yes."

Did he find him sleeping?

"Oh, yes."

Did he take his watch?

"I cannot deny it."

Did he want to leave the room with it?

"Also this has its truth."

So, now it is clear that he wanted to steal.

"Heaven forbid, how can you say that? I just wanted to go down and show Schmul who was down there what time it was. If they had let me come down quietly, I would certainly have taken it back up, but I was detained." [90–91]

293. A rich Jewish banker in B—— married off a daughter to a Jewish doctor in H——.

A few years after the wedding, the young couple converted to the Christian religion and this caused a downright tension between the banker and his daughter.

The son-in-law and his wife did everything to bring about a reconciliation, but the old guy insisted on his grudge.

Finally, someone suggested to the son-in-law to send his two sons, two boys age four and five, to the father-in-law in B——. Perhaps this would create a favorable impression in the heart of the aggrieved.

This happened, the kids arrived. The grandfather took them into his home, but he barely looked at them and didn't concern himself anymore with the children.

After a few weeks he accidentally entered a room where the kids were sitting on the floor playing with each other.

They had pieces of paper that they passed back and forth to each other.

"What are you doing?" the grandfather asked grumpily.

"We're playing with little draft notes," the oldest boy replied happily.

Tears of joy poured out of the old man's eyes as he hurried toward his grandchildren, swept them up in his arms, pressed them gently to his heart and cried out, "In that I recognize my blood!" [92–93]

297. A Jew in Göttingen had himself baptized. A few months after the conversion of this Jew to the Christian religion someone asked Professor Lichtenberg, who knew this baptized Jew: "Apropos, how does N—— N—— behave since he has professed Christianity?

"Nothing can be said of him," replied Lichtenberg. "He is like the white page between the Old and New Testament." [96]

299. A student once asked a very orthodox Jew: "Tell me, Bendix, if you would find a pouch with 100 ducats on the Sabbath, would you pick it up?"

"Oh, my, how shall I answer," replied the Jew. "I don't see the pouch, and today is not the Sabbath." [97]

NOTE: It is forbidden to handle money or carry it on the Sabbath.

301. An old Jew, who was a pawnbroker, was asked by a man to lend him a small sum for a crucifix on which was a Christ in silver.

"Oy vay," said the Jew, "I can't get involved with that. That could be from a church and that would be on my conscience. You know what, go to my son; he may do that. I will send my man with you. He'll take you there."

This happened, but as the servant was about to go, he called him back.

"Listen, I want to remind you to tell my son that he should not forget to deduct the wood from the silver." [98]

∼

307. Two Jews stood in a wax museum in front of a small figure of the Emperor Napoleon and asked: "Who is that?" [Yiddish: *doos*] someone answered: "The Emperor Napoleon."

"Oy vay!" said the one. "People said he was such a big man!" [101]

∼

317. In a city where a distinguished civil servant had died, through whom Jews had achieved great advantages, someone said to a Jew, "I am sorry that you all have lost your great benefactor."

"Well," said he, "He is bound to have a successor. And if he has no money, we will give him some, and if he has some, we will invest it for him." [106]

∼

320. Each Jewish cantor in the synagogue receives two underlings who only sing individual notes to make the song full bodied. They are called supporters [*Zuhalter*].

A cantor, newly arrived in ——, was heard to sing in the synagogue to further his future prospects, but the supporters were too proud to accompany the stranger with their voices, so he had to sing alone.

The trip had weakened the man, which is why he succumbed to a colic attack in mid-song.

He had to stop his activity and, holding his body with both hands, very anxiously asked: "Is there no supporter here?" [109–10]

NOTE: *Zuhalter* also means "pimp," but it is not clear that the joke turns on this double entendre.

∼

323. A Christian merchant and a proselyte from Judaism had undertaken a contract. The latter demanded, out of a lack of trust, some relevant documents from his partner, and since these were not forthcoming, he wanted to annul the whole contract. The merchant therefore wrote him an insulting letter in which he mainly attacked his origins. The proselyte demanded written satisfaction whereupon he received only these laconic lines:

"Pilate said to the Jews, what I have written, I have written [John 19:22]." [111–12]

∼

325. A minister said impertinently to a Jew: "We have much too much leniency with you Jews. One should limit you more. You are way too many."

"Begging your pardon, Your Excellency, I don't believe that."

"Why not?"

"Would there be so many usurers among Christians if there were enough Jews?" [113]

∼

326. A young Jewish man of letters ordered his servant to get a catalog from the library.

"What is a catalog?" asked the servant.

"Well, a catalog is a catalog."

The servant was not satisfied with this description and demanded a better explanation.

"You simpleton!" yelled the man very disappointed at the ignorance of his servant. "I will make it very clear to you.

"Catalog is the continence of books." [*Enthaltsamkeit* = continence, instead of *Inhalt* = contents]. [113–114]

∼

328. A young Jewish woman from the country came to visit a relative in Berlin who welcomed her very warmly and showed her all the sights of this beautiful town.

After six weeks the visitor had to return home.

This is what she wrote to her relative in Berlin.

"Berlin is quite a town!

"When I remember the police market [*Jandarmenmarkt*] (*Gensd'armen Markt*), I am gripped by nostalgia." [114–15]

NOTE: The Gendarmenmarkt is an area in Berlin that was built as a market in the late seventeenth century and redesigned in the late eighteenth century. It was named after a cavalry regiment (*Gens d'Armes*) that had stables there until its redevelopment.

∼

329. Many Jews live in —— and among them are some quite wealthy families who pretend to have an aesthetic education. The young Jewish dandies dedicate themselves to poetry, painting, and music and do know enough for one of them to rhyme a screwball sonnet, to splash a landscape quite colorfully onto some paper, or to pick out some songs on the piano.

One evening a young man in one of these Jewish family circles played the flute.

The night watchman called out and rasped out the hour.

Suddenly a window opened and a young woman called to him:

"Mr. Nightwatchman, Mr. Nightwatchman! Let him shut up. Mr. Quieter [*Leiser*] is playing the flite" [mispronunciation: *Fleit* instead of *Flöte*]. [115]

∼

331. A Jew was recounting his talent of finding the right thing to do at the critical moment.

"I you give example," he said [in broken German]. "Went I did in middle of street; has come from one side the king, has come from other side the rabbi, did I greet no one, so that no one could annoyed be, if greet I the other." [117]

∼

332. A young Jewish scholar had fallen desperately in love with the actress at the National Theater in Berlin, Demoiselle Weber, and he did not miss an opportunity to acquaint her with his heartfelt feelings, sometimes in prose, sometimes in verse.

Once he chose an original means that would scarcely have occurred to any lover before him. He had a goose roasted, filled it with Borsdorfer's apples, and sent it to the object of his adoration in her dressing room as a light repast. On top of one of the apples there was a sheet of paper with the following rhyme:

Roast goose, goose liver
Had long not the pleasure
As from Mam'selle Weber
A single friendly kiss [117–118]

∼

333. The deceased Jewish philosopher, Salomon Maimon, lived in constant discord with his wife, a very rough creature. Even when he was away from her, their correspondence contained nothing but mutual recriminations. Once he wrote to her in response to a letter where she demanded his return,

"Dear Wife!

"I am not smart, because if I would write, 'you' are not clever, you'd read, 'I' am not clever. So I write, 'I' am not clever, and you will read correctly: 'You' are not clever."

He once wrote her a similar letter that began with the words: "May the devil take me!" and when she assured him that she would follow him wherever he might be, he answered her:

"If you come from Warsaw to Berlin, then I'll go to Hamburg. If you come to Hamburg, I'll go to London. If you followed me, I'll go to Paris from there back to Germany and finally to Warsaw. If I find you there, I'll say: 'You could have stayed there all along.'" [118]

NOTE: Solomon Maimon (1753–1800) was a Talmudic scholar as a boy, but he left his home in the Duchy of Lithuania for Germany, where he learned German and philosophy. For a time he entered the circle of Moses Mendelssohn in Berlin. He corresponded with Immanuel Kant and wrote essays on philosophy as well as his own autobiography. He was married at the age of eleven and had a child at the age of fourteen. He was separated from his wife for many years, and when she eventually tracked him down, he granted her a divorce.

336. When Justice Commissioner Grattenauer published his writings against the Jews in Berlin, it created quite a sensation. The Jewish community was especially up in arms over it.

The deceased chamber assessor Cosmann used this occasion to seek favor with the Jewish community in order to gain advantage for himself and published a small pamphlet challenging the attacks of Justice Commissioner Grattenauer.

The refutation, however, was so superficial and shallow that the following satirical verse came together:

Grattenauer insulted us
Oh well;
Cosman defended us,
Oy vay [120–21]

NOTE: Carl Wilhelm Friedrich Grattenauer (1773–1838) in his youth wrote a number of anonymous anti-Semitic tracts and published *Wider die Juden: Ein Wort der Warnung an alle christliche Mitbürger* [Against the Jews: A word of warning to all Christian fellow-citizens] in 1803. It attracted considerable attention. The same year, Johann Wilhelm Andreas Kosmann (1761–1804) defended the Jews in his *Für die Juden* (For the Jews).

337. In reading the writing of Hufeland that brandy is very harmful—yes, even a real poison—a Jew spouted the following words: "Now I no longer wonder why the brandy drinkers have so little interest in money and belongings, and why they build their brandy merchants splendid houses. They recognize that they have so much poison in their body that they are going to die, and that therefore they have no use for Mammon." [121]

NOTE: Physician Christoph Wilhem Hufeland (1762–1836) was famous throughout Europe and wrote many books on practical medicine, including *Die Kunst, das menschliche Leben zu verlängern* (The art of extending human life) (1796).

339. The cook of a lady educated in the Old Testament came and asked her, "Madam, how I must write a friend, 'thee' [*Dich*] or 'thou' [*Dir*]. To me I know well, I say 'me' [*mich*], but to a friend I just don't know."

The lady was quite surprised by this difficult grammatical question, and after a long pause, she finally said:

"Let her write 'thou.'"

"I thought so, that it had to be 'thou,'" replied the girl. "So my mother also learned me, but I wasn't sure" [broken syntax]. [123]

∼

340. A Jew by the name of Saul Ascher published a journal under the title *Pharus* [Latin: lighthouse].

When this was displayed in the museum with the rest of the journals and magazines, a prankster wrote on the title page of the first piece, "How does Saul come among the prophets?" [123]

NOTE: In the Bible, Saul is a king, but he is not counted among the prophets. Saul Ascher (1767–1822) was a very active Jewish writer, editor, and publisher who argued for Jewish emancipation and attacked German folk nationalism and its anti-Semitic ideology. He was a friend of Heinrich Heine, Eduard Gans, and Salomon Maimon.

∼

343. The famous philologist, privy counselor Wolf in Berlin, announced via the newspaper that in the autumn of 1809, he was considering giving a free lecture on Aristophanes and that those interested in participating should let him know in order to receive a free admission ticket from him.

As a result of this announcement a young Israelite came to him and asked for such an admission ticket. Upon receiving it, the privy counselor wanted to ask him, "Which edition of Aristophanes will you use for your study?"

He had barely said *Ausgabe* [edition, expense], when the Jew interrupted him, shocked:

"What expenses are there with this? I thought it was gratis. If there are expenditures, I can't profit from it. Take my ticket back."

He left in a big hurry. [124–25]

NOTE: Friedrich August Wolf (1759–1824) established the discipline of philology in Germany. He published important works on Homer, Demosthenes, and Plato.

∼

344. The confessor asked a sick, converted Jew if he believed what was in the articles of the Christian faith.

He answered: "Yes,"

The clergyman further asked him if he also believed that Jesus would come to judge.

"I have a hard time believing that," answered the Jew, "because when he came the first time my ancestors behaved so badly against him that they are not worthy of a second coming."

∼

346. "Oh, my," said Saul Bechor Moses to an acquaintance of his nation. "You are a scholarly guy. You know everything. So tell me, what does it mean when someone says 'aesthetic' [*ästhetisch*]? The whole world speaks of 'aesthetic.' What do they mean?"

The learned scholar beat his chest and replied:

"Aesthetic? Well, I'll tell you what it is. It's a thing out of which one can make everything, for example, out of it I can make a dining- [*Ess*] and a tea- [*Thee*] table [*Tisch*, all together *ästhetisch*]. Now do you understand?"

"When you ask like that, of course I understand," answered Saul Bechor Moses, and admired the scholarship of his clever fellow-believer. [126–27]

∼

347. People in a community believed that the poet Duplessis came from a Jewish family. The Count von Rivoral [*sic*] demurred and as proof cited that Duplessis produced a play that had no interest at all. [127]

NOTE: Probably Antoine de Rivarol (1753–1801), who assumed the title of count claiming a connection with a noble Italian family. He published a translation of Dante's *Inferno* but was known mainly as an epigrammatist. He fled the Terror in 1792 and eventually settled in Berlin. He was critical of young authors.

∼

348. In a provincial town not far from B——, a Jew who owned his own home and in addition had some wealth, was ordered to quarter a soldier. Since the Jew shunned everything called a public burden, he tried to free himself thereof by even the most illicit of means. He plotted night and day how he could politely get rid of his guest, whom he already had been forced to lodge for seven weeks.

To this end he had in the past few days decreased the small ration daily, bemoaned and lamented about the bad times and the lack of income, grimaced in despair, and finally said that he could now not get one more crumb of bread, and he begged, in the name of the patriarchs Abraham, Isaac, and Jacob that "the Master soldier should find other quarters since in this village there were enough well-to-do people who would count themselves as honored to have such a polite, noble sir, as the soldier was, lodge with them." Whereby, he in all possible speed named a dozen, where he could count on having delicious soup, roast, and wine every day.

The soldier let himself be convinced and promised to leave the next day. The Jew smirked happily as if he had made a bargain for something secret at the tenth of its price, and he put on a very lavish supper for which he claimed to have borrowed the money.

The exaggerated amiability of the Jew, however, made the soldier suspicious, and he decided to watch his host more closely. At night the Jew did not go to bed, because he was so happy, and when the clock struck four in the morning, he reminded his guest to wake up. The night watch had barely announced the time, but the soldier didn't want to hear of it since it was still pitch-dark and no one was up. That did not keep the Jew from warning him that it was time to get ready for his departure.

"Sir soldier, sir soldier, did you hear? On my life! It's early! Are you listening? It's early; just now the cock crowed and all my hens are cackling; are you listening?"

"Hey, you damned Jew!" screamed the soldier. "Now your rooster is crowing and your hens are cackling, and yesterday you didn't know where to get a bit of bread for today. Now pull together breakfast and then butcher your fowl, and when that is gone and you can't get anything else only then will I leave your house."

The outsmarter was caught and had to obey! [127–29]

NOTE: Mendelsohn 1951, 170; Learsi 1961, 218; Spalding 1969, 35.

349. At the beginning of the reign of Friedrich II, a rich Jew in Berlin called Ephraim had an ineradicable hate against another Jew called David Posen because he had crossed his path in some transactions.

At that time, the Jew Posen allowed himself significant liberty by having his beard cut off, and Ephraim took advantage of this situation to make fun of his enemy.

He lodged a complaint with the chief rabbi that he, against the customs of the Jewish people, had had his beard shaved, and for punishment he was informed that in the future he had to let his beard grow.

The Jew Posen was unhappy with this order and immediately sought permission from King Friedrich to be allowed to shave his beard as before.

But Friedrich wrote in the margin of the presentation:

"Posen shall leave me and his beard untouched [*ungeschoren*]. [130]

NOTE: Figuratively, *ungeschoren* can mean "unfleeced," as in an economic transaction, but as there is no indication that Posen is in any economic relationship with Friedrich II, it seems an unlikely element in the joke.

350. An elegant young man from the tribe of Judah took a stroll with an even more elegantly made-up lady during the noon hour in order to catch some sun. A beggar boy had barely noticed the strolling pair when he followed them with entreaties for alms, all in the hope that with begging for alms, he would instantly receive a gift from an elegantly clothed gentlemen in the company of a lady, just so that he would leave them alone.

"Gracious sir, a three-pence, only a three-pence, dear Baron, I beg, Lord Count, I am so hungry, my father has died, my mother is sick. We haven't eaten one piece of bread since yesterday, gracious Lord Prince, have mercy on us!"

This is how the boy followed the Israelite, who had nothing better to do but to zealously reject the begging companion with threats and curses.

But the boy dressed in rags remained steadfast, and the dandy fought constantly with his greed and his better nature as to whether he should allow himself and his lady to be hounded further or if he should take a small token out of his pocket.

Finally he had had enough, and he decided to buy his freedom from the irritating pursuer.

Angrily he put his hand in his pocket and pulled out a lot of coins. With a careful eye, he examined the money and dug around for a low value coin, but in vain; nothing but large coins. How could he separate himself from the beautiful money? He decided quickly and put it all back into his pocket and turned to the lady with the words:

"I'd give a fortune for a groschen!" [131–32]

~

351. A young merchant in Hamburg owed a Jew a sum of money. The due date passed and the lender appeared.

The merchant couldn't pay promptly but didn't want to compromise his credit. He called the Jew into his room and said; "Friend, I have here a note from Malaga and will give it to you. But you can't say a word; the shipper gave it to me secretly, and he is still in quarantine. Not even the note is disinfected."

In shock the Jew ran away and, out of fear, wasn't seen for fourteen days, during which time the merchant could finally pay. [132–33]

~

353. The Baron von S—— had been in contact with a Jewish trader for quite some years who took care of all of his financial transactions.

When the baron's son was scheduled to attend the University of Göttingen, the father had the Jew come to him and asked him for an open letter of credit in a certain amount for his son from the Jewish enterprise in Göttingen.

"Gladly!" said the Jew. "But what's the honorable son going to study?"

"Well, that's self-evident; he shall become a lawyer and study the law."

"Oh my, what do you do with that, dear sir!" cried the Jew. "Better you have him study power, because might makes right." [133–34]

∼

354. The director of music was teaching a young Jew music. Many of his fellow believers were making a powerful noise over the great talent of the young man.

An acquaintance once asked the director if his Jewish pupil was really a great musical genius.

"Talent he certainly has," replied the music director. "Only he cannot hold the rhythm"

"How's that?"

"Yes, he plays everything too fast, and makes out of a quarter note, an eighth, because with that he has a hundred percent profit." [134–35]

∼

355. Among the many strangers who visited Baden Baden in the summer of 1807 was one Emanuel Dreyfuss, a Jewish trader from Strassburg. On the evening of the twenty-ninth of July at around ten o'clock, he went with the butcher Heymann, who was visiting him, to the Inn Hirsch to give a coachman a letter for Strassburg, and there met another Jewish trader, Jastro, from west Prussia.

Dreyfuss ordered a bottle of red wine and some sweets and encouraged the other trader to come drink with him. Afterward they watched the games of Faro without playing themselves and then had another bottle of red wine.

Near midnight, talk turned to going to bed, but Heymann Seligmann said he couldn't go home any more since while taking the baths, he was lodging with the local Jewish innkeeper, Low Simson from Rastadt, and that house would now be closed.

Jastro responded that he couldn't sleep with him either since he had to go to Geresbach very early, and he also refused Heymann's request to accompany him there since he had already ordered a porter for his merchandise. Dreyfuss on the other hand offered Heymann a bed for the night, which he accepted.

Early in the morning, it aroused suspicion when Dreyfuss did not appear from the locked room. Finally the room was forced open, and Dreyfuss's body was found stiff and lying close to the door in his own blood. The bedcover of the murdered man was pierced, covered in blood. Bloody slippers were under the bed and the wall by the open luggage was splattered with blood. A rough shirt was next to the body from which the name had been cut out. On the murder victim twenty-eight cuts were discovered. The first one through the bedcover had not been mortal, and he had to have jumped up and fought with the murderer because he had, among others, cuts in the nape, one in the calf muscle, and two deep cuts in the right hand, but the main wound was through the heart. Since Dreyfuss came to his room without having been noticed by anyone at the inn, one couldn't shed any light on a possible murderer. A few neighbors remembered hearing a frightening screaming resembling the fighting of some drunks or the bellowing of animals. Meanwhile the suspicion arose against the butcher Heymann. For example, the local cutler reported that he had recently sharpened a stiletto for Heymann, and he was also seen at midnight standing with Dreyfuss in the street in front of the inn, and the report of Jastro coming back from Geresbach free of wares added to the suspicion. The latter also announced that he urged him to go on some remote paths, and that he proposed taking a walk into the deep forested mountain range to the old Baden castle. The butcher could also have gone to his quarters during the night since he came in after one o'clock and got up in the morning at six o'clock to butcher a calf and after that he went to Rastadt.

Now a police officer was sent to Rastadt to bring in the butcher Heymann. He was found in the local Jewish tavern unabashedly gambling, and in the evening, he was returned to Baden under arrest. He brazenly denied everything and put the suspicion onto a poor Jew from Fürth.

During his physical examination a bloody spot under the arch of the heel was found, proof that he must have stepped into blood with his bare feet. Also the laundress and Dreyfuss's wife, just returned from Strassburg, recognized the shirt he was wearing, despite the fact that the name was cut out, as that of the murder victim. He was taken into the room of the victim and it was noticed that his footprints completely matched those still visible in the room in a couple of places. After much persistent denial, he finally admitted the murder committed on August 4 with all the circumstances.

His admission was as follows:

He reportedly went home with Dreyfuss and still watched the light of the moon and stars for three-quarters of an hour. Whereupon the latter undressed, removed his money pouch from under the covers, put it in his suitcase, went to bed, and fell asleep. He himself also undressed and went to bed on the far side against the wall. After half an hour, he got up and took his stiletto knife out of his pocket and gave Dreyfuss one thrust through his covers into his chest. The latter jumped up, let out a terrible scream, and fought with him until he finally fell down after many cuts. Thereupon he took off his shirt, which had become bloody; cut out the name; washed himself; took a shirt out of the suitcase; and put it on. Then he took the money pouch out of the suitcase, with seven gold and one silver watch, dressed himself, locked the room, and said he left. The money, consisting of 311 guilders and 9 Kreuzer, and the watches, estimated as costing 384 guilders, were found, as he had declared, in the Jewish tavern in Rastadt hidden under the roof.

As soon as Heymann acknowledged his deed, he apparently underwent a quick transformation of character. The frequent visits of the officials in his prison, sometimes in the company of curious strangers, were welcomed by him, and they liked being entertained by him. At times he was alert and moody and seemed to forget his circumstances, until a sigh from his depths betrayed his grief again.

He made two unusual requests during his incarceration. He wanted to see the widow of the murdered man so that he could beg her for forgiveness and request that she and her children not curse him after his execution. This curse he feared as a most frightening thing for a Jew. One tried to console him with the suggestion that he could make his request in writing, and that calmed him to some extent. His second request concerned his beloved, a young Jewish woman working in Bühl in Neufreistadt. For her he had two golden rings in his box, which he had made to reimburse her parents for the food and favors he had received from them, as well as other little things that he was keeping for her and that he wanted to declare as her property and asked they be given to her. This young woman was very close to his heart, and whenever the opportunity presented itself, he sent her his regards and begged that she would forgive him for all the pain his evil caused her. He wanted to soothe her so that her grief would not cause her harm.

As confidant or confessor, he asked for an upright Jew from Bühl who also came to him. With him he sought to lighten his conscience, acknowledge his strong regret for his evil deed, chastised his thoughtlessness and the neglect of the laws of his religion in which he had been raised, and the neglect of which he recognized as the sole cause for his crime. He assured that he had never been an evildoer and, aside from the murder, had never committed a crime in his life and had never hurt a child. On the first of October, he was executed by the sword. [135–42]

∽

358. At the University of —— a young Jew studied medicine, and since his father was a rich banker, and had an open line of credit with his uncle while he was at the university, he indulged a bit too much with all of his wealth.

Some of his acquaintances, from their own self-interest, forgave his presumption, but the result was that his arrogance increased so significantly that some students agreed to teach him a lesson.

When he once became too overbearing in public with a student of his acquaintance, the latter vehemently attacked him and showered him with insulting abuses.

The concerned Jew was shocked, gave in, and removed himself quickly. But when the following day he appeared again in the company of his friends, no one wanted to put up with him because according to academic technical terms, he had made a fool of himself. Unanimously it was explained to him that he could no longer be seen in public if he didn't challenge his offender to a duel and demand satisfaction.

The whole thing was awkward. The Jewish student was afraid for his life, even more so since he could not fence, and his opponent was known as one of the best fencers.

He presented this to his friends. One of them suggested that it would be best if he chose pistols instead of swords. With those it wouldn't be a matter of speed; rather it would be a matter of chance, and so he would not be in as much danger as in a duel with rapiers, because bullets rarely hit their mark but in a fencing match he would at least be wounded.

The Jewish student fought a long battle with himself, deciding whether he would speedily leave the university or if he should endanger his life to save his honor. Ultimately ambition triumphed over timidity, and he decided to challenge his opponent to pistols.

Everyone had hoped for this. Another student immediately offered to be his second. The offender was challenged and accepted the deal.

The duelists met at the fixed time and place, and since the seconds had loaded the pistols only with powder, no misfortune could occur.

Extremely happy, the Jew returned from the battle and hurried to his uncle, to whom he recounted the course of the duel with the following words:

"Here I am. Heavenly miracle! It all unfolded better than I had thought. I came to the place. The seconds measured the distance, loaded the pistols, and I, as the aggrieved, had the first shot. I placed myself there, closed my eyes, and pulled the trigger. When I opened them, I thought my opponent was dead, but how did it happen, he was still standing in the same place. I thought now he will shoot me dead. I was shaking all over, but was horribly brave; he came to me, slapped my face a couple of times and said: 'For now the matter is settled'—and left." [143–46]

360. It's well known that Frederick the Great, during the Seven Years' War, ordered that eight-groschen pieces be minted with very little content, which were immediately taken out of circulation.

For this financial operation he used the very rich Jewish banker in Berlin called Ephraim.

This caused a joker at that time to compose an epigram to this newly minted money:

"Beautiful on the outside; bad on the inside
Frederick on the outside; Ephraim on the inside." [147–48]

To the Publisher of the Anecdotes of Noble Jews

You want to tell us of noble Jews?
Fill eight folios!—Had you chosen
As material the bad ones
You'd certainly not have enough paper [176]

∼

Song of the Jewish Trader at the Leipzig Fair [some Yiddish diction and syntax]

Here are some rare things,
O look at my stuff,
If I could make a trade,
What grief I would have.

I'll give it to you cheaply,
Mademoiselles, come closer,
I'll let you, on my life,
Not go by like that.

I bring the best wares,
From Frankfurt and Berlin,
Linen, borders, schnapps,
Calico and muslin.

You are connoisseurs,
Just look at my goods,
I don't want to gain anything,
As long as I can trade.

Vay! it's not a life,
Earnings nowhere!
What do you want to pay,
Who says a golden word?

This cloth, what shall I get
I'm only asking for two dollars,
I don't want to cheat you,
It's without finish.

It's a fine weaving
Made in Berlin.
What will I get as profit?
Nothing, absolutely nothing?—Woe is screamed!

Who wants to give two guilders?
Not even one? Heaven forbid,
Who can live from trading,
Not one cent profit.

So heaven help me, I am no braggart,
It's a splendor and a decoration.
I myself paid a thaler,
I'll let it go for that.

What shall I do with these things,
Dear Madam, just for you,
I'll make it cheap,
One guilder, make it fast.

Eight pennies!—Divine miracle,
As I am truly honest,
It isn't junk!
Well, so take it already. [176–78]

Complaint of a Pigtail-Ribbon Jew

How you can feel sorry for poor me,
I have to slave away day after day
And barely have enough bread;
The unfaithful change of fashion
Cruelly destroyed my business
And caused me to fall into dire need.

Once there were long, thick braids,
Now you only get to see bald heads
And all napes are bare.
How the times have changed.
Before I sold a lot of my ribbons,
Now I can't get rid of one yard.

O please change, dear fashion,
Or I'll die of starvation
And that would indeed be wicked!
Won't the hair of men be combed
And not the braid replaced,
I call in vain: Buy a ribbon, buy a ribbon!

Instead of Titus—and of Swedish heads [hair or wig styles]
Put coarse, long powdered braids

Again on the impostors;
Because only then can I exist,
Else I will surely be ruined
I am already half a beggar.

Have mercy on me, Goddess Fashion,
Then I'll also praise you in an ode,
In many a strange assonance.
Beware of where your insanity leads,
May the braid of man decorate the earth
Like the baboon his tail. [178–79]

Thoughts of a Jew at Sunset

Even used she still maintains luster and shine
That must be some rare gold plating. [179]

Consolation of the Jews

Sonnet

We children of Israel are truly to be pitied,
We're hated by priesthood, nobility, citizens, peasants,

The rabble ridicules us always, now a Grattenauer
Wants to beat us down to the ground with his cautionary writings.

Only because one is already used to the yoke, all of this can be carried,
Only our business remains with which we acquire treasure;
Through writings no Jew has been ruined, although often a Christian,
Honor is empty trash, we care for the stomach.

If the ransom decreases, we see patience shine,
We will be enlightened and feed on pig and sow,
And drink kosher wine, like our Christian brothers.
They have to go to war, and we can pay for it,
Only one thing dampens our courage in this crisis,
Alas! Only a Cosmann and a Merkel are defending us. [179–80]

Appendix I: Büschenthal Texts Taken from Judas Ascher, *Der Judenfreund*

(Page numbers in the table refer to the original German texts and not the translations published here.)

Büschenthal			Ascher	
Joke Number	Page	Description	Joke Number	Page
27	19–22	Watchmaker hides in chest	207	9–14
28	22	Jews and asses in Turkey	211	15
29	22–24	Rich man in Meseritz	213	16–18
30	24–25	Pilates and Herods	214	18–19
31	25	Officer refuses to pay debt	215	19
32	25–26	Three-cornered hat	216	19–20
33	26	Die Neuberin	218	22
34	26–27	Frenchman accurately depicted	220	24–25
35	27	Jew with fake ring	229	36
36	27–28	Armor on back	232	37
37	28–30	Deceptive borrowing of Abraham Moses	233	37–40
38	30–32	Bribing city guard	234	40–41
39	32–33	What Jew doesn't like about Mainz	235	41–43
40	34	Borrower has no coat but the reckoning is right	237	44–45

(*Continued*)

Büschenthal			Ascher	
Joke Number	Page	Description	Joke Number	Page
41	35–36	Rabbi can neither read nor write	239	46–48
42	37	Commentary on Lamentations	240	48
43	37–39	Talmud prodigy after four years	241	48–50
44	39–42	Gloves and stocking	242	51–53
45	42–44	Jews beaten by coachmen want good relations	244	54–55
46	44–45	Cure toothache	246	57–59
47	45–46	Where there is nothing, there is Moses	248	60
48	46	Disgusting pinch	255	65–66
49	46–47	Watching others' hands	256	66
50	47–48	Mannheim beer	257	66–67
51	48	Not even for twenty strokes	258	67
52	48–49	Wanted elders to say he wasn't mad	259	67–68
53	50	Already ate on a fast day	261	70
54	50	Milk and blood	262	70
55	50–51	Wishing verdict was awaiting the file	266	72–73
56	51–52	Musikalisch	267	73–74
57	52	We carry our own skin	270	75
58	52–53	Your son will be a courier	272	76
59	53–54	Slaps friend at chess move	273	77
60	54	Can't waste a theater ticket	274	77–78
61	54–55	Mendelssohn: "I couldn't use him"	275	78
62	55	My face must be a mirror	276	78–79
63	55–56	Birds have no written notes	277	79
64	56	Mendelssohn: "Can't even insult a Jew"	278	79–80
65	56–58	Saw person who lived without a heart	281	81–83
66*	58–59	Animal doctor	283	83–84
67	59–60	Shoots percent down	285	85–86
68	60–61	Mendelssohn: Demosthenes and Aesop	286	85–86
69	61	Mendelssohn trades in "Intelligence"	287	86–87
70	61–62	I'm the master of the house	290	88–89
71	63–64	Clink clink	294	93–94
72	64–65	Going for a walk while sitting	295	94–95
73	65	Laws developed, tricks were made	296	95–96
74	66	Easter eggs "Christ has risen"	298	96–97
75	66–67	Kept H. A. H initials on conversion	300	97–98
76	67	Jewess says she was always pious	302	98–99

(Continued)

Appendix I

Büschenthal			Ascher	
Joke Number	Page	Description	Joke Number	Page
77	67	Pay cash? I'm not a crook	303	99
78	68	Finds out whether lender is secure	304	99–100
79	68–69	Nürenberg gingerbread	305	100
80	69	What are false oaths for?	306	101
81	69	Ask the wolf	308	101–2
82	70	Horse will run too far	309	102
83	70–71	Bureaucrat/witchcraft	310	102–3
84	71	Passenger half out of coach	311	103
85	71–72	What is justice doing here?	312	103–4
86	72	That's the worse coat	313	104
87	72–73	Old baron never rushes to pay	314	104–5
88	73	Lump/Paper	315	105
89	73–74	Blindness not a flaw but a misfortune	316	105–6
90	74	Two halves of discount make a whole	318	106–8
91	75–77	Signs document in Chaldean	319	108–9
92	77	Six-finger child will be pianist	321	110
93	77–78	Soldier's widow as maid gets pregnant	322	110–11
94	78–79	Jew mistakes someone on street for actor	324	112–13
95	79–80	The pauses on the piano are different	327	114
96	80–81	Why do you need a temperament?	330	115–17
97	81	Maid criticizes employer for reading *Agathon*	334	119
98	82	Child expresses its pure nature	335	119–20
99	83–84	Rather not give a speech	338	121–22
100	84	Daughter loves geography but can't be coachman	341	123–24
101	84	Paper ruined him, he will ruin paper	342	124
102	85	There's the meat, where's the cat?	345	126
103	85–86	The Jew gives in to horse because smarter	352	133
104	86	Mendelssohn and chess	356	142
105	87–88	Undressed/gone out	357	142–43
106	88–89	Politician is sheath around a crook	359	146–47
	89–99	Biography of Nehemie Jehuda Leib		148–58
	100–119	Autobiography of Nehmie Jehuda Leib		158–75

Note: Eighty jokes are taken from Ascher's *Der Judenfreund*.
*Joke 66 is a variant of 283 but is included in this table.
Thus, 75.5 percent of Buschenthal's total jokes are from Ascher.

Appendix II: Sources of Joke Analogues

Below is a list of those joke anthologies and publications that are cited in the annotations accompanying the jokes in Lippmann Moses Büschenthal's *Sammlung* (Collection) and in Judas Ascher's *Der Judenfreund* (The friend of the Jews). Following these sources is a list of books and periodicals that were consulted but in which no analogues to the jokes in these collections were found.

Adler, Hermann. 1893. "Jewish Wit and Humour." *Nineteenth Century* 33: 457–69.
"Anekdoten." 1812. *Sulamith: Eine Zeitschrift für Beförderung der Kultur und Humanität unter den Israeliten* (Sulamith: Journal for the advancement of culture and humanism among the Israelites). 1:354–55.
Anekdotitut. n.d. https://anekdotitut.ru/pro_muja_i_jenu13.php.
Anekdotov. n.d. anekdotov.net/anekdot/pro_muzha_i_zhenu/p 105/.
Anek-dotov. n.d. http://anek-dot.ucoz.ru/news/pjanyj_muzh_i_zhena_kto_v_dome_khozjain/2012-04-05-5070.
Anekdoty.ru. n.d. http://anekdoty.ru/pro-femidu/.
Ausubel, Nathan, ed. 1948. *A Treasury of Jewish Folklore*. New York: Crown.
Beiwagen zum Volksboten für Bürger und Landmann (Addendum to the people's courier for town and country folk). 1851. 50 (December 21): 107–8.
Best Jewish Jokes. 2014. http://evrofilm.com/luchshie-evrejskie-anekdoty-raznoe-assorti-chast-3.html.
Bez zaglavija radi potehi: Sobranie anekdotov, kalamburov, ostrot, glupostej, scen; Iz russkogo, everjskogo, armanianskogo, bytov, aforizmov i proch (Without a title for fun: A collection of jokes, puns, witticisms, foolishness, and scenes; From Russian, Jewish, Armenian everyday life, aphorisms, etc.). 1880b, Part 2. St. Petersburg: Krakovskij.
Bluestein, Gene. 1962. "'The Arkansas Traveler' and the Strategy of American Humor." *Western Folklore* 21 (3): 153–60.

Clements, William M. 1973. *The Types of the Polack Joke*. Rev. ed. Bibliographic and Special Series No. 3. Bloomington, IN: Folklore Forum.
Downing, Charles. 1965. *Tales of the Hodja*. New York: Henry Z. Walck.
Druyanow, Alter. 1963. *Sefer ha-bediḥah ve-ha-ḥidud* (The book of the joke and the witticism). 3 vols. Tel Aviv: Dvir.
Ernst, Shimon. 1933. *Meotzar habediḥa* (From the treasury of the joke). Tel Aviv: P. Anev.
Freedman, Harry, and Maurice Simon, eds. 1977. *The Midrash Rabbah*. Translated by Harry Freedman and Maurice Simon. 5 vols. London: Soncino.
Freud, Sigmund. 1954. *The Origins of Psychoanalysis: Letters to Wilhelm Fliess, 1887–1902*. Translated by Eric Mossbacher and James Strachey. New York: Basic.
Freud, Sigmund. 1960. *Jokes and their Relation to the Unconscious*. Translated by James Strachey. New York: W. W. Norton.
Gross, Naftoli. 1955. *Maaselech un Mesholim* (Tales and parables). New York: Aber.
Heine, Heinrich. 1856. *Pictures of Travel*. Translated by Charles G. Leland. 2nd ed. Philadelphia: John Weik.
Herschfield, Harry. 1932. *Harry Herschfield's Jewish Jokes*. New York: Simon and Schuster.
Joe Miller's Jests or the Wits Vade-mecum. 1963 [1739]. New York: Dover.
Landmann, Salcia. 1962. *Der Jüdische Witz*. Olten und Freiburg im Breisgau: Walter.
Landmann, Salcia. 1972. *Neues von Salcia Landmann: Jüdischer Witz*. Berlin: Herbig.
Landman[n], Salcia. 2006. *Evrejskoe ostroumie* (Jewish witticism). Translated by U. Gusev and N. Mikhelevich. Moscow: Text.
Learsi, Rufus. 1961. *Filled with Laughter: A Fiesta of Jewish Folk Humor*. New York: Thomas Yoseloff.
Lolanekdot. n.d. https://www.anekdot.ru/id/10890/.
Meatprikol. n.d. http://meatprikol.narod.ru/anekmeat.htm.
Mendelsohn, S. Felix. 1935. *The Jew Laughs*. Chicago: L. M. Stein.
Mendelsohn, S. Felix. 1947. *Here's a Good One: Stories of Jewish Wit and Wisdom*. New York: Bloch.
Mendelsohn, S. Felix. 1951. *The Merry Heart: Wit and Wisdom from Jewish Folklore*. New York: Bookman Associates.
Mendelsohn, S. Felix. 1952. *Let Laughter Ring*. Philadelphia: Jewish Publication Society of America.
Milburn, George, ed. 1926. *The Best of Jewish Jokes*. Girard, KS: Haldeman-Julius.
Novak, William, and Moshe Waldoks, eds. 1981. *The Big Book of Jewish Humor*. New York: Harper & Row.
Olsvanger, Immanuel. 1931. *Rosinkess mit Mandlen: Aus der Volksliteratur der Ostjuden; Schwänke, Erzählungen, Sprichwörter, und Rätsel* (Raisins with almonds: From the folk literature of eastern Jews; Comic tales, stories, proverbs, and riddles). Basel: Schweizerischen Gessellschaft für Volkskunde.
Oring, Elliott. 1981. *Israeli Humor: The Content and Structure of the Chizbat of the Palmah*. Albany: State University of New York Press.
Poggio Bracciolini, Giovanni Francesco. 1968. *The Facetiae*. Translated by Bernhardt J. Hurwood. New York: Award.

Rawnitzki, J[ehoshua] Ch[ana]. 1950 [1922]. *Yidishe Witzn*. 2 vols. New York: Morris S. Sklarsky.
Richman, Jacob. 1952. *Jewish Wit and Wisdom*. New York: Pardes.
Richman, Jacob. 1954. *Laughs from Jewish Lore*. New York: Hebrew Publishing Company.
Sadan, Dov. 1950. *Ka'arat Tzemukim* (A bowl of raisins). Tel Aviv: Mordeḥai Neuman.
Sadan, Dov. 1953. *Ka'arat Egozim* (A bowl of nuts). Tel Aviv: Mordeḥai Neuman.
Schwarzbaum, Haim. 1968. *Studies in Jewish and World Folklore*. Berlin: Walter de Gruyter.
Shmerka i Shlemka. 1906. *Sbornik evrejskih jumoristicheskih kupletov, scen, rasskazov, anekdotov i shutok: Veselye pohozhdenija znamenitogo evrejskogo shuta Gershko iz Ostropolya* (The collection of Jewish humorous songs, scenes, stories, anecdotes and jokes: Merry adventures of a famous Jewish jester Gershko from Ostropol). Odessa: N. M. Gubanov.
Spalding, Henry D. 1969. *Encyclopedia of Jewish Humor*. New York: Jonathan David.
Teitelbaum, Elsa. 1945. *An Anthology of Jewish Humor and Maxims*. New York: Pardes.
Uther, Hans-Jörg. 2011. *The Types of International Folktales: Classification and Bibliography*. 3 vols. Helsinki: Academia Scientiarum Fennica.
Vejnberg, Pavel Isaevich. 1870. *Sceny iz evrejskogo byta* (Scenes from everyday Jewish life). St. Petersburg: A. Kaspari.
Vejnberg, Pavel Isaevich. 1874. *Sceny iz evrejskago byta* (Scenes from everyday Jewish life). 5th ed. St. Petersburg: Plotnikov.
Vejnberg, Pavel Isaevich. 1880. *Novye sceny i anekdoty iz evrejskogo, armianskogo, grescheskogo, nemeckogo i russkogo byta* (New scenes and jokes from Jewish, Armenian, Greek, German, and Russian everyday life). St. Petersburg: I. A. Tuzov.
Vkontakte. 2011. https://vk.com/topic-12938769_22367824?offset=40.
Vysokovskiy. 2004. http://www.vysokovskiy.ru/anekdot/perebegal/.
Znamenityj evrejskij shut Gershko iz Ostropolya: Ostroty etogo chudaka, shutki, kalambury, anekdoty i rasskazy iz evrejskoj zhizni (The famous Jewish jester Gershko from Ostropol: The witticisms of this character, jokes, puns, anecdotes and tales from Jewish life). 1902. Translated from Yiddish by Jak. Sirkes. Odessa: O. L. Akkershtejn.
Znamenityj evrejskij shut Haskel' iz Berdicheva: Veselye pohozhdenija ego, shutki, ostroty i rasskazy iz evrejskoj zhizni (Famous Jewish jester Haskel from Berdichev: Funny adventures of his, jokes, witticisms, and tales from Jewish life). 1902. Translated from Yiddish. Odessa: O. L. Akkershtejn.

Sources Containing No Joke Analogues

Alexandrov, D. A., comp. 1880. *Deklamator i komik: Sbornik izbrannyh stihitvirenij, kupletov, shansonetok i rasskazov iz russkogo i evrejskogo bytov, chitannyh i petyh na scenah stolichnyh i provincialnyh Nikitinym, Monakhovym, Ozerovym . . . i dr* (Reciter and comedian: The collection of selected poems, satirical songs, cabaret songs and stories from Russian and Jewish everyday life read and sung at the capital and provincial stages by Nikitin, Monakhov, Ozerov and others). Vol. 1 with printed music. Vilna: A. G. Syrkin.

Arkhipova, Alexandra, and Mikhail Melnichenko. 2010. *Anekdoty o Staline: Texty, kommentarii, issledovanija* (Jokes about Stalin: Texts, comments, research). Moscow: OGI.

Balys, Jonas. 1937. *Lietuvių samojus : Liaudies anekdotai* (Lithuanian wit: Folk anecdotes). Kaunas, Lithuania: Sakalas.

Birkerts, Pēteris. 1929–30. *Latvju tautas anekdotes: Ilūstrēts izdevums ar variantiem un zinātniskiem apcerējumiem* (Latvian folk anecdotes: Illustrated publication with variants and scholarly essays). 4 vols. Riga: Literātūra.

Bez zaglavija radi potehi: Sobranie anekdotov, kalamburov, ostrot, glupostej, scen; Iz russkogo, everjskogo, armanianskogo, bytov, aforizmov i proch (Without a title for fun: A collection of jokes, puns, witticisms, foolishness, and scenes; From Russian, Jewish, Armenian everyday life, aphorisms, etc.). 1880a, Part 1. St. Petersburg: Krakovskij.

Borev, Yuri. 1990. *Staliniada: Istorii, svidetelstva, apokrify, anekdoty* (Staliniada: Histories, testemonies, apocryphas, anecdotes). Riga: Paritet.

Budilnik (Alarm clock). 1873–1917. St. Petersburg, Russia.

Dahl, Vladimir. 1861. "Evrei i tsygane" (Jews and gypsies). In *Kartiny iz russkogo byta* (Pictures from Russian everyday life), 2 vols., by Vladimir Dahl. St. Petersburg: M. O. Wolf.

Davydov-Ganaropulo, Jurij Afanasjevich. 1886. *Sceny, rasskazy i vodevil iz evrejskogo byta* (Scenes, stories, and vaudeville from Jewish everyday life). Composed by Ju. A. Davydov (pseud.). Kharkov: F. I. Mikhajlov.

Evrej (A Jew). 1912–14. Odessa, Russia.

Evrejskaja mysl': Organ evrejskoj natsional 'noj mysli na juge Rossii (Jewish thought: The apparatus of Jewish national thought in the south of Russia). 1906–7. Odessa, Russia.

Evrejskaja obschina (Jewish community). 1917. Moscow: Moscow Committee of the United Jewish Socialist Labour Party for the Elections.

Evrejskaja rabochaja khronika (Jewish Labour Chronicles). 1917–18. Petrograd, Russia.

Evrejskaja zhizn' (Jewish life). 1915–17. Moscow, Russia.

Evrejskaja zhizn' v izobrazhenii evrejskih bytopisatelej (Jewish life depicted by Jewish writers of everyday life). 1903. St. Petersburg: Voskhod.

Evrejskie izvestija (Jewish news). 1907–11. St. Petersburg, Russia.

Evrejskij golos (Jewish voice). 1906–7. Odessa, Russia.

Evrejskij narod (Jewish people). 1906. St. Petersburg, Russia.

Evrejskij proletarij (Jewish proletarian). 1917. Petrograd, Russia.

Evrejskij put' (Jewish way). 1917. Ekaterinoslav, Russia.

Evrejskoe obozrenie (Jewish review). 1910. St. Petersburg, Russia.

Evrejskoe slovo (Jewish word). 1917. Aleksandrovsk, Russia.

Evrej v Varshave vo vremya poslednego polskogo myatezha (Ocherk iz evrejskogo byta) (Jews in Warsaw during the latest Polish uprising [Sketch from Jewish everyday life]). 1896. Vilna: Romma M. R.

Evstigneev, Mikhail Evdokimovich. 1872. *Sceny iz narodnogo byta raznyh stran in obschestv, sostavlennye M. Evstigneevym* (Scenes from the folk everyday life of different countries and societies). Moscow: D. I. Presnov..

Fortunov, Stephan, and Pyotr Prodanov. 1978. *Gabrovskie ulovki* (Gabrovo tricks). Sofia: Sofia Press.

Frug, Semen Grigorjevich. 1898a. *Eskizy i skazki: Iz evrejskogo byta* (Sketches and tales: From Jewish everyday life). St. Petersburg: fast printing by Ja. I. Liberman.

Frug, Semen Grigorjevich. 1898b. *Vstechi i vpechatlenija: Iz evrejskogo byta* (Meetings and impressions: From Jewish everyday life). St. Petersburg: Ja. I. Liberman.

Galler, Alexander Nikolaevich. 1876. *Sceny iz narodnogo russkogo i evrejskogo byta sochinennye A.N. fon-Gallerom* (Scenes from folk Russian and Jewish everyday life composed by A.N. von-Galler). St. Petersburg: R. Golike.

Gejm, Mojshe. 1871. *Illustrirovannye jumoristicheskie sceny iz evrejskogo i nemetskogo byta.* (Illustrated humorous scenes from Jewish and German everyday life). Part 1 and 2. Composed by Mojshe Gejm and Baron Shperling. Moscow: Shuman.

Gejm, Mojshe. 1876. *Illustrirovannye jumoristicheskie i satiricheskie sceny iz evrejskogo i nemetskogo byta: S prilozheniem zabavnyh kupletov, shansonetok i komiheskih rasskazov dlya semejnyh vecherov, domashnih spektaklej i teatralnyh scen; S portretami znamenitostej kaskadnogo mira i avtorov knigi* (Illustrated humorous scenes from Jewish and German everyday life: With appendix of funny satirical songs, cabaret songs, and comical stories for the family evenings, home performances, and theatrical scenes; With portraits of the celebrities from the cascade world and the authors of the book). 2nd ed. Composed by Mojshe Gejm and Baron Shperling. Moscow: Indrih.

Gulevich, Alexander. 1870. *Sceny iz evrejskogo byta* (Scenes from Jewish everyday life). Moscow: Kosogorov's Printing House.

Holodov, I. A. 1901. *Veselchak: Novyj sbornik scen, rasskazov, anekdotov i parodij iz mirskoj, ulichnoj, salonnoj i zakulisnoj zhizni russkih, malorossijan, armian, nemcev i evreev; Sobesednik ot skuki* (Merry fellow: The new collection of scenes, sketches, stories, jokes and parodies from mundane, street, salon and backstage life of Russians, Ukrainians, Armenians, Germans and Jews; The interlocutor against the boredom). Moscow: Vilde.

Ischenko, I. A. 1897. *Sobranie rasskazov iz evrejskogo byta Leonidova, Vejnberga, Davydove, Dmitrieva, Vilde i pr* (The collection of stories from Jewish everyday life by Leonidov, Vejnberg, Davydov, Dmitriev, Vilde, etc.). Kiev: T. A. Gubanov.

Krasovskij, Nikolaj Ivanovich. 1905. *Evrejskij sbornik zlobodnevnyh evrejskih kupletov, pesen, shutok i razskazov iz evrejskoj zhizni Zhidochek* (Jewish collection of topical Jewish satirical songs and tales from Jewish life in *A small Jew*). Moscow: Filatov.

Krikmann, Arvo. 2004. *Netinalji Stalinist* (Internet humor about Stalin). Tartu: Eesti Kirjandusmuuseum.

Krikmann, Arvo. n.d. *Collection of Soviet Jokes: Estonian and Russian Variants.* http://www.folklore.ee/~kriku/TRANSPORT/SovEstRus.doc.

K-skij, Gr. 1903. *Veselye rasskazy i sceny iz evrejskogo, armianskogo i malorusskogo narodnogo byta* (Merry stories and scenes from Jewish, Armenian and Ukrainian everyday folk life). Poltava: M. L. Starozhitskij.

Kurganov, E., and N. Ohotin, comps. 1990. *Russkij literaturnyj anekdot XVIII – nachala XIX vv* (Russian literary anecdote eighteenth–beginning of the nineteenth century). Moscow: Hudozhestvennaja literatura.

Kurganov, Efim. 1995. "Literaturnyj anekdot pushkinskoj pory" (The literary anecdote of the Pushkin epoch). PhD diss. Department of Slavonic language, University of Helsinki, Helsinki.

Leonidov, L. A. 1876. *Sceny iz evrejskogo byta: Ne hochesh, da hohochesh* (Scenes from Jewish everyday life: You cannot help laughing). St. Petersburg: R. Golike.

M-l' M. 1891. *V Ameriku (Kartinki iz evrejskoj zhizni)* (To America [Pictures from Jewish Life]). Vilna: Syrkin.

Mejervejn. 1898. *Rasskazchik jumoristicheskih i satiricheskih scen iz byta: Russkogo, nemeckogo, evrejskogo, armianskogo, tureckogo, tsyganskogo, polskogo i drugih i komicheskie illustririvannye rasskazy s celju provodit vremia v udovolstvii. V 3 chastiah.* (The teller of humorous and satirical scenes from everyday life: Russian, German, Jewish, Armenian, Turkish, Roma, Polish, and other comic illustrated stories for a pleasant pastime. In three parts). Composed by Mejervejn and Galchenko. Moscow: Ioganson.

Melnichenko, Misha. 2014. *Sovetskij anekdot (Ukazatel' siuzhetov)* (Soviet anecdote [The plot index]). Moscow: Novoe literaturnoe obozrenie.

Morozovskij, A. P. 1876. *Sceny iz evrejskogo byta* (Scenes from Jewish everyday life). Kiev: Fiodorov.

Polatus, S. S., coll. and comp. 1902a. *Ios'ka akter: Podrazhemyj kupletist, na vse ruki artist. Sbornik jumoristicheskij: Sovershenno novye kuplety I rasskazy iz evrejskogo i armianskogo byta luchshih avtorov; Ju.A. Davydova, Vejnberga i dr* (Ios'ka the actor: Imitating comic singer, skillfull actor. The humorous collection: Totally new satirical songs and tales from Jewish and Armenian everyday life of the best authors; Ju.A. Davydov, Vejnberg, etc.). Odessa: Galperin and Shvejcer.

Polatus, S. S., coll. and comp. 1902b. *Ios'ka akter: Podrazhemyj kupletist, na vse ruki artist. Sbornik jumoristicheskij: Sovershenno novye kuplety I rasskazy iz evrejskogo i armianskogo byta luchshih avtorov; Ju.A. Davydova, Vejnberga i dr* (Ios'ka the actor: Imitating comic singer, skillfull actor. The humorous collection: Totally new satirical songs and tales from Jewish and Armenian everyday life of the best authors; Ju.A. Davydov, Vejnberg, etc.). 2nd ed. Odessa: Galperin and Shvejcer.

Rajkova, Irina. 1993. *Petr I: Predanija, legendy, skazki i anekdoty* (Peter I: Stories, legends, tales and anecdotes). Moscow: Izdatelsto Sabashnikovyh.

Raskin, Iosif. 1994. *Entsiklopedia huliganstvujuschego ortodoksa* (The encyclopaedia of the hooligan orthodox). Moscow: Knizhnyj Klub 36.6.

Rassvet (Dawn). 1879–84. St. Petersburg, Russia.

Rassvet (Dawn). 1907–17. Petrograd, Russia.

Sbornik luchshih novyh scen, rasskazov i anekdotov iz russkogo, evrejskogo, malorusskogo, tsyganskogo i nemeckogo byta: Luchshih avtorov (The collection of the best new scenes, stories and jokes from Jewish, Ukrainian, Roma, and German everyday life: By the best authors). 1893. Kiev: T. A. Gubanov.

Sceny iz evrejskogo i malorossijskogo byta (Scenes from Jewish and Ukrainian everyday life). 1871. Compositions of Ios'ka and Gritsko with the portraits of the authors. Moscow: N. A. Kalashnikov.

Shut: Hudozhestvennyj zhurnal karikatur (Jester: The artistic journal of cartoons). 1879–1914. St. Petersburg, Russia.

Sovrasov, I. A. 1901. *Sobranie komicheskih kupletov iz evrejskogo byta* (Collection of comic satiric songs from Jewish everyday life). Composed by actor I. A. Sovrasov. Odessa: A. M. Dyhno.

Strekoza (Dragonfly). 1875–1918. St. Petersburg, Russia.

Suchilin, N. 1895. *Novye sceny, rasskazy i anekdoty iz russkogo, evrejskogo, malorossijskogo, nemeckogo, armianskogo i tsyganskogo byta, sobrannye iz sbornikov russkih pisatelej* (New scenes, stories, and jokes from Russian, Jewish, Ukrainian, German, Armenian, and Roma everyday life collected from the collections of Russian writers). Moscow: E. A. Gubanov.

Telushkin, Joseph. 1992. *Jewish Humor: What the Best Jewish Jokes Say about the Jews.* New York: William Morrow.

Vejnberg, A. 1878a. *Evrejskij rekrutskij nabor i esche koe-chto iz evrejskogo byta* (Recruiting Jews and a bit more of everyday Jewish life). 3rd ed. Kiev: F. A. Ioganson.

Vejnberg, A. 1878b. *Nashi zhidki na vojne* (Our Jews at war). 2nd ed. Kiev: K. N. Milevsky.

Vejnberg, Pavel Isaevich. 1883. *Polnyj sbornik jumoristicheskih scen iz evrejskogo I armianskogo byta* (The full collection of humorous scenes from Jewish and Armenian everyday life). Moscow: T. Ris.

Vejnberg, Pavel Isaevich. 1886. *Novye rasskazy i sceny* (New stories and scenes). St. Petersburg: V. Kirshbaum.

Vestnik evrejskoj emigracii i kolonizacii (The bulletin of Jewish emigration and colonization). 1911–14. Elec, Russia.

Viazemsky, Pyotr. 1883. *Staraja zapisnaja knizhka* (Old notebook). In *Polnoe sobranie sochinenij* (The complete works), vol. 8., by P. A. Viazemsky. St. Petersburg: S. D. Sheremetev.

Voskhod (Sunrise). 1899–1906. St. Petersburg, Russia.

Zaher-Mazoh, Leopold. 1889. *Neslyhannoe zaveschanie: Rasskazy iz evrejskogo byta.* (Unprecedented testament: The stories of Jewish everyday life). Translated from German. St. Petersburg: V. V. Lepehin.

Zhivye strunki. *Jumoristicheskij sbornik scen iz russkogo, evrejskogo i armianskogo byta, satiricheskih stihotvorenij i kupletov, anekdotov, shutok i prochee* (Life strings. A humorous collection of scenes from Russian, Jewish, and Armenian everyday life, satirical poems and songs, anecdotes, jokes, etc.). 1879. St. Petersburg: Shataev.

References

Abramowicz, Hirsz. 1999. *Profiles of a Lost World: Memoirs of East European Jewish Life before World War II*. Edited by Dina Abramowicz and Jeffrey Shandler. Translated by Eva Zeitlin Dobkin. Detroit, MI: Wayne State University Press.
Adler, Hermann. 1893. "Jewish Wit and Humor." *The Nineteenth Century* 33: 457–69.
Alter, Robert. 1987. "Jewish Humor and the Domestication of Myth." In *Jewish Wry: Essays on Jewish Humor*, edited by Sarah Blacher Cohen, 25–36. Detroit, MI: Wayne State University Press.
Altman, Sig. 1971. *The Comic Image of the Jew: Explorations of a Pop Culture Phenomenon*. Rutherford, NJ: Farleigh Dickinson Press.
"Anekdoten." 1812. *Sulamith: Eine Zeitschrift für Beförderung der Kultur und Humanität unter den Israeliten* 1:354–55.
An-ski, S. [Shlomo Zanvil Rappoport]. 1920–25. *Gezamelte Schriften*. Warsaw: Ferlag An-ski.
Ascher, Judas. 1810. *Der Judenfreund, oder auserlese Anekdoten, Schwänke, und Einfälle von den Kindern Israels* (The friend of the Jews, or selected anecdotes, pranks, and notions of the Children of Israel). Leipzig: Baumgartner Buchhandlung.
"Assembly of Jewish Notables." http://people.ucalgary.ca/~elsegal/363_Transp/Sanhedrin.html.
Ausubel, Nathan, ed. 1948. *A Treasury of Jewish Folklore*. New York: Crown.
Ausubel, Nathan, ed. 1967. *A Treasury of Jewish Humor*. New York: Paperback Library.
Bar-Itzhak, Haya. 2010. *Pioneers of Jewish Ethnography and Folkloristics in Eastern Europe*. Ljubljana: Scientific Research Center of the Slovenian Academy of Sciences and Arts.
Ben-Amos, Dan. 1991. "Jewish Folklore Studies." *Modern Judaism* 11 (1): 17–66.
Bergler, Edmund. 1956. *Laughter and the Sense of Humor*. New York: Grune and Stratton.
Bermant, Chaim. 1986. *What's the Joke? A Study of Jewish Humor through the Ages*. London: Weidenfeld and Nicolson.
Bisberg-Youkelson, Feigl, and Rubin Youkelson. 2000. *The Life and Death of a Polish Shtetl*. Translated by Gene Bluestein. Lincoln: University of Nebraska Press.

Brinton, Crane. 1967. "Enlightenment." *The Encyclopedia of Philosophy*, edited by Paul Edwards, 1:519–25. 4 vols. New York: Macmillan and the Free Press.
Brodsky, David. 2011. "Why Did the Widow Have a Goat in Her Bed? Jewish Humor and Its Roots in the Talmud and Midrash." In *Jews and Humor*, edited by Leonard J. Greenspoon, Studies in Jewish Civilization, 22:13–32. West Lafayette, IN: Purdue University Press.
Broers, Michael. 2014. *Napoleon: Soldier of Destiny*. New York: Pegasus.
Büschenthal, Lippmann Moses. 1812. *Sammlung witziger Einfälle von Juden, als Beyträge zur characteristik der Jüdischen Nation* (Collection of funny incidents about Jews, as a contribution to the characterization of the Jewish nation). Elberfeld: H. Büschler in Kommission.
"Büschenthal." 1840. *Allgemeine Zeitung des Judentums* (General journal of Judaism) 4 (4): 60.
Chase, Jefferson S. 2000. *Inciting Laughter: The Development of "Jewish Humor" in 19th Century German Culture*. Berlin: Walter de Gruyter.
Chisick, Harvey. 2002. "Ethics and History in Voltaire's Attitudes toward the Jews." *Eighteenth-Century Studies* 35 (4): 577–600.
Chotzner, Joseph. 1905. *Hebrew Humor and Other Essays*. London: Luzac.
Clouston, William Alexander. 1888. *The Book of Noodles: Stories of Simpletons; or, Fools and Their Follies*. London: Elliott Stock.
Cohen, Ted. 1999. *Jokes: Philosophical Thoughts on Joking Matters*. Chicago: University of Chicago Press.
Cray, Ed. 1964. "The Rabbi Trickster." *Journal of American Folklore* 77 (306): 341–45.
Davidson, Israel. 1907. *Parody in Jewish Literature*. New York: Printed in Leipzig by W. Drugulin.
Davies, Christie. 1986. "Jewish Jokes, Anti-Semitic Jokes and Hebredonian Jokes." In *Jewish Humor*, edited by Avner Ziv, 75–96. Tel Aviv: Papyrus.
Davies, Christie. 2002. *The Mirth of Nations*. New Brunswick, NJ: Transaction.
Declaration of the Rights of Man and of the Citizen. 1789. http://oll.libertyfund.org/pages/declaration-of-the-rights-of-man-and-of-the-citizen.
"Décret infâme." http://www.juif.org/imprimer-blog-7026.php.
Deutsch, Nathaniel. 2011. *The Jewish Dark Continent: Life and Death in the Russian Pale of Settlement*. Cambridge, MA: Harvard University Press.
Dohm, Christian Wilhelm, von. 1957. "Concerning the Amelioration of the Civil Status of the Jews." In *Readings in Modern Jewish History*, edited by Ellis Rivkin. Translated by Helen Lederer, 12–69. Cincinnati, OH: Hebrew Union College–Jewish Institute of Religion.
Downing, Charles. 1965. *Tales of the Hodja*. New York: Henry Z. Walck.
Druyanow, Alter. 1963. *Sefer ha-bediḥah ve-ha-ḥidud* (The book of the joke and the witticism). 3 vols. Tel Aviv: Dvir.
Dubnov, Simon. 1971 *The History of the Jews*. 5 vols. Rev. ed. Translated by Moshe Spiegel. New York: Thomas Yoseloff.
"Edict of Toleration for the Jews of Lower Austria." 1782. http://germanhistorydocs.ghi-dc.org/sub_document.cfm?document_id=3648.
Eilbirt, Henry. 1993. *What Is a Jewish Joke?: An Excursion into Jewish Humor*. Northvale, NJ: Jason Aronson.

Elon, Amos. 2002. *The Pity of It All: A Portrait of the German-Jewish Epoch, 1743–1933*. New York: Picador.
Finkin, Jordan. 2011. "Jewish Jokes, Yiddish Storytelling, and Sholem Aleichem: A Discursive Approach." In *Jews and Humor*, edited by Leonard J. Greenspoon, Studies in Jewish Civilization, 22:83–106. West Lafayette, IN: Purdue University Press.
Fischman, Fernando. 2011. "Using Yiddish: Language Ideologies, Verbal Art, and Identity among Argentinian Jews." *Journal of Folklore Research* 48 (1): 37–61.
"French Revolution." Wikipedia. https://en.wikipedia.org/wiki/French_Revolution.
Freud, Sigmund. 1960. *Jokes and Their Relation to the Unconscious*. Translated by James Strachey. New York: W. W. Norton.
Friedman, Hershey H., and Linda Weiser Friedman. 2014. *God Laughed: Sources of Jewish Humor*. New Brunswick, NJ: Transaction.
Gay, Peter. 1966. *The Enlightenment: An Interpretation*. New York: Alfred A. Knopf.
Gay, Peter, and the editors of Time-Life Books. 1969. *The Enlightenment*. Rev. ed. New York: Time-Life.
Gilman, Sander. 1996. *Smart Jews: The Construction of the Image of Jewish Superior Intelligence*. Lincoln: University of Nebraska Press.
Gilman, Sander. 2012. "'Jewish Humour' and the Terms by which Jews and Muslims Join Western Civilization." *Leo Baeck Institute Yearbook* 57 (1): 53–65.
Glückel of Hameln. 1977. *The Memoirs of Glückel of Hameln*. Translated by Marvin Lowenthal. New York: Schocken.
Goedeke, Karl. 1938. *Grundrisz zur Geschichte der deutschen Dichtung aus den Quellen* (Outline of the history of German poetry from the sources). Vol. 13. Dresden: L. Ehlermann.
Golden, Harry. 1972. *The Golden Book of Jewish Humor*. New York: G. P. Putnam's Sons.
Goldschmidt, Hermann Levin. 2007. *The Legacy of German Jewry*. Translated by David Suchoff. New York: Fordham University Press.
Gottesman, Itzik Nakhmen. 2003. *Defining the Yiddish Nation: The Jewish Folklorists of Poland*. Detroit, MI: Wayne State University Press.
Grotjahn, Martin. 1966. *Beyond Laughter: Humor and the Subconscious*. New York: McGraw Hill.
Heine, Heinrich. 1893. *Heinrich Heine's Life Told in His Own Words*. Edited by Gustav Karpeles. Translated by Arthur Dexter. New York: Henry Holt.
Hertzberg, Arthur. 1968. *The French Enlightenment and the Jews*. New York: Columbia University Press.
Heuer, Renate, ed. 1996. *Lexicon deutsch-jüdischer Autoren* (Dictionary of German-Jewish authors). Vol. 4. München: K. G. Saur.
Honderich, Ted, ed. 1995. *The Oxford Companion to Philosophy*. Oxford: Oxford University Press.
Ilan, Tal. 2009. "The Joke in Rabbinic Literature: Home-Born or Diaspora Humor." In *Humor in arabischen Kultur* (Humor in Arab culture), edited by G. Tamer, 57–75. Berlin: Walter de Gruyter.
Isaacs, Abram S. 1911. *Stories from the Rabbis*. New York: Bloch.
Jacobs, Joseph. 1906. "Hep! Hep!" *Jewish Encylcopedia*. http://www.jewishencyclopedia.com/ articles/7578-hep-hep.

Keller, Werner. 1966. *Diaspora: The Post-Biblical History of the Jews*. New York: Harcourt Brace & World.
Kilcher, Andreas B. 2007. *Geteilte Freude: Schiller-Rezeption in der jüdischen Moderne*. (Shared joy: Schiller's reception in Jewish modernity). München: Stiftung Lyric Kabinett.
Killy, Walther, ed. 1995–2003. *Deutsche Biographische Enzyklopädie* (German biographical encyclopedia). 12 vols. Darmstadt: Wissenschaftliche Buchgesellschaft.
King, David. 2008. *Vienna 1815: How the Conquerors of Napoleon Made Love, War, and Peace at the Congress of Vienna*. New York: Harmony.
Klein, Ernst Ferdinand, ed. 1791. *Annalen der Gesetzgebung und Rechtsgelehrsamkeit* (Annals of legislation and legal scholarship). Vol. 17. Berlin: Friedrich Nicolai.
Kriminalgeschichten: Aus gerichtlichen Akten gezogen (Stories of criminals: Drawn from court records). 1792. Vol. 1. Berlin: Friedrich Bieweg, dem ältern.
Kugelmass, Jack. 2006. "The Father of Jewish Ethnography." In *The Worlds of S. An-Sky: A Russian Intellectual at the Turn of the Century*, edited by Gabriella Safran and Steven J. Zipperstein, 346–59. Stanford: Stanford University Press.
Landmann, Salcia. 1962. "On Jewish Humor." *Jewish Journal of Sociology* 4: 193–204.
Learsi, Rufus. 1961. *Filled with Laughter: Fiesta of Jewish Folk Humor*. New York: Thomas Yoseloff.
Lefebvre, George. 1969. *Napoleon: From Tilsit to Waterloo*. Translated by J. E. Anderson. New York: Columbia University Press.
Lifschutz, Ezekiel. 1952. "Merry Makers and Jesters among Jews." In *YIVO Annual of Jewish Social Science*, edited by Koppel S. Pinson, 7:43–83. New York: YIVO.
Lindfors, Tommi. "Jean Bodin (c. 1529–1596)." *Internet Encyclopedia of Philosophy*. http://www.iep.utm.edu/bodin/.
Locke, John. 1824 [1689]. "A Letter Concerning Toleration, Being a Translation of the Epistola de Tolerantia." Vol. 5. In *The Works of John Locke in 9 Volumes*, 1–58. London: For G. and J. Rivington.
Lukes, Steven. 1973. *Individualism*. Oxford: Basil Blackwell.
Margolis, Max L., and Alexander Marx. 1927. *A History of the Jewish People*. Philadelphia: Jewish Publication Society.
Marshall, John. 2006. *John Locke, Toleration and Early Enlightenment Culture: Religious Intolerance and Arguments for Religious Toleration in Early Modern and "Early Enlightenment" Europe*. Cambridge: Cambridge University Press.
Meyer, Michael A. 1967. *The Origins of the Modern Jew: Jewish Identity and European Culture in Germany, 1749–1824*. Detroit, MI: Wayne State University Press.
Mikes, George. 1971. *Laughing Matter: Towards a Personal Philosophy of Wit and Humor*. New York: Library Press.
Miller, Saul. 1980. *Dobromil: Life in a Galician Shtetl, 1890–1907*. New York: Lowenthal.
Nador, Georg. 1975. *Zur philosophie des jüdischen Witzes* (On the philosophy of Jewish jokes). Publication der Academia Maimonideana, Kurzmonographien Nr. 3. Northwood, Middlesex: Bina.
"Napoleon Bonaparte." 1801. *Allgemeiner Litterarischer Anzeiger* (General literary gazette). 49 (27 March).
Nevo, Ofra. 1991. "What's in a Jewish Joke?" *Humor: International Journal of Humor Studies* 4 (2): 251–60.

Nevo, Ofra, and Jacob Levine. 1994. "Jewish Humor Strikes Again: The Outburst of Humor in Israel during the Gulf War." *Western Folklore* 53 (2): 125–46.
Niger, Shmuel. 1972. "The Humor of Sholom Aleichem." In *Voices from the Yiddish: Essays, Memoirs, Diaries*, edited by Irving Howe and Eliezer Greenberg, 41–50. Ann Arbor: University of Michigan Press.
Novak, William, and Moshe Waldoks, eds. 1981. *The Big Book of Jewish Humor*. New York: Harper and Row.
Omar, Ifran A. 2004. "Humor." In *Encyclopedia of Islam and the Muslim World*, edited by Richard C. Martin. 2 vols. New York: Thompson Gale.
Oring, Elliott. 1981. *Israeli Humor: The Content and Structure of the Chizbat of the Palmah*. Albany: State University of New York Press.
Oring, Elliott. 1983. "The People of the Joke: On the Conceptualization of a Jewish Humor." *Western Folklore* 42 (4): 261–71.
Oring, Elliott. 1984. *The Jokes of Sigmund Freud: A Study in Humor and Jewish Identity*. Philadelphia: University of Pennsylvania Press.
Oring, Elliott. 1989. "Between Jokes and Tales: On the Nature of Punch Lines." *Humor: International Journal of Humor Research* 4 (2): 349–64.
Oring, Elliott. 1992. *Jokes and Their Relations*. Lexington: University Press of Kentucky.
Oring, Elliott. 2003. *Engaging Humor*. Urbana: University of Illinois Press.
Oring, Elliott. 2015. "Review of *God Laughed: Sources of Jewish Humor* by Hershey H. Friedman and Linda Weiser Friedman." *Western Folklore* 74 (3/4): 404–7.
Pagden, Anthony. 2013. *The Enlightenment and Why It Still Matters*. New York: Random House.
"Parlement." Wikipedia. https://en.wikipedia.org/wiki/Parlement.
Posener, S. 1945. "The Social Life of the Jewish Communities in France in the 18th Century." *Jewish Social Studies* 7: 195–232.
Radday, Yehuda T. 1990. "On Missing Humour in the Bible." In *On Humour and the Comic in the Hebrew Bible*, edited by Yehuda T. Radday and Athalya Brenner, 21–38. Sheffield, UK: Almond.
Radday, Yehuda T., and Athalya Brenner, eds. 1990. *On Humour and the Comic in the Hebrew Bible*. Sheffield, UK: Almond.
Raskin, Richard. 1992. *Life Is Like a Glass of Tea: Studies of Classic Jewish Jokes*. Aarhus, Denmark: Aarhus University Press.
Reik, Theodor. 1962. *Jewish Wit*. New York: Gamut.
Revel, Hirschel. 1943. "Wit and Humor." In *The Universal Jewish Encyclopedia*, edited by Isaac Landmann, 10:545–48. New York: Universal Jewish Encyclopedia.
"Review of Life and Opinions of Heinrich Heine." 1878. *Athenaeum*, January 15, 81–82.
Richman, Jacob. 1952. *Jewish Wit and Wisdom*. New York: Pardes.
Richman, Jacob. 1954. *Laughs from Jewish Lore*. New York: Hebrew Publishing.
Roberts, Andrew. 2014. *Napoleon: A Life*. New York: Penguin.
Robertson, Ritchie, ed. 1999. *The German-Jewish Dialogue: An Anthology of Literary Texts, 1749–1993*. Oxford: Oxford University Press.
Rogow, Arnold A., ed. 1961. *The Jew in a Gentile World*. New York: Macmillan.
Rohatyn, B. 1911. "Die Geschtatlen des juedischen Volkshumor I" (Forms of Jewish folk humor I). *Ost und West* 11: 122–126.
Roskies, Diane K., and David G. Roskies. 1975. *The Shtetl Book*. New York: Ktav.

Rosten, Leo. 1970. *The Joys of Yiddish*. New York: Pocket Books.
Roth, Cecil, ed. 1972. *Encyclopaedia Judaica*. 16 vols. Jerusalem: Keter.
Sa'di Shirazi. 1258. *Gulistan* (The rose garden]). Chapter 4, story 10. http://classics.mit.edu/Sadi/gulistan.5.iv.html.
Samuel, Maurice. 1971. *In Praise of Yiddish*. New York: Cowles.
Schechter, Ronald. 2003. *Obstinate Hebrews: Representations of Jews in France, 1715–1815*. Berkeley: University of California Press.
Schwarzbaum, Haim. 1968. *Studies in Jewish and World Folklore*. Berlin: Walter de Gruyter.
Schwarzfuchs, Simon. 1979. *Napoleon, the Jews, and the Sanhedrin*. London: Routledge & Kegan Paul.
Simon, Edith. 1974. "Frederick II the Great, of Prussia." *Encyclopedia Britannica: Macropedia*. 15th edition. 19 vols. Chicago: Helen Hemingway Benton.
Simon, Ernst. 1948. "Notes on Jewish Wit." *Jewish Frontier* 15 (October): 42–48.
Singer, Isadore, and Emil G. Hirsch. 1906. "Zunz." *Jewish Encyclopedia*. http://www.jewishencyclopedia.com/articles/15299-zunz-leopold.
Skikne, Maurice. 2009. "*Vitzen, Meises, Kloggen und Humor*: A Brief History of Yiddish Humor." *Jewish Affairs* 64 (1): 44–46.
Sorkin, David. 1987. *The Transformation of German Jewry, 1780–1840*. New York: Oxford University Press.
Spalding, Henry D. 1969. *Encyclopedia of Jewish Humor: From Biblical Times to the Modern Age*. New York: Jonathan David.
Stern-Taeubler, Selma. 1949. "The Jews in the Economic Policy of Frederick the Great." *Jewish Social Studies* 11 (2): 129–52.
Sutcliffe, Adam. 1998. "Myth, Origins, Identity: Voltaire, the Jews and the Enlightenment Notion of Toleration." *The Eighteenth Century* 39 (2): 107–26.
Szajkowski, Zosa. 1954. "The Jewish Problem in Alsace, Metz, and Lorraine on the Eve of 1789." *The Jewish Quarterly Review* 44 (3): 205–43.
Teitelbaum, Elsa. 1945. *An Anthology of Jewish Humor and Maxims*. New York: Pardes.
Telushkin Joseph. 1992. *Jewish Humor: What the Best Jewish Jokes Say about the Jews*. New York: William Morrow.
Toland, John. 1714. *Reasons for Naturalising the Jews in Great Brittain and Ireland on the Same Footing with All Other Nations*. London: for J. Roberts. https://archive.org/stream/reasonsfornaturootolagoog#page/n6/mode/2up.
Untermeyer, Louis. 1946. *A Treasury of Laughter*. New York: Simon and Schuster.
Uther, Hans-Jörg. 2011. *The Types of the International Folktale: A Classification and Bibliography*. 3 vols. Helsinki: Academia Scientiarum Fennica.
Wengeroff, Pauline. 2010. *Memories of a Grandmother: Scenes from the Cultural History of the Jews of Russia in the Nineteenth Century*. Translated by Shulamit S. Magnus. Stanford Studies in Jewish History and Culture. Palo Alto, CA: Stanford University Press.
Williams, Roger. 1867 [1644]. *The Bloudy Tenent of Persecution*. Publications of the Narragansett Club, edited by Samuel L. Caldwell. First Series, vol. 3. Providence: Rhode Island. https://books.google.com/books?id=IL8MAAAAIAAJ&pg=PR3&source= gbs_toc_r&cad=3#v=onepage&q&f=false.

Wisse, Ruth R. 2013. *No Joke: Making Jewish Humor.* Princeton, NJ: Princeton University Press.

YIVO Vilna. https://vilnacollections.yivo.org/What-Was-Considered-Funny-Two-Hundred-Years-Ago.

Ziv, Avner. 1986. Introduction to *Jewish Humor*, edited by Avner Ziv, 7–15. Tel Aviv: Papyrus.

Zunz, Leopold. 1818–19. "Nekrolog." *Jedidja: Eine religiöse, morlaische und pädagogische Zeitschrift* (Jedidja: a religious, moral, and pedigogical journal). 1: 265–67.

Index

Abramowicz, Hirsz, 24n9
Adler, Hermann, 3
Aleinu (prayer), 35, 46n8
Anecdotes, 12
Anekdoten von guten Juden, vii
Arab and Persian jokes, 7
Ascher, Judas, vii–viii, 11
Assembly of Jewish Notables, 10, 41

Baden, 42
Badkhonim (wedding jesters), 8
Bayle, Pierre, 31
Bildung (education), 36, 43, 45
Bischheim, 10
Blood libel, 28
Bloudy Tenets of Persecution, The, 31
Bodin, Jean, 31, 32
Bonaparte, Jerome, 42
Bonaparte, Napoleon: conquests, 40; decrees about Jews, 41–42; defeat, 43; elevation of Karl von Dalberg, 10, 42–43; escape from assassination, 10, 24n13; redraws map of Europe, 40–41; visit to lower Rhine, 10. *See also* Assembly of Jewish Notables; Grand Sanhedrin
Börne, Ludwig, 9
Büschenthal, Lippmann Moses, vii–viii; and Heidenheim, 10; biography of, 9–11, 37, 45; on negative characteristics of Jews, 11–12, 23; on women, 24n16; poetry of, 10, 41; theory of Jewish joke, 11–12; use of *Der Judenfreund*, 19, 20
Büschler, Heinrich (bookseller), 20

Carlyle, Thomas, 3
Colloquium heptaplomeres de rerum sublimium arcanes abditis (Colloquium of the seven about the secrets of the divine), 31
Confederation of the Rhine, 10, 40–41
Congress of Vienna, 43–44
Consistorial system, 10, 41, 42, 43
Conversion, 34–35, 44, 47n16
Conversos (converts), 30, 46n3
Cri de Citoyen (Outcry of a citizen), 24n15
Custine, Adam Phillipe Comte de, 40

Dalberg, Karl von, 10, 42–43
Déclaration des droits de l'homme et du citoyen (Declaration of the Rights of Man and of the Citizen), 38, 39, 40, 42, 46nn12–13, 46n15
Décret infâme (infamous decree), 42–43, 44
Der Judenfreund, vii–viii; viii n3; 11, 12; interactions in, 16; jokescape of, 17–18; serious texts in, 12, 18–19; numbering of texts in, 16, 19; poems in, 19
Descartes, René, 31
Die Juden (The Jews), 32
Dohm, Wilhelm von, 37
Druyanow, Alter, 24n27

Edict against the Jews, 30
Elberfeld, 10, 20, 30, 41
Enlightenment: and French Revolution, 38–39; beginnings of, 31; nature of, 31–31, 33; terms for, 31. *See also Haskalah* (Jewish Enlightenment)

155

Fichte, Johann Gottlieb, 47n22
Firt, 29
Folksongs, 9
Fränkel, Rabbi David, 33
Frederick II the Great, 35, 37; relation to Jews, 29, 33, 34–45
Freischule (free school), 33
French Revolution, 10, 22, 37–39
Freud, Sigmund, 3, 23n1, 24n4
Friedländer, David, 34
Friedrich Wilhelm I, 29

Galileo Galilei, 31
Gans, Eduard, 22
Ghettos: Frankfurt, 28, 43; Rome, 30, 40
Grand Duchy of Berg, 10, 41
Grand Sanhedrin, 41
Grégoire, Abbé Henri Jean-Baptiste, 22, 40
Gulistan (The rose garden), 8

Hardenberg, Karl August von, 43–44
Haskalah (Jewish Enlightenment), 11, 21, 22, 33, 34
Hebrew, 33, 37
Heidenheim, Wolf, 10
Heine, Heinrich, 9, 45
Hell, François, 24n15, 47n19
Hep! Hep! riots, 45, 47nn20–21
Herder, Johann Gottfried von, 44
Ḥerem (excommunication), 34
Hobbes, Thomas, 31
Hodja Nasreddin, 15
Humboldt, Wilhelm von, 43–44
Humor, 9
Hundert un eyni anekdotin (One hundred and one anecdotes), 8, 24n6

Inquisition, 29, 30, 46n3

Jehuda Leib, Nehemie: autobiography of, 19–20; 91–97; biography of, 19–20, 88–91
Jewish education, 33–34
Jews: assimilation of, 44–45; assumption of family names, 42; as race, 45; autonomous communities, 27, 37, 40; 45nn1–2; as virtuous, 32; bodies of, 25n23; civil rights of, 27, 36, 43, 44, 47n22; connection with jokes and humor, 5, 7, 12; conversion of, 22, 30, 34–35, 36, 44, 45; cunningness of, 12, 21; defense of, 3, 21, 22, 24n15, 34, 36, 37, 46n7; deformed character of, 21–22; emancipation of, 21, 30–31, 36–37, 39–40, 42, 43–44, 45; expulsions of, 29, 30, 38, 44, 46n9, 46–47n15; extraordinary, 28, 35; intelligence of, 12, 24n15; limiting population of, 29, 37, 47n17; marriage of, 28, 38; memoirs by, 8–9; military service, 42, 44; Napoleon and, 10, 40, 41–42; occupations of, 15, 27–28, 29, 35, 37, 40; of Alsace, 30, 38, 39, 42; of Altona, 30; of Avignon, 39; of Bayonne, 29, 39; of Bordeaux, 29, 39; of Holland, 30, 40; of Rome, 30; of Sweden, 30; ordinary, 28; population in France, 30, 46n9; restrictions on domiciles, 28, 29, 35, 37, 38, 40, 43, 45–46n2; restrictions on movement, 28, 30, 40, 42; riots against, 45, 46–47n15; rollback of rights, 44; Sephardic ("Portuguese"), 29, 39; taxes on, 27, 28, 37; Voltaire on, 33
Joke texts in *Der Judenfreund*: aesthetic (*Ess+Thee+Tisch*), 124; animal doctor, 115–16; armed Jews ask for protection, 108; army officer quartered in Jew's home, 124–25; artist won't sell paintings of Christ, 108; bargaining for clothes of hanged, 109; beard should be untouched, 125; begging boy hounds couple, 126; blank page between testaments, 118; brandy drinkers have no use for money, 122; brother buried in shabby grave, 103; buyer doesn't show up, 117; cantor and *Zuhalter*, 119; catalog is "continence" of books, 120; child encouraged to pass coin, 110–11; coin is Frederick outside, Ephraim inside, 130; convert leaves bequest to those he cheated, 101; cook asks mistress about grammar, 123; deduct for wood on silver crucifix, 118–19; don't cut on the Sabbath, 115; ducking thrown stone, 101; duel with empty pistols, 129–30; eating pickled body, 100; edition vs. expense, 123; eighth notes give profit, 127; fake jewels as security, 103–4; false note is said to be "abbreviated," 109; Fenchified Jew at border, 113; fraud by pretending to burn note, 106–7; fraud over repurchase of note, 104–5; giving money to benefactor, 119; grandchildren play with drafts, 118; Grattenauer attacks and Cosman defends, 122; greets neither king nor rabbi, 121; grunting with rich Jew, 114; Handel and Gluck, 116; hanged body counts as credit, 110; ichthyologist overcomes fear of water, 102; Jesus won't return because of ill treatment, 123–24; Jew made to stay in ditch, 100; Jew murders another Jew, 127–29; Jewish peddler used to scare child, 111; Jewish regiment echoes orders, 108–9; Jews and asses in England, 115; Jews debauched like

Christians, 116; Jews do not give change, 102; Jews of Posen greet king, 107–8; king beats Jews who fear him, 102; lawyer advises father to covert, 101–2; Lessing praised and manager criticized, 99; marshal receives Jews because of gift, 108; might makes right, 126–27; Moslem puts out eye of Jew, 106; Napoleon not so big, 119; not shaving to avoid debt, 106; note from quarantined ship, 126; officer is honest man, 113; old man encouraged to remarry, 112; picking up money on Sabbath, 118; playing the flite, 120–21; plays holds no interest, 124; police market, 120; praising ring to painter, 115; punishment but not reform, 113–14; repayment to court musician, 112; responds like Pilate, 119; Rienzi's body roasted, 100; roast goose sent to actress, 121; salesmen return with each other's goods, 116; Salomon Maimon and his wife, 121; Saul among the prophets, 123; scholars separated in afterlife, 109–10; schoolmaster has 37 children, 112; shoot/advance money, 114–15; Simon Ox and Abraham Cow, 114; small trading on credit, 108; stealing watch to show friend, 117; student wounded in duel, 114; thief branded against will, 111; thief requests quick beating, 112–13; too many Christian moneylenders, 120

Jokes texts in *Sammlung*: animal doctor, 75; armor on back, 62; ask the wolf, 80; ate on fast day, 71; banner eaten by mice, 69; baron never rushes to pay, 81; birds have no written notes, 73; birth after 4½ months, 57; blindness not a flaw, 81–82; borrower has no coat but reckoning is right, 64–65; bribing city guard, 63–64; bureaucrat/witchcraft, 80; can't waste a theater ticket, 73; carry our own skin, 72; Chaldean document, 82–83; checking if goose is fat, 57; child expresses pure nature, 85; coat is worse, 81; commentary on Lamentations, 66; convinced Christian is a Jew, 54; credit for an eternal father, 55; crucify our Lord, 55; cures toothache, 68–69; daughter can't be coachman, 86; deceptive borrowing of Abraham Moses, 62–63; *die Neuberin*, 62–63; difference between Jew and ass, 53; disgusting pinch, 69; dislikes about Mainz, 64; dropping cow's tail, 57; Easter eggs, 78; elders to say he wasn't mad, 70–71; face must be a mirror, 73; fake ring, 62; false oath, 79; Frenchman accurately depicted, 62; garden height praised, 52; girl accosted in theater, 52; giving rat the bill, 58; gloves and stockings, 67; God has a son? 53; going for a walk while sitting, 77–78; H. A. H initials, 78; horse will run too far, 80; "I should be the devil," 56; impromptu lie, 54; Jew gives in to horse, 87; Jew hides in sack, 77; Jew mistakes actor, 83–84; Jew sent across border, 58; Jewess always pious, 78; Jews and asses in Spain, 57; Jews and asses in Turkey, 60; Jews beaten by coachmen, 68; laws developed, tricks made, 78; lump/paper, 81; Mannheim beer, 70; master of the house, 76; Mendelssohn and chess, 87; Mendelssohn trades in intelligence, 76; Mendelssohn: "I couldn't use him," 73; Mendelssohn: "Can't even insult a Jew," 74; Mendelssohn: Demosthenes and Aesop, 75–76; milk and blood, 71; *musikalisch*, 71–72; no need to leave with 100 horses, 53; not even for twenty strokes, 70; not old until married, 55; not shooting but hitting, 58; Nürenberg gingerbread, 79; officer refuses to pay debt, 61; passenger half out of coach, 80–81; pauses on piano are different, 84; pays cash, 79; Pilates and Herods, 61; politician is sheath around a crook, 88; promises to shit across border, 55; rabbi can't read or write, 65; rabbi orders not obeyed, 54; rascal is an honest man, 51; rather not give speech, 85–86; reading *Agathon*, 85; rich man in Meseritz, 60–61; ruin paper, 86; security of lender, 79; shoots percent down, 75; six-fingered child will be pianist, 83; slaps friend at chess, 72–73; soldier's widow gets pregnant, 83; son will be a courier, 72; stealing eggs, 54–55; student rewarded for slapping, 56; stuttering Jew in court, 58; Talmud prodigy, 66–67; temperament, 84–85; three-cornered hat, 61; two fasts at once, 52; two half discounts make a whole, 82; undressed/gone out, 87; verdict awaiting file, 71; watching others' hands, 69–70; watchmaker in chest, 59–60; weighing the cat, 86; what is justice doing here? 81; when did "we" arrive? 56; without a heart, 74

Joke texts, other: Battle of Minorca, 8; stones frozen in ground, 8

Jokes: transformation of negative characteristics in, 24n10

Jokes, Jewish: 3–9; absence in Middle Ages, 7; aesthetics of, 5; and oppression, 6; as consolation, 6; as defense, 6; as Jewish trait, 9, 11; as mythology, 7; as psychological, 4; as self-critical, 3, 6, 15; as social fact, 3; definition

Jokes (cont.)
  of, 4, 7, 21; eastern European origin of, 4, 5, 8, 9, 21; history of, 23; in Bible, Talmud, and Midrash, 5, 7, 23n2; in ethnographic program, 8; in Israel, 4; in Middle East, 4; in Yiddish, 4, 8, 9, 11; logic of, 5–6, 15; masochism of, 4
Jokescape, 13
Joseph II Habsburg, 36
Judenwitz (Jewish wit), 9

Kepler, Johannes, 31
Kingdom of Westphalia, 42
Kriminalgeschichten (Stories of criminals), 19, 20

Lacretelle, Pierre-Louis, 21–22
Latour-Foissac, Philippe-François de, 24n15
Laughter through tears, 6
Leibzoll (body tax), 20, 25n28
Lessing, Gotthold Ephraim, 32, 33
Locke, John, 31, 32, 36

Machiavelli, Niccoló, 31
Maria Theresa, 29
Mecklenburg, Duchy of, 29
Mendelssohn, Moses, 29, 33, 34, 35, 37; anecdotes about, 11, 25n23; Bible translation by, 33; descendants of, 35; election to Academy, 33; made *parnas*, 34; opposition to, 34; religious observance by, 34
Metternich, Klemens von, 44
Metz, 29
Mirabeau, Honoré Gabriel Riquetti, Comte de, 40
Moneylending, 33, 35, 39, 41, 42, 47n19
Montesquieu, Charles-Louis de, 45n7
Moser, Moses, 22

Napoleon. See Bonaparte, Napoleon
Nathan der Weise (Nathan the Wise), 32, 45n6
National (Constituent) Assembly, 38
Naturalization bill, 36
Neuwied, 10
New Christians, 29. See also *conversos*
Newton, Isaac, 31
Nicolai, Friedrich, 33
Novalis (George Phillip Friedrich von Hardenberg), 47n22

Oath *more judaico*, 43
Observations d'un Alsacien sur l'affaire présente des Juifs d'Alsace (Observations of an Alsatian on the present matter of the Jews of Alsace), 24n15
"Ode to Joy," 10

Pale of Settlement, 4, 8, 9
parlements, 38, 46n10
Péage. See *Leibzoll*
Phaedon, or the Immortality of the Soul in Three Dialogues, 33
Philosophical Dialogues, 33
Poem texts in *Der Judenfreund*: "Complaint of a Pigtail-ribbon Jew," 132–3; "Consolation of the Jews," 133; "Song of a Jewish Trader at the Leipzig Fair," 131–2; "Thoughts of a Jew at Sunset," 133; "To the Publisher of the Anecdotes of Noble Jews," 131
Poland, partitions of, 29
Pope Pius VI, 30, 40
Pranks, 8
Protestants, 31, 34, 38, 41, 44, 46n13
Prussian Academy of Science, 33
Purim shpiln (Purim plays), 8

Reasons for Naturalizing the Jews in Great Britain and Ireland (Toland), 36
Reform Judaism, 34
Renan, Ernest, 3
Romantic-nationalism, 44, 45, 47n22

S. An-ski, (Shlomo Zanvil Rappoport), 8, 24n8
Sa'di Shirazi, 8
Sammlung, vii–viii, viiinn1–2, 9–10; absent topics in, 13; and Jewish character, 11–12; and Jewish cunning, 12; as revision of *Der Judenfreund*, 20; audience for, 11; importance of, 11; interactions in, 11–12; jokescape of, 13–15; language of, 11; numbering of texts in, 16; relation to *Der Judenfreund*, 11, 16, 20–21
Saphir, Moritz Gottlieb, 9, 24n10, 25n29
Schiller, Friedrich, 10
Schlegel, Friedrich, 45
Sinzheim, Rabbi David, 10
Spinoza, Baruch, 31, 33
Stadlan (intercessor), 27, 28
Strasbourg, 10, 30, 40, 41
Sulamith (journal), 10, 11, 24n12

Taylor, John, 8
Teller, Wilhelm Abraham, 34
Thirty Years' War, 31
Toland, John, 36
Toleranzpatent (Edict of toleration), 36–37

toleration: legal, 36, 37; religious: 12, 31, 32, 36, 46n4
Tugend (virtue), 36, 45

Über die bürgerliche Verbesserung des Juden (On the civil improvement of the Jews) (Dohm), 37
Usury, 33, 39, 41. *See also* moneylending

Verein für Kultur und Wissenschaft des Judens (Society for Jewish culture and science), 22
Voltaire, 32–33, 35, 45n7

Williams, Roger, 31
Wit and Mirth, 8
Witz (wisecrack), 9

Yiddish, 19, 30, 33, 37. See also *jokes in Yiddish folklore*, 9
YIVO (Institute for Jewish Research), 24n26

Zunz, Leopold, 22, 25n30

ELLIOTT ORING

is Professor Emeritus of Anthropology at California State University, Los Angeles. He is author of *Joking Asides: The Theory, Analysis, and Aesthetics of Humor*; *Engaging Humor*; *Jokes and Their Relations*; *The Jokes of Sigmund Freud: A Study in Humor and Jewish Identity*; and *Israeli Humor: The Content and Structure of the Chizbat of the Palmah*. He is also past editor of *Western Folklore* and is currently on the editorial boards of *Humor: International Journal for Humor Research* and *Journal of Folklore Research*.

www.ingramcontent.com/pod-product-compliance
Lightning Source LLC
Chambersburg PA
CBHW020932180426
43192CB00036B/896